The Royal Burgh of
INVERARAY

ALEXANDER FRASER, M.A., B.D.

THE SAINT ANDREW PRESS
EDINBURGH

1SBN 0 7152 0354 1

To

The Provosts, Bailies and Councillors who gave disinterested service in their day and generation, century after century, for the weil and standing of the Royal Burgh of Inveraray.

Printed and bound in Great Britain
by T. & A. Constable Ltd., Edinburgh

CONTENTS

Chapter   Page

Acknowledgments   5

1. The Burgh of Inveraray   7

      Its Origins
      The Sixteenth Century
      The Seventeenth Century
      The Eighteenth Century: First part
      The Eighteenth Century: Second part
      The Nineteenth Century
      The Twentieth Century
      The End of the Burgh
      References

2. The Old Town   92

      References

3. The New Town   117

      References

4. The Churches   143

      The Early Church
      The Reformation
      The Establishment of Episcopacy
      The Marquis as Churchman
      The Restoration
      The Eighteenth Century: The Early Years
      Glenaray and Inveraray: A Collegiate Charge

CONTENTS

New Ministries, New Churches and New Manses
Two Very Different Ministers
The Nineteenth Century
Church Union
The United Presbyterian Church, Inveraray
The Free Church
The United Free Church of Scotland, Inveraray
Inveraray (Argyll) All Saints
Appendix
References

5. Inveraray Grammar School   193

    References

6. Other Schools   210

    The English-speaking School
    The Free Church School
    Education for Girls
    The Parochial School at Glen Douglas
    Glenaray School
    Creggans School
    Glen Shira School
    References

ACKNOWLEDGMENTS

I have much pleasure in acknowledging my obligation to the former Town Council of the Royal Burgh of Inveraray and to the Argyll and Bute District Council for giving me access to the Minutes of the Council; to Mr R.P.K. Campbell, B.L., Director of Administration, Argyll and Bute District Council; to Miss C. Ramsay and Miss A. Steer, Local Office, Inveraray, Argyll and Bute District Council; to Provost Helen Buntain, Inveraray; to Mr. H. Graham, The Oban Times for permission to quote, occasionally at some length; to Mr. Donald MacKechnie, O.B.E., M.A., Bridge of Douglas; to Major Ron. Smith, M.B.E., Argyll Estates, Inveraray; to Members of Staff, The National Library of Scotland, and The General Register House, Edinburgh; to the Rev. James Bulloch, D.D., Stobo, for reading the chapter on the Churches; and to my wife Doctor E. M. Fraser for reading the proofs. Grateful acknowledgment is also made to the Scottish Tourist Board for providing the photographs for the frontispiece and cover.

Alexander Fraser

Manse of Cumlodden,
Inveraray,
Argyll.

20 August 1976

A Burgh most large and wonderful.

Neil Munro

There is a charm about anything old.

W. R. Inge: The End of an Age

I

THE BURGH OF INVERARAY

Its Origins

The Burgh of Inveraray owed its origin to a combination of those factors which are generally recognised as causes of the rise and growth of a burgh. Although Inveraray did not have a good natural harbour, it had at least an estuary, off which the ships of the Middle Ages might anchor and unload. It was the marketing centre of an alluvial plain. It grew up on the banks of the River Aray, the glen of which acted as a trade route into and out of the hinterland, while the river itself served as an hindrance to transverse traffic. The settlement grew up at the lowest fordable point of the river. There was also the element of "attractive growth": the burgh sheltered under the shadow of the baron's castle. The Castle of Inveraray was built in the first half of the fifteenth century (about 1432). It became the home of Colin, second Lord Campbell, created first Earl of Argyll in 1457, and without doubt this development caused the community to increase rapidly. The castle afforded protection to those in its vicinity and the presence of the Earl and his lady created a demand for and a supply of commodities. The occupations of fishing, hunting, agriculture, cattle and sheep rearing, curing of hides and iron working received encouragement.

Inveraray however could not make progress in trade until it evolved from a village into a burgh. It was not in order to hold a fair or a market within the township. Inveraray must be raised to the dignity of a burgh, and the times were propitious for such a development. During the second half of the fifteenth century (1450-1516), the king set up many burghs (51 burghs in barony; 4 royal burghs) and Inveraray received benefit from this policy. In 1474, King James III for his singular favour towards Colin, Earl of Ergile, Lord Campbell and Lorne, Master of his Household, and for the Earl's gratuitous and faithful services to the King's late

7

father and to himself, erected his town into a free burgh of barony,[1] with the usual liberties, a weekly market on Saturday and two yearly fairs, one at the Feast of Michael the Archangel (29th September), the other on the Feast of St. Brandan (16th May) and during the eight days which succeeded these festivals.

This charter promoted the development of Inveraray. The burgesses who were farmers held their property of the Earl of Argyll: they were his vassals. Bailies, aldermen and provosts were appointed by the Earl. A burghal court was constituted at least twice yearly. This was presided over by the baron (the Earl of Argyll) or by his baron bailie when the Earl was in Edinburgh or abroad. All the burgesses attended on the baron court: infringements of the law were dealt with, and statutes were promulgated concerning the conduct and administration of the burgh.

Like many other burghs in barony at this period, the erection of the Burgh of Inveraray was partly a commercial speculation.

In line with this policy markets and fairs were held. A market cross was erected.[2]

Ale houses were opened and travellers could find refreshment and supplies. Traders brought their merchandise to a Toll House and paid toll on their goods. There were stands and tents at the fairs, and each week country people carried wool, cheese, feathers, eggs, broom, salmon, milk and skins to the market. Good order was ensured by the proximity of the Castle, the seat of the Justiciary of Scotland and the Lord-High-Chancellor of Scotland. There was an enlargement in the range of ideas and a rise in the standard of living of those who dwelt in the burgh.

The Sixteenth Century

During the regency of Mary of Lorraine, which began on 12 April 1554, there was the possibility that Inveraray might become a Royal

1 Register of the Great Seal of Scotland (later R.M.S.G.S.) No. 1168, A.D.1474.

2 The Mercat Cross in the old town was ecclesiastical in origin. It dates from about 1400. It is a monolith. There is a floriated cross at the top; the stem is carved on front with a creeping vine motif; on the sides there is a Latin inscription which reads: This is the Cross of the nobleman Duncan McGillecomghan, Patrick his son and MacImuire the son of Patrick who caused this cross to be erected.

Burgh. A letter and a precept under the Privy Seal,[3] dated 6 October 1554, indicate an intention to create a Royal Burgh "in liberum burgum regalem", but this seems to have been ineffective, and Inveraray continued as a burgh of barony.

On 10th February 1572, in the Register of the Great Seal of the Kings of the Scots, the town is referred to as the Royal Burgh of Inveraray, and subsequently in the Proceedings of the Lords of the Articles there is a reference to the town as "Ane brugh royall". But in the sixteenth century, Inveraray was not raised to this dignity.

Tradition tells of one family of this period, descendants of which ultimately became provosts of Inveraray. About 1560, there was a glovemaker in the burgh called Little Duncanson. There was small demand for his wares: riding gloves, prelate's gloves, gantlets for hawking, ladies' gloves, gloves for enfeoffing vassals, or simply gloves to keep one's hands warm - there was no sale for them. After one hard winter Little Duncanson, his wife and family in despair were leaving Inveraray for the South Country. The Parson of Cilmalieu met them on the outskirts of the town. He bade them turn again as the morrow was the Feast of St. Brandan (16th May) on which one of the yearly fairs was about to be held and at which they would have good trade. And with his gift of the second sight, he foretold that from the family of Little Duncanson there would arise provosts of the burgh. The prophecy came true. In the graveyard of Cilmalieu is a standing stone with the words, "Mente manuque" over the gloved palm of a hand. Here are buried the Duncansons who did indeed become provosts of Inveraray.

The Seventeenth Century

It was on 28 January 1648, that the promotion of Inveraray to be a royal burgh was effective. On that date, Charles, by the grace of God, King of Great Britain, France and Ireland; Defender of the Faith created, made, erected and incorporated the Burgh of Inveraray into one whole and Free Royal Burgh to be called the Burgh of Inveraray in all time coming.

Next year, on 17 July 1649, Inveraray was enrolled among the free royal burghs of Scotland. One that day, Donald Cameron,

3   George S. Pryde, The Burghs of Scotland.

9

commissioner for the Burgh of Inveraray, with Maister James
Campbell commissioner for the Burgh of Dumbarton as cautioner
or surety, compeared before the commissioners of burghs convened at Edinburgh, and "desyred that Inveraray be inrolled amongst
the number of the free royall burrowis of Scotland."

James Campbell, commissioner for the Burgh of Dumbarton
entered a caveat that the enrolment of the Burgh of Inveraray
among the free royal burghs should not be prejudicial to the liberty
of the Burgh of Dumbarton.

Inveraray thereupon had the privilege of being represented at
the Convention of Royal Burghs, and for his diligence Donald
Cameron received an allowance for hospitality and the cost of his
travelling, paid by Inveraray, but fixed by the Commission of
Royal Burghs.

The charter which had been granted in 1648 and the enrolment which took place in 1649 gradually and radically affected the
corporate life of Inveraray.

The boundaries of the Burgh were defined by the charter. The
marches and limits of the Burgh were the Cromallt Burn on the
south; the yard dykes of the castle of the Marquiss, and Kilmalew
on the north; Lochfyne on the east; and the park dyke of the Marquess and the common mure on the west.

The burgesses were given powers. They had the full liberty
and power of choosing a provost, four bailies, a dean of guild, a
treasurer and twelve persons as counsellors, which office-bearers
were to be chosen from leets given in yearly by the Marquess.
These dignitaries had power to elect commissioners for the Burgh
to the Parliaments of Scotland and to the Convention of Royal
Burghs. They had power of making regulations, acts and statutes
for the just governance of Inveraray and of creating burgesses and
guild brothers.

As a Royal Burgh, Inveraray had a liberty of trade. There
might be within its marches all merchants and craftsmen whatsoever, pertaining to a free royal burgh. The Marquess encouraged
merchants and tradesmen to settle in the town. They were given
meat and wages and they had money in comparison with the
natives.[4] The Burgh had the power of enjoying traffic and trade
within the Kingdom of Scotland, as in other kingdoms beyond the

4 Minutes of the Kirk Session of the Highland Congregation, Glenaray.

same; and of exporting and importing all lawful merchandise and commodities. It had the liberty of possessing "schipis, barkis and boates" with sailors and other mariners, and of issuing and directing "cocquetts",[5] and of buying and selling wine, wax, woollen and linen cloth, broad and narrow, and all other merchandise.

Not only did Inveraray have a liberty of trade; it had a regality. The Provost and bailies were given power of holding burgh courts, of appointing their own court days, clerks, officers and other necessary members of court. The Provost and bailies were constituted justices of the peace with the power of appointing constables, a power which they continued to exercise in the twentieth century. There was conveyed to the magistrates the whole forfeits, fines and amercements of the courts to be applied for the common good of the burgh and its inhabitants.

The Dean of Guild was authorized to decide in all causes between merchants, and between merchant and mariner. He took care that buildings within the burgh were carried on according to law; that encroachments were not made on the streets. He judged in disputes between proprietors and considered the state of buildings, whether they were in a safe condition. He could grant warrant for repairing, pulling down or rebuilding according to the circumstances of the case.

The provost, magistrates and councillors met regularly within the Tolbooth, which was also known as the Town House, and their proceedings were recorded in the Minute Books of the Council which are extant from the year 1655. The Tolbooth served as a Court House, in which Campbell, Younger of Glenurchy, sheriff depute of Argyll and provost and bailies of Inveraray having received a royal commission, tried and judged malefactors.[6] The

5 A cocquet was a parchment writ with its seal. It was an important part of what we call a "Ship's papers": the official certificate that all customs duties and Governments imports had been adjusted, and that the vessel was free upon the seas. There was the possibility that a vessel being destitute of cocquet might be treated as a pirate's ship.

6 Register of the Privy Council of Scotland, (later R.P.C.S.) Third Series. Vol. 1. (Such malefactors as Duncan McKellar, son to Patrick McKellar in Maam, who in the month of March or April 1662 most cruelly murdered his own brother german.)

Tolbooth was employed as a prison, but was not at all secure.[7] As its name implies it was originally a booth for collecting tolls. A tron which was a heavy beam or balance used for weighing heavy wares, was set up in the vicinity of the Tolbooth and all weights and measures were sealed in the Tolbooth with the Town seal.

Note

The Tron was the public weighing machine; it was a place where malefactors were punished, being nailed by their lugs to the Tron; it was also a series of weights, quite different from and much heavier that the Troye series.

The basis of all liquid and dry measures was the Scottish pint (26,300 grains, 104.2 cubic inches, 2 lb 9 oz trois of clear water, 3 lb 7oz troye of clear running Water of Leith). The capacity of the Scottish pint to all intents and purposes remained constant. In Inveraray, the Magistrates used the water of the River Aray.

The two main measures of capacity were the firlot (21¼ Scotch pints) and the boll which contained 4 firlots.

In 1618, there were two firlots of different capacities, one of 21¼ Scotch pints, the other of 31 Scotch pints. In Mid-Argyll, the firlot in use was the Auchenbreck firlot. (From Clan Campbell Abstracts, Vol. II, p.83) This firlot the Magistrates filled with Aray water.

The chalder was 16 bolls: there was a great Chalder of 12 Troye stones and a little chalder of 6 Troye stones.

The Scottish standard measure of length was the Ell, Elne or Ellwand: this measure remained more or less constant, being 37 Scotch inches. The inch was the breadth of the thumb of a middle sized man, measured at the root of the nail. The Burgh of Inveraray was required to have an iron or copper ell, hung up at the Tolbooth.

In actual fact, there were innumerable local and customary measures in use throughout the country, every burgh having its own variation of the standard.

The magistrates of Inveraray had power to take trial of false metts, wechts and measures and the users of the said fals wechts to amit and tine their haill goods and gear which were to be forfeited for the King's use. But everyone made a choice of measures according to their unruly appetites and as their avaritious and greedy humour led them. (L. Burrell 'The Standards of Scotland' in The Monthly Review, March 1961.)

---

7   "Duncan McKellar being incarcerat within the tolbuith of Inveraray in 1662 did shortly thereafter make his escape."

The provost, bailies and councillors of the new royal burgh were given power of erecting a market cross (there was a cross in the burgh of barony). The mercant croce of Inveraray was a sign of the status of the burgh, and of its authority in matters of trade. Its base was designed with a view to the reading of proclamations and other magisterial duties.

The burgh was given the right of having ports or harbores in the mouth of the river Aray, or in any other part within the bounds. As goods were loaded and unloaded at the town on the banks of the river, the delta required to be kept from silting up. The citizens of the burgh therefore laboured in relays from time to time to clear stones from the estuary and to deepén the channel.[8]

One of the responsibilities which the Town Council asumed was the provision of a ferry. Without doubt, boats ferried passengers from one shore of Loch Fyne to the other from time immemorial. Mary, Queen of Scots crossed the loch in July 1563 by the ferry from West to East Creggans. In September 1591, the Thane of Cawdor gave 6/8d. to the ferrier for taking him from Inveraray to Dunderave.[9]

In 1654, birlings, boats of shallow draft, were used to ferry people between Inveraray and Strachur.[10] The ferry at Inveraray was known as the Royal Ferry. The right of ferry especially on sea

8   In 1675, the harbour became a scene of magisterial activity. In 1673, an embargo was put on Irish commodities and the bailies of Inveraray were required to give undertakings to the Earl of Argyll that they would not import victual from Ireland. The object of this embargo on Irish cattle, salt beef, meal and all kinds of corn was the encouragement of home industries, but the prohibition was not regarded with favour and was not effective. In order to enforce the law, offices were established at the port of Inverary in 1676; deputy commissioners were authorised by the Earl of Argyll and empowered to search all barks, boats or other vessels whether Irish or Scots, wherein any Irish victual or cattle were suspected to be, and to receive declarations from the merchants, skippers or owners of boats. The bailies of Inveraray were ordered to assist the commissioners to search vessels by night or by day, to open and patent doors, to search cellars, to seize victuals, and having brought suspects before a magistrate to send to prison those guilty of contravening the laws. (R.P.C.S., 1673, 1676).

9   Cosmo Innes, Sketches of Early Scotch History and Social Progress (later Innes: S.E.S.H.)

10   Minutes of the English Congregation, Inveraray.

lochs is one of the regalia, that is one of the rights pertaining to the King. The right however is alienable and may be erected into a heritable estate by direct grant from the Crown in favour of a person such as the Earl of Argyll, in favour of a burgh of barony or of a royal burgh. After the town became a royal burgh, Inveraray claimed (although it is not mentioned in the charter of 1648) the exclusive right of ferrying pasengers and cattle from Inveraray to the opposite side of Loch Fyne. This claim entailed the obligation to serve the ferry, the right to exact reasonable dues for the service, and the privilege of protection against competition within the immediate vicinity.

The monopoly of the ferry was one source of income. Other sources of burghal income were defined in the charter. Not only was the Burgh to have the forfeits, fines and amercements of the burgh courts, but it was to have the petty customs of the fairs and markets, [11] the anchorage dues and tolls of vessels, [12] "roades and harbories" of the burgh, to be applied for the good and benefit of the said burgh.

11. A Table of Petty Customs was drawn up.

There was paid on a boll of great oats	6d
a boll of small oats	4d
a boll of groats (the grain of oats deprived of the husks)	1s
a gallon of aqua vitae	1s
a boll of salt	8d
a roll of tobacco	4d
a stone of butter	6d
a stone of wool	4d
a rood of plaiding	4d

There was set down also a Table of the Bridge and Water Customs, the proceeds of which were used in the first instance for repairing the bridge, the causey and the ferry. The sums required were much the same as those of Petty Customs. On imported goods there was paid

on a boll of malt	9d
on a boll of meal	8d
on a boll of great oats	6d
on a boll of small oats	4d
on a gallon of aqua vitae	1s
on a boll of groats	1s

In 1655, the Bridge and Water Customs were sett for a year to George Duncanson (perhaps a descendant of Little Duncanson, the glovemaker) for the sum of forty merks.

In return for so many liberties and privileges, the Burgh of Inveraray was required to pay to the Crown the sum of six pounds, thirteen shillings and four pence, coin of the Kingdom of Scotland, at the festival of the Purification of the Blessed Virgin Mary (2nd February) in the name of burgh mail with service use and wont only.

Inveraray having been erected to be a royal burgh, two important, involved and obscure questions required to be clarified. One was the superiority of the houses in the burgh: was the land lying within the boundaries of the burgh to be held of and under the Crown in free burgage? The other question was that of the taxes for which the burgh was to be assessed.

The first Gordian knot was the question of the superiority of the houses in the burgh. When the Town of Inveraray was a burgh of barony, the whole houses of the burgh heretably appertained to the baron, the Earl of Argyll. On the erection of Inveraray into a Royal Burgh in 1648, all duties and rights in use to have been paid to the Marquis were reserved to him. When the burgh was enrolled in the Convention of Royal Burghs, the Marquis promised that "he wold quyt his superiorite of the saidis houssis and to suffer them to hold in free burgage".[13] In 1651, the Marquis agreed to convey to the Provost, bailies and Council of the Burgh the duties and rights with the whole houses and tenements within the bounds of the burgh as their own property and proper heritage for the common good of the Burgh. This Renunciation was made in acknowledgement of certain sums of money, manufully paid in the name of the community. In 1657, the commissioners of burghs

---

12   The Town Council charged anchorage and shore dues:

for a ship of grave burden	30s
for a bark with two top sails	20s
for a bark with one top sail	13s
for a gabbart	6s
for a herring boat	4s
for a boat with a rudder	3s
for a boat without a rudder	2s

The usual payment from the schipper for his anckerage at this period was 6/8d. Part of this revenue was used in keeping the harbour in repair.

13   Extracts from the Records of the Convention of the Royal Burghs of Scotland (later, R.C.R.B.) 1615-1676 Vol. III, p. 456.

were informed to their surprise, that the whole houses of the Burgh of Inveraray heritably appertained to the Marquis. On 24 May 1661, the Marquess departed this life, leaving a son, Archibald, Lord Lorne. In September 1662, the Town Council of Inveraray, "considering how useful and advantageious the said family was to the Burgh and the inhabitants, and may be in time, if they shall be restored to their former dignities ... therefore the Magistrates consent that the Renuniciation made by the late Marquess shall be void and null."

The decision of the Magistrates of Inveraray, however, did not affect Government policy and practice. In January 1663, Charles II ratified the Renunciation made by the late Marquess.

Later in the same year, the estates of his House were restored to Archibald, Lord Lorne. The nobleman was in need of money to journey to London, in order to his restoration and the Magistrates and Town Council agreed to pay a large sum of money in three instalments to Lord Lorne, if he would obtain from the King a ratification of the Renunciation made by the late Marquess.

The Magistrates and Town Council resorted to borrowing. By 13 July 1663, they had borrowed 3,000 merks [14] from Jon Rowans, merchant in Grainock and 1,000 merks from Alexander Gordon, the minister. In return for this sum of money, Archibald, now become 9th Earl, handed over the King's Majesty's Ratification under the Privy Seal of that writ issued in the Town's favour by the deceased Marquis of Argyll, which was appointed "to be keipit in the Charter Kist" [15]

It is not clear whether the balance of the money was ever paid or not. It does seem however that the Magistrates and Town Council had the right to receive certain rents which may indicate that part of the property within the bounds of the Burgh was held in free burgage.

The other Gordian knot which required to be unravelled was the question of the taxes for which the Burgh was to be assessed and, more perplexing, how they were to be paid. On 17 July 1649, Inveraray was "inrolled amongst the number of the free royall burrowis of Scotland". The royal burghs paid a sixth part of the

---

14   A Scottish silver coin formerly current = 13⅓d. sterling.

15   Donald Mackechnie: 'Inveraray - The Beginnings' in The Kist, No. 9, Spring 1975.

sum imposed as a land tax upon the counties of Scotland. The proportion payable by individual burghs was assessed by the Convention of Royal Burghs, which met annually and consisted of two deputies from each burgh. After 1649, the Convention had the power to consider the state of trade and revenues of Inveraray, and to assess the Burgh according to its ability to pay. At first, the obligations of Inveraray were referred to only in a general way: the burgesses were to bear all such burdens as might be imposed upon them according to their part in the tax roll, and for this purpose they were to send a commissioner sufficiently instructed for stenting of (or making an assessment on) the Burgh of Inveraray.

Nothing was done for five years concerning the proportion of the tax roll payable by Inveraray, but in July 1654 the commissioners of burghs appointed Inveraray's proportion of the tax roll to be in all time hereafter four shillings Scots money of the hundred lib.[16]

Despite the fact that the burgh was represented regularly in the Convention of Royal Burghs after 1661, Inveraray did not appear in the tax roll of 1665, 1670 and 1683.[17] In 1689, the convention found that Inveraray had not made any payment of the four shillings of the hundred pounds payable as its proportion of the tax-roll. Wherefore in that year the Convention of Royal Burghs appointed an agent to exact from the Burgh of Inveraray the four shillings of the hundred pounds which is their proportion they are to pay by the tax roll, and that for all by-gones since the year 1649. This exaction came to an overwhelming sum which the Burgh could not pay, particularly as there had been much interference with trade during the Rebellion of 1685. The exaction of this money was delayed till the next general convention.

In 1690 the Convention of Royal Burghs appointed visitations of the whole royal burghs with a view to ascertaining authoritatively the condition, trade and commond good of each. But Inveraray with three other royal burghs was excepted, "because of the difficulty of access to these places". In this year, 1690, the Burgh of Inveraray was entered in the tax roll, it was believed, for the first time.

16   Pound Scots: a twelfth of the value of the pound sterling, or 1/8d.

17   Index, R.C.R.B., under "Tax Roll". also Robert S. Rait: The Parliaments of Scotland, Glasgow, 1924.

In 1692, exemption was granted to the Burgh from appearing at meetings of the Convention for the space of three years unless specially required.[18] In 1694, the Convention of Royal Burghs attempted to help the insolvent member in the west. It was agreed that the Burgh of Falkland relieve the Burgh of Inveraray of two shillings of the stent roll; and that the agent of the Convention of Royal Burghs advance this sum upon condition that Inveraray should pay the remainder. Inveraray was unable to pay.

At the end of the century, 1697 the Convention, having heard the case of the town of Inveraray and the representation of their commissioner and because the town had not patrimony or casualty, appointed the agent to discharge them of the sum of one hundred and forty four pounds Scots resting of the bygone missive dues [19] preceding July 1697 years instant. [20]

The status of a free Royal Burgh was a dignity which Inveraray at this period was scarcely able to support, financially.

To conclude: the first fifty years of Inveraray's history as a free royal burgh were difficult. The magistrates and council were involved in heavy financial obligations which they were not able to discharge, while the benefits conferred upon them were not real in terms of income. But the foundations of the institutions of a royal burgh were laid, and despite the poverty and debt there was the hope that in future generations the town might enjoy the increase of polity, commerce and traffic, promised in its charter.

The Eighteenth Century: First Part

When the eighteenth century began, the Royal Burgh of Inveraray

---

18 R.C.R.B., Vol. iv, p. 162.

19 Often by way of addition to the Land Tax or Cess (which was part of the national taxation) the Convention of Royal Burghs imposed extra taxes on the whole of the burghs for special purposes, and as the Convention had no funds of its own, it ordered the magistrates by missive letter to raise the money under the title of "missive dues". The chief purpose for which these additional taxes were imposed was for aiding various burghs in the execution of public works such as harbours.

Because Inveraray had not paid the missive dues, the commissioner representing that Burgh did not have the right to vote in the Convention.

20 R.C.R.B., Vol. iv, p.233.

was in process of achieving development and adjustment to larger corporations.

One of the most important of these was the Convention of Royal Burghs. In the previous century, the position of Inveraray with respect to other Royal Burghs had been that of a poor relation, and in the first part of the eighteenth century there was not much improvement in its standing. In 1697, the Convention of Royal Burghs had appointed an agent to discharge the Town of Inveraray of the by-gone missive dues. But in 1705 the situation was no easier. The proportion of the tax roll payable by Inveraray had been augmented by one shilling of the hundred pounds. Inveraray sent a petition by its commissioner to the Convention of Royal Burghs, craving the Convention to take their indigent case into consideration. The Convention did so and appointed an agent to pay to the Burgh an equivalent to the present augmentation of their proportion of the tax roll. More than a quarter of a century passed, but Inveraray was in no better case. On 6th July 1732, the Convention of Royal Burghs allowed to Inveraray £20 stg. to enable that burgh to pay two years cess[21] to the General Receiver and in June 1733, the Agent was authorised to pay the commissioner for Inveraray the above mentioned sum.[22]

While struggling in these difficulties, the Burgh endeavoured to take part in the work of the Convention. In 1726, the Convention offered opposition to the project of the African Company which sought a monopoly of trade with that continent; also to the project of the South Sea Company, which had survived the failure of 1720 and was participating unsuccessfully in the whale fisheries and in trade with Spanish America.[23] In this opposition, the Burgh of Inveraray loyally played its part. James Nimmo, commissioner for Inveraray, was appointed a member of the sub-committee of the Convention ''to prepare a draught (sic) of a letter to be sent by the committee to the representatives of the burrows in parliament, praying to them as they regard the welfare of the trade of this island and particularly this part thereof to use their utmost

21   The Land Tax or Cess was part of the general national taxation which was levied at irregular intervals for a long time and then became an annual tax. Turner: History of Local Taxation in Scotland, 1908.

22   R.C.R.B., Vol. v, pp. 536-548.

23   E. Lipson: The Economic History of England, Vol II pp. 358, 369, 370.

endeavours to obstruct one exclusive trade so detrimental to the nation and which is an infringement on the liberty of the subject"[24]

Despite the care of the Convention to secure the payment of cess and to protect rights conferred by royal charter, burghs of barony and burghs of regality were encroaching on the trading privileges of royal burghs. These burghs which were not members of the Convention of Royal Burghs paid no share of the national taxation. In 1690, there was an act of the Parliament of Scotland to restore the privileges of Royal Burghs, but at the same time negotiations were begun with burghs of barony and burghs of regality to permit them to share in the privilege of trade, provided that these bodies undertook to pay ten per cent of the burghs' cess.[25] The exclusive position of the Royal Burghs was weakened further by the Treaty of Union, 1707, in which it was provided that the whole United Kingdom enjoy the same trade privileges. As the eighteenth century passed, it became increasingly evident that the privileges of the Royal Burgh of Inveraray were slipping away and that freedom of trade was becoming more extensive. The Town Council continued to send their commissioner[26] to Edinburgh every year, however, to nominate an assesor and faithfully to cooperate in the work of the Convention.

Another external body of which Inveraray was become a member was the District of Royal Burghs, a privilege involving responsibilities. Inveraray along with other royal burghs of the west, Campbeltown, Rothesay, Ayr and Irvine made up a District. Each one of these burghs elected a commissioner and these commissioners in turn elected a burgess for the Parliament of Great Britain to represent the burghs of the district. In July 1748, the Magistrates and Town Council of Inveraray chose Mr. John Campbell, merchant and provost of the town to meet with the other commissioners of the royal burghs in the district. Mr. Campbell was qualified conform to law; a man fearing God, of the true Protestant religion, publicly professed and authorised by the laws of the kingdom, without suspicion on the contrary expert in the

---

24 R.C.R.B., Vol. v, pp. 379-381.

25 George S. Pryde, Burghal Administration.

26 In 1742, the commissioner was John McLea: he paid 5 shillings when he gave in his commission to the Convention of Royal Burghs; and he paid 9/4d. missive dues.

common affairs of the burrows, a merchant and inhabitant within the said Burgh, bearing all portable charges with his neighbours and a part of the public burdens and can tyne and winn in all their affairs, and a merchant and trafficker within the said Burgh, to be their commissioner or delegate to meet with the rest of the commissioners of the said district to elect a burgess or commissioner to the ensuing Parliament of Great Britain. The Town Council appointed the clerk to give an extract of this minute to the said commissioner and to append thereto the Town Seal. The Burgess chosen to represent the Western Burrows in Parliament was Charles Erskine, Esq., who died in the following year.

While it was important that the Royal Burgh of Inveraray should take part in the work of corporations larger than itself, nevertheless, much the greater part of its time was occupied with the internal administration of the burgh.

The provost, bailies and councillors were concerned at all times with matters affecting the health and good name of the town. One such matter was the danger to health from infected brandy. On 28th January 1721, the Magistrates and Town Council took to their serious consideration the plague they were threatened with from other countries and designed after the laudable example of neighbouring burrows to use all manner of precautions to prevent their being infected with the same. They had received information that there was brandy and other French liquor being brought from these countries to this nation and at present some was imported to this burgh. They therefore enacted that henceforth no persons of whatever degree or quality should take upon them to import into this burgh any French brandy or any other commodities of that country, without quarantine. They enacted likewise that none of the inhabitants of the burgh should retail any such liquors without consent of the magistrates and ordained that any of the inhabitants must give in to the Lord's Magistrates a particular account of what brandy they had in their custody. It was certified, if any should contravene this Act, that, after clear evidence, whatever brandy or any other liquors found in their custody, should be spilled and the casks staved and burned, and the importers and retailers thereof to be amerciate in one hundred pounds, Scots, and severely punished in their persons at the discretion of the Magistrates.

Despite the precautions and prohibitions of the Town Council, plague did come to the Burgh from time to time, if not through

French brandy in particular, then through contact and commerce with foreign traders in general.

In the same year, 1721, the Magistrates and Town Council, under considerable and sustained pressure, made enactments to preserve the good name of the Burgh in respect of the payment of excise. Excise, a tax on articles of home manufacture dating from January 1644 when the first act was passed by the Edinburgh parliament, was collected with great difficulty in the Highlands. At the Union of 1707, the excise system was managed by a board of commissioners who appointed collectors of H.M. Excise. The collector in this area frequently represented to the Magistrates and Town Council of Inveraray the great loss H.M. Revenue of Excise in the Burgh sustained by allowing several poor people, inhabitants in the burgh, to brew, vend and retail ale, aquavity and other excisable liquors, who were altogether insolvent and unable to pay H.M. Excise or entertain strangers, to the great prejudice of such persons as were willing to keep publick change houses and pay the duties of Excise.

Moved by these repeated representations, the Magistrates and Town Council on 1st May 1721 discharged insolvent brewers and retailers in time coming and gave the sole liberty and privilege of brewing, selling and retailing of ale, acquavity and other excisable liquors and of keeping publick change houses to certain persons licensed by the Magistrates. The Magistrates and Council granted to Henry Oswald, Alex. Lambie, Donald Campbell, Merchant, Archibald Roy McVicar, Malcolm McLaurine, Widow Clerk, Widow Murray, Niven McInturner, Charles Stewart, Angus McNokair, John McDougall, Gilbert Munroe, Alice McKay, Margaret Strachan, John Munroe Smith, John Bane McKellar, Bailie Donald Campbell, Alex. Roy Campbell, Donald McNicol, Dugald Logan and John Campbell, maltman, with such persons as hereafter might be licensed by the magistrates, the sole liberty and privilege of keeping publick change houses and victualing houses and of brewing, vending and retailing excisable liquors within the burgh. They were ordained to keep strangers and passengers, and furnish them with meat, drink and lodgings at reasonable prices. If they should fail therein, they were to be fined in twenty pounds, Scots money. At the same time, the Magistrates and Council discharged all other persons within the burgh to brew, vend or retail in greater or lesser quantities any excisable liquors for sale, under the penalty of being banished furth of the burgh in all time coming.

Rightly to order the weekly markets was one of the preoccupations of the Magistrates and Town Council. They enacted that goods for sale be brought into the town and sold at the Mercat Cross, not disposed of in the outskirts; that goods be sold only on market days; and that the coins exchanged be legal currency. There were abuses to be rectified in the sale of fuel. While it was quite in order that some citizens should go to houses in the country and buy peats where they were stacked, it was not equable that the inhabitants living at the ends of the town should buy up several loads of peat as they were brought into the burgh, leaving nothing for those who were waiting at the Market Cross. It was therefore enacted on 9th January 1721 that peats were not to be bought up by any of the inhabitants until they were brought to the Cross, and that not above one load should be bought at once by any of the inhabitants till others were equally served. Irregularities in the sizes of creels in which the peats were sold caused discontent. On 13th September, 1723, and that not for the first time, the Magistrates and Council appointed a new peat creel to be made as a measure for buying and selling peat within the burgh, according to the dimensions of the standard formerly appointed by the Magistrates and Council. Alexander Lambie and John Reid were to see to the making thereof, and to deliver the same to the Town Officer. The carelessness or wilfulness of country people, who brought their produce into the town and sold it on other than market days, was a recurrent source of annoyance to the burgh authorities. The Magistrates and Town Council considering the inconveniences that attend the practice of buying and selling provisions which come from the country to the town, without any regard to the weekly mercat days appointed by their charter of erection, did therefore give publick notice that all beef, mutton, goat, veal, lamb, kid, eggs, meal, potatoes and other provisions, not water borne, should be brought to the town only upon Tuesday or Friday weekly and then not sold or bargained for but in the mercat place, which was erected for that purpose in 1749 at the south end of the deceased John M'Lea's tenement.

It was necessary to prohibit the use of debased coins. On 18th August 1725 the Magistrates and Council forbade and discharged the whole inhabitants of the burgh in all time coming to take or give in change for any kind of merchandise, meat or drink, the little money pieces called doites and the halfpennys called Wood's halfpennys [27], under pain of forefauting them wheresoever or in whose custody they are found, and otherwise punished at the Magistrates' pleasure: in respect the said halfpennys and doits are by reason of the badness of the metal, and for other reasons, certified and declared by the Magistrates not current and discharged.

The town council was responsible for ordering the daily life and work of the people. This was done in part by the ringing of the church bell or bells. These were used for the customary purpose, according to immemorial usage, of warning people to proceed to or leave their work in the morning and evening, or on occasions of national rejoicing. For these purposes the magistrates might use the bell of the church without permission of the Kirk Sesion.[28] The corporation was somewhat hampered in the fulfilment of this civic duty, by the fact that in 1725 the two bells in the steeple of the church were broken. It was resolved to have the bells recast. Campbell of Stonefield, Sheriff Depute of Argyll, asumed responsibility and the new bell was made by Robert Maxwell in Edinburgh in 1728, bearing the imprimatur of the Burgh Coat of Arms. On 28th January, 1729 the provost reported to the Council that he and Asknish had agreed with Duncan Clerk, officer, for ringing the bell daily, at six of the clock in the morning and at ten at night, which the Council approved of.

Another service for which the Magistrates and Council accepted responsibility was the collection and delivery of letters. In the first half of the eighteenth century, the flow of letters to and from Inveraray was increasing in volume. Between 27th April and 31st

27 The doit was a Dutch coin of the value of a penny, or (some say) a penny and a third of a penny, Scots. The doit was the twelfth part of an English penny. Wood's halfpennys were Irish halfpennies minted by George I (1714-1727). In 1722 a patent was granted to William Wood for the coining of copper halfpennies and farthings for use in Ireland. The coins appear to have been minted at Bristol, and the issue only lasted from 1722-1724. The coins were known also as Hibernias and harps, because on the reverse was Hibernia seated left, holding a harp.

28 Dunlop's Parochial Law, third edition, p. 62n.

December, 1734, more than 2,450 letters passed through the hands of the Inveraray Postmaster.[29]

On 11th July, 1734 at Inveraray, the Magistrates authorised John M'Neur in the Parkhead of Inveraray to be their post or runner for carrying the packet between Inveraray and Dumbarton from that date to the first of July, 1735, he always behaving himself faithfully and honestly in the said office.

It has been said that the poor we have always with us. This was a truth which the Magistrates and Council accepted, and about which they were prepared to take action. But it was necessary to distinguish between the deserving and the undeserving poor. On 2nd April, 1736, they took preventive measures concerning the undeserving poor. The Magistrates and Council appointed that no stranger beggars, sturdy beggars or vagabonds be harboured or allowed to stay in any house in the town above two nights under the penalty of five pounds, Scots, to be paid by the harbourers. On 28th June, 1746, they provided for the relief of the deserving poor by imposing a compulsory contribution on the citizens. The Magistrates and Town Council, considering that for a considerable time past the inhabitants of the place have paid a monthly stent towards supporting the poor beggars that formerly went from door to door, and judging it highly proper to continue the same for some time longer, and that the arrears there of be paid and applied as usual, they therefore appoint the persons at present in arrears forthwith to pay up the same, otherwise they grant warrant to the town officers to poind and arrest, and recommend to the ministers to intimate this to their congregations next Lord's Day.

The Magistrates and Town Council of necessity enforced the somewhat vexatious regulations connected with mill.[5] The lands cultivated by the people of Inveraray were astricted or thirled to the Miln of Carlunnan: the grain grown on these lands must be taken to the miln to be ground, and for this service every eleventh peck was exacted out of every boll by the miller while the servant took one fourth of a peck from the boll. In 1679, the Town Council had enacted that the tenants pay either conform to use and wont,

29 Manuscript Notebook of Archibald Campbell, Postmaster at Inveraray, 1734-35 (see also A.R.B.Haldane: Three Centuries of Scottish Posts).

or that they pay for each boll of dry corn, five lippies [30] and one lippie meal from the miln eye,[31] in satisfaction to the miller and his servants, of all duties that can be enacted from them, and likewise that there be twelve shillings, Scots, enacted for each mash of malt. It appears that the tenants were unwilling to make these payments, for on 15th June, 1742 the Magistrates and Town Council appointed a memorandum to be made of the act of 1679, and that it should be entered in their Council books. There was of course need that adequate payment be made to the miller for his services, because the miller in his turn required to pay more than 300 merks in rent yearly to the superior, or £16.13.4d. sterling in 1760. Those who took oats to be ground at the mill were put to considerable costs: not only did they require to satisfy the miller, but they had to pay workmen who kept horses to carry the meal to the mill, and these carriers either demanded a high price or refused their services. The mill on the River Aray was necessary to the parish: in 1747, it was rebuilt and slated and in 1749-51 new machinery was installed.

Sanitation and the water supply were of necessity the business of the Magistrates and Town Council. On the third day of May 1723, the Council recommended to the Magistrates to agree with fit persons for removing and carrying away the great midden betwixt the Cross and the Tolbooth and for making the same clean and redd, and for laying the same with sand or gravel. Fines imposed by the Magistrates were to defray the charges of the work, which was to be carried on without delay, and the Magistrates and Council charged all persons whatsoever from putting dung, redd or filth on this dunghill or midden or making any addition thereto under the penalty of three pounds, Scots. The Town Officer made intimation of this decision to the adjacent inhabitants, that they might not pretend ignorance.

Like so many acts of the Council, this required to be renewed. On 17th February, 1744, the Magistrates and Town Council prohibited and discharged any of the inhabitants of the burgh to put dung, ashes or other nastiness upon any part of the public streets and particularly upon the midden stead before the house of one of

30   An old Scottish dry measure, the fourth of a peck.

31   Miln eye or mully: this word was applied sometimes to the whole mill and its pertinents. The miln eye or mully was the equivalent of 1 31/32 of a Scottish pint. (Scottish National Dictionary)

the burgesses under the penalty of half a crown to be paid into the Town Treasurer.[32]

Not only did the Magistrates endeavour to keep the burgh clean and decent, they also sought to provide a water supply. This was a well from which water was raised by means of a windlass. The people with their pitchers used to gather in lines early in the morning, and each had to wait his or her turn. In 1743, the well was in need of repair. The windlass was not working properly, and it may be that the coping required attention. On 7th October of that year, sixteen men worked at the well, for which they were paid the sum of 8 shillings and Donald and Archibald McNeilage worked about the windlass for 5/6d.

If Inveraray were to prosper, there must be access for shipping, and in the first half of the eighteenth century, this access was at the mouth of the River Aray. The mouth of the river, therefore, required continual attention. In 1743, the Town Treasurer paid ten pence for drink to people redding the water.

After the goods had been landed at the harbour, they must be transported to the Town. This service was performed by workmen who kept horses for the common work of the Town. These workmen however finding that their assistance was indispensable began to exact exorbitant prices for their services, for themselves and for their horses. The Magistrates and Town Council, having had several complaints made to them by the inhabitants of the Burgh, enacted that each draught or load from the harbour to the Brae or to Provost Duncanson's house be six pennys Scots, and below that, to be only four pennys money, and that for drawing a barrel of water from the far end of the bridge, they have only six pennys, Scots.

The ferry from Inveraray to the east side of Loch Fyne was a service which continued from generation to generation. On 1st May, 1744, the Magistrates sett, set or let to William McGibbon and to Donald McNicoll, both in Inveraray, the ferry and ferryboat of the Burgh, with the house and garden belonging thereto, with the fees and emoluments belonging to the ferry, for one year.

---

32 On one occasion, in the Burgh of Glasgow, when the town manure had been sold to a farmer, and was being removed by two carters in the early morning, one of the carters, an Irishman, being sleepy, fell backwards into the cart full of nastiness. The other carter pulled him out by the head, threw him into a horse trough, and left him.

There was a big ferry boat worth fifty pounds, Scots, belonging to the Town Council, while the ferriers kept a small yawl at their own charges. The tenants of the ferry were to serve the lieges diligently and faithfully as ferriers upon payment of the ordinary freights, and they must ferry the Magistrates and Councillors gratis. They were to pay two pounds Scots money of yearly rent. William McGibbon, among his many other interests and activities, continued to carry people to and fro for many years.

In 1745, but not due to the Rebellion, the spectre of famine appeared at the door. On 14th May 1745, the Magistrates, Town Council and a dozen other gentlemen considering that victual was so scarce and the prospect of being supplied so distant and precarious that if some way were not fallen upon for a speedy relief, the people must be reduced to the utmost distress, they therefore to prevent this misfortune, as far as it lay in their power, collected the sum of eighty eight pounds, sterling money, which they put into the hands of Duncan Ochiltree, merchant in Inveraray (who himself contributed £5) and instructed him forthwith to repair to Glasgow and purchase any quantity of meal that was to be had, and failing meal of any kind, flour or biscuit, to be transported to this place in such a manner as he should judge best without loss of time.[33]

In the charter granted by King Charles, power was given to the Provost and bailies of Inveraray of holding burgh courts and the king made and constituted these officials to be Justices of the Peace. It was necessary for the Provost and bailies to exercise their judicial powers.

On 4th November, 1747, the Magistrates considering that Mary Semple, spouse to William Smith, soldier, did lately when called before them to answer for immoral practices, shew the utmost contempt of their authority by giving very abusive language and resisting their officers and having also learnt from several of the inhabitants of this place that the said Mary Semple is a contentious and offensive neighbour, and harbours bad company in her house, and is in several respects an unworthy member of society, they do therefore appoint her to be banished out of this burgh and limits thereof not to return under the pain of imprisonment and such other punishments as the Magistrates shall think

---

33 Similar situations arose in 1772-73, 1795-96 and in 1800.

fit, and they appoint the town officers on the morrow at twelve of the clock to put this sentence into execution.

Next year on 1st October, 1748, eight persons, six of which were women, were convened within the Tolbooth before the Provost for entering into the Duke of Argyll's enclosures in that park called the Wintertown[34] and for gathering and attempting to carry off part of the timber newly cut in the enclose. They all judicially confessed and one Angus Campbell was dealt with particularly severely, presumably on the ground that he should have known better. Considering that the said Angus Campbell was one of the Duke's common workmen, the Provost banished him from residing within the Town's liberties, never to return in order to remain therein, under the penalty of five pounds, sterling. The Provost fined all the other persons and each of them in five shillings money.

The office of Magistrate was not without its pitfalls. John Bell, tailor in Inveraray, commenced a process of alleged wrongous imprisonment against James Campbell of Silvercraigs, one of the bailies of Inveraray, and John Bell obtained a decreet for the sum of thirty pounds, sterling. James Campbell expended in defending the process the sum of forty one pounds making up together the sum of seventy one pounds. The Magistrates and Town Council unanimously resolved that the expenses of the process should be repaid to James Campbell out of the Town's revenues.

The provost, Bailies and council on whom these various responsibilities rested were chosen each year and nominated each year, usually by a leet subscribed by H.G. the Duke of Argyll as in 1744; but occasionally no leet was given as in 1743. On 10th October, 1743, the Magistrates and Town Council of the burgh convened within the Tolbooth for the election of magistrates for the ensuing year. No leet having been given in, the Council accordingly elected, nominated and appointed Alexander Duncanson, merchant in Inveraray to be provost, John Campbell of Kintraw and John McLea of Limecraig to be bailies and Patrick Campbell, wigmaker in Inveraray to be Dean of Guild of the Burgh till Michaelmas next, who accepted of the said office respective. Thereafter, the Magistrates and Council did nominate and appoint

34 Wintertown, in Gaelic Bail' a' Gheamhraidh. This may suggest that there was a township of this name, or of a name which sounded similar, on this spot, in the past. (Local tradition)

Patrick Reid, maltster in Inveraray to be Treasurer, John Campbell, Sheriff Clerk of Argyll to be Clerk, and Duncan and John Clerk to be officers. These took the oath de Fidele. Thereupon, the following persons were appointed councillors. They are to say:-

> Sir James Campbell of Ardkinglass
> Sir James Campbell of Auchenbreck
> Mr. Archibald Campbell of Stonefield
> James Fisher, late provost
> John Campbell, late provost
> Angus Campbell of Asknish
> John Campbell, Chamberlain
> Duncan Campbell of Loch-head
> Dugald Murray, late bailie
> Duncan Fisher, writer
> John Campbell, clerk
> Archibald Campbell of Jura
> John McNab, chirurgeon in Inveraray

It is evident that if the retiring provosts, magistrates and council chose the succeeding magistrates and council, the Burgh of Inveraray was administered by a self-perpetuating oligarchy.

The Magistrates and Council employed certain officials to carry out their decisions. One of these was the Town Officer or Town Officers.[35] It was the duty of this functionary to fix and toll the Town bell at six of the clock in the morning and at ten at night daily from Michaelmas to Michaelmas, for which he received twenty shillings sterling. For this purpose he carried a lanthorn to light him at ringing the bell. The Officer made public intimation of the Acts of the Magistrates and Council which concerned the adjacent inhabitants, that none might pretend ignorance. Attendant upon the Town Officer on these occasions was the Town Drummer usually a discharged veteran of the foreign wars, who gave notice by tuck of drum that a proclamation was about to be made. The Town Officer also served as gaoler and sheriff-officer. He searched for stolen goods and apprehended petty thieves. He duly and orderly lit the oil lamps of the town and was given a frock

---

35 At a later date (1805), the Town Officer was given a colleague on account of the number of his duties. The Officers were provided with full suits of clothing of scarlet cloth, with a pair of white worsted stockings, to be worn by them when officially on public duty.

to save his clothes at the lighting of them. For this purpose also, he carried a lanthorn. He was suitably clad for his important office, being presented with a suit of livery, stockings and a wig. For his various services he received five pounds sterling per annum and his house rent. When he came to the period of his service, an allowance was made to him in charity on account of his old age and infirmity.

Another henchman of the Council was the executioner or lockman. He was called lockman because of the small quantity of meal (or lock a ladleful) which he was allowed to take out of every boll, set out for sale in the market. This man performed and executed the ofice of dempster, lockman and executioner within the Burgh and in the County. He obeyed the orders and commands of the magistrates and all other Sovereign Lords' Judges, when required. For these services, he received £1 sterling from the Burgh in 1749, and at a later date an allowance of £5.11.1⅓d. called "the Rogue Money"[36] was made to him by the County. He also received a suit of clothes from the Burgh. The person who discharged this sinister office at the end of the eighteenth century was one William Stewart. The tools of his grim trade required to be kept in repair: in 1749, the Town paid 7/6d. for making a ladder to the gibbet.[37]

A retainer with more cheerful associations was John McIlchonnel, the piper in the Burgh. A boat carpenter, in consideration of his services done and to be done as piper to the Burgh, he was admitted burgess thereof. There was also the Town fiddler called MacPhee.

The Town Herd was a kenspeckle figure. His place of work was the Town Muir which was separated from the parks of the Duke by the Park Dyke. The herd carried off the cattle belonging to the inhabitants to their pasture daily by seven o'clock in the morning from May till the first of September, and after that date at nine o'clock daily. He advertised the inhabitants by sounding a horn in the morning. His charge varied in numbers being 43 cows and 7 horses in 1743; he was also in charge of the town bull, which was

---

36   A popular name for a tax levied in counties and burghs for the expenses of arrest and detention of criminals, authorised by Act of Parliament in 1725, and abolished in 1868.

37   Was the gibbet kept in the Tolbooth? In Glasgow the gibbet was stored in the Cathedral.

sold for £1.14.6d. at Martinmas, 1751. He kept the Park Dyke next to the Common in repair, preventing the cattle from breaking it down and feeding on the sweeter grass on the other side of the fence. For his work, he received five firlots of meal which was worth 17s. sterling and a house, being compensated when he left, for repairs done by him to the fabric. When the house became ruinous in 1754, he was obliged to build another house for himself, for which he received three cows' grass from the Council.

The Town Guard carried out the services of watching and warding within the Burgh. The Watch was made up by citizens, two of which, or their proper substitutes employed by them, were to be on guard from ten at night till six o'clock the next morning. The head quarters of the Town Guard was the Tolbooth, where they were supplied with peats, coals, candles and oil for the lamps by the Town Council. Armed with halberds, the night watchmen came round with heavy tread telling (without anybody asking them) that day was breaking or that there was a house on fire about a mile away.[38]

As generation succeeded generation, these picturesque figures became obsolete one by one. Although the demand for their services gradually withered away and they were unnecessary, the way of life in the Burgh was the poorer for their passing.

One of the chief preoccupations of the Council was finance. The income of the Burgh in the seventeen forties was small. In 1741, the rents of crofts in the Town Muir and Parkhead of Inveraray and the rent of the ferrier's house was £5.4.5⅓d. sterling,[39] and the pasturage of thirty nine cows and four horses on the Town's Common Muir came to £2.19.8⅔d. sterling. The Petty Customs of the Burgh were sett to Archibald Campbell, vintner, for 1741 and 1742 at £33.10s. sterling, and he made what profit he could, but usually suffered loss. In 1745, the ferry and ferryboat of the Burgh were sett in tack to William MacGibbon for payment of eight pounds Scots money of rent.

Each year the sums received by the Town Council became larger in terms of pounds, shillings and pence. This probably indicated that currency was circulating more freely, but not necessar-

38 Norman MacLeod: Caraid nan Gaidheal, O Chuairtear nan Gleann, p. 106, Edinburgh, 1910.

39 ⅓d. sterling represented a certain sum in terms of Scots currency.

ily that there was an increase in real wealth. Despite a yearly rise in charges, the income of the Burgh remained small.

In the period from Michaelmas 1747 to Michaelmas 1749, the income from the usual sources received by the Burgh treasurer was £60.7.-⅔d. sterling. Against this sum certain charges had to be placed. There was payment to the Town herd for keeping up the Park dyke next to the Muir; payment for foddering the Town's bull; payment for rebuilding the gable of the school master's house, for turf and thatch there to and for thatching the school-master's house; there was payment to the Town Officer for tolling the bell; there were missive dues and payment made by the commissioner when he gave in his commission to the Convention of Royal Burghs; there was charity to a distressed seaman; there was the price of drink given to people deepening the mouth of the river; there were payments to men working at the Town well; there was payment for drink at the annual roup of the Petty Customs and Anchorage; and the price of drink at the creation of new bur-gesses.

The balance in the Treasurer's hands at Michaelmas 1749 was £5.5s. The position of Burgh Treasurer was no sinecure and the Magistrates and Town Council in some years had a struggle to make ends meet.

The third Duke was well aware of the indigence of the Burgh and in 1750, he came to its help. For the weil and standing of the Burgh of Inveraray and in order to make up a common good to them for the necessary uses and support of the community, he settled upon them a free annuity of twenty pounds sterling money yearly to be always applied for the common good and profit of the Burgh and for the support and maintenance of the common bur-dens there of and for the preservation and standing of the same. This subvention was of help to the Treasurer and Council for many generations to come.

In these and other weighty concerns, the provosts, magis-trates and councillors spent the early part of the eighteenth cen-tury. There were many signs that change and development were taking place, both in the life of the nation and of the burghs. The Union of Parliaments had made great differences; the old Scots currency was being replaced by sterling; irresponsible brewing and distilling were being made more difficult; the privileges of royal burghs were becoming less exclusive and less advantageous;

communication between one part of the country and another was easier; representation in Parliament was provided for, if not in a very democratic manner. But these indications of change were as nothing compared with the upheaval which was about to take place in the Burgh of Inveraray, of which change intimations in plenty had already been clearly given.

The Eighteenth Century: The Second Part

Great alterations took place in the Burgh of Inveraray because the third Duke of Argyll decided to build a new castle. The old castle raised about 1432 was become ruinous, inconvenient for the accommodation of the Duke and his guests. It was used to house a few old servants and for the storage of halberds for the Town Guard. A residence known as the Pavilion, built in 1720-21, was occupied by His Grace during his autumn visits, but this could be no more than a temporary arrangement.

When the erection of the new castle was taking place, it became obvious that it would be unsuitable to have thatched cottages at the front door; herds of cows, horses, pigs and poultry under the windows; and cargo vessels loading and unloading at the mouth of the river. Plans were, therefore, put in hand to re-erect the Burgh and harbour in a more convenient situation.

The first step was to send a summons of removing to a large number of the citizens including the Provost himself, in 1746. The Magistrates and Town Council did not minute a debate or decision on the project, but Alexander Duncanson, Provost of Inveraray was instructed by the Duke to urge the people of the Town who were His Grace's tacksmen to give in proposals to His Grace about building in the New Town.[40]

In 1750, the concession of pasturage on the Town Muir was reviewed. For many generations, the cows belonging to the burgesses were indulged to pasture on a commonty belonging to the Duke and which made part of his estate. In 1750, the Duke apprised the Magistrates and Town Council of taking the Town Muir or Common into his own hands and enclosing the same within his policy. At the same time as he converted the Muir to other uses and purposes for himself and his family, he allowed the cattle belonging to the inhabitants of the town to pasture on the Farm of

40   Duncan C. MacTavish: Inveraray Papers, p. 52.

34

Auchenbreck. The Provost on behalf of the Town Council thanked the Duke for what had been allowed in the past and at present, and hinted delicately that His Grace might bear in mind the insufficiency of their public funds to answer their exigencies. The annuity of £20 stg. made by disposition for the common good of the Burgh was partly an acknowledgement of this tactful suggestion.

Another centre of public life and work to be affected was the Tolbooth. Much of civic life revolved around the Town House. If there were going to be a new town, there would have to be a new Tolbooth. Like so much else in the old town, the old Tolbooth was become ruinous and was insufficient for the purposes of a Town House, Court House and Prison. (When James of the Glens was tried for the Appin Murder in 1752, the trial was held not in the Court House, but in the Parish Church). The new Town House, variously referred to as the Tolbooth and the Town Hall, was begun on the North Front in 1775. The Architect was John Adam; the type of architecture was Georgian; it was of three storeys and was completed in 1761. It served as a Customs House, a County Court House and a prison. There was a debtors' room which was strengthened with stanchers or stanchions; in the room was a fire, and the vents were swept from time to time. The doors of the prison were re-inforced with iron; some prisoners were fastened with irons and a ponderous key was turned in the lock.

The Magistrates met in the new Tolbooth but retained an interest in the old Tolbooth. In 1758, they let the old Town House for £2 stg. and repaired the fabric from time to time.

The demolition of the old Castle necessitated the removal of the Town's Arms which were stored there. A letter was sent by the Duke of Argyll's chamberlain to the Provost, desiring him to acquaint the Magistrates in His Grace's name, that at their request and at the request of their predecessors in office, he had hitherto accommodated them with a room in the Little Old Tower for holding the arms allowed by law to the Royal Burgh of Inveraray. But as that edifice was to be taken down, His Grace desired that they might in due time, provide some proper and secure place for holding and preserving their arms. This put the Magistrates in difficulty. From time to time, they paid John Allan, armourer, for cleaning the arms, but they had nowhere else to put them. They appointed Bailie James Campbell immediately to wait on His Grace, and to return him their thanks for having hitherto given them a proper place for preserving the arms, and considering the expense they were and must be at in making their harbour suffic- ient, they were not in a condition to build a proper and secure place for preserving the arms. Another concern of the Bailies and Town Council was the Magazine, where the powder was kept in casks, which required to be repaired at intervals.

The harbour at the mouth of the River Aray was affected by the new layout of the Burgh. The harbour was removed, as the Charter of 1648 provided that it could be, to the point called the Gallowfarland, where it is situated at this present time. So early as 1748, £8 stg. was collected from the inhabitants of the Burgh for a Quay. In 1758, James Potter, mason, represented to the Provost of the Burgh concerning the new Quay, that for every cubical foot of the facing there must be paid at the rate of one shilling, stg. for cutting stone in the quarry, shipping, unloading, dressing and building, the Town Council always furnishing the lime or fog. The proposal was laid before the Duke of Agyll and His Grace allowed £30 stg. towards making a pier, the work to be set about with all convenient dispatch. In 1758, the Town Council borrowed £13 stg. for the new quay; William McGibbon, ferrier, bound himself to pay £2 stg. towards the building of the new quay in the Fisherland; and in 1763, Sir Adam Ferguson gave a present of £5 stg. for the same object. No sum, however small, from whatever source, was refused.

The work went on apace: plans were made; stones were quarried and shipped; labourers were employed; rocks were blasted; timber was fetched. But the sea was merciless. In 1760, in 1763 and in 1764, the quay was in need of repair. As the work went on, the Town Council became more ambitious. In 1765, an addition was made to the new quay in height and length at a cost of £26 stg. with which the Magistrates reported themselves satisfied.

The cruel sea continued to undo the work of man. In Decem- ber 1771, the Magistrates and Town Council, having taken into their consideration the present ruinous state of the quay by its having been frequently overflowed by the sea in the repeated viol- ent storms of last harvest, unanimously resolved that the same be forthwith repaired and heightened, particularly on the south-east side to prevent it being overflowed in the same manner in time coming and likewise to make and affix so many cruives as maybe found necessary at the end of the quay to prevent the sands being driven round the same to the west side thereof.

The administrative side of the harbour work early received attention. In May 1752, a table of the Petty Customs and Anchorage of the Burgh of Inveraray was agreed upon by the Magistrates and Town Council.

A ship of 60 tuns and upwards to pay.....................	£0. 3. 6d. stg.
A ship of 40 to 60 tuns......................................	0. 3. 0d.
A ship of 30 to 40 tuns......................................	0.2.6d.
A ship of 20 to 30 tuns......................................	0.2.0d.
A vessel of 12 to 20 tuns...................................	0. 1. 3d.
Any vessel from the size of a fishing boat to 12 tuns	0. 0. 9d.
A fishing boat for a season's fishing	0. 0. 6d.
A vessel that comes upon freight or merchandize for each trip..	0. 0. 4d.

BRIDGE DUES

For each horse, cow or ox passing the river on the bridge from the southward to the northward...........	0. 0. 0⅔d.
For the score of sheep and goats and so in proportion..	0. 0. 3⅓d.

VICTUAL DUES

	Sterling
To the boll of Malt, Bear, Meal, Great Oats, Groats, Wheat, Pease, Potatoes, Salt..............................	0. 0. 1½d.
For every tun of coals imported and measured, the inhabitants to pay a penny per tun for the use of the barrell and strangers to pay 2d. for custom and barrells.. It was inserted in an act of Council that the farmer of the Customs, having a coal barrell, he is to deliver the same to the next farmer, who is to pay for it conform to comprisement.	0. 0. 2d.
For each gallon of aquavitae................................	0. 0. 2d.

For each roll of tobacco, stone of iron, butter cheese or wool... £0. 0. 0½d.

For each barrell or hides of beef, mutton or herring   0. 0. 3d.

For every 100 daills and in proportion for a lesser quantity... 0. 0. 8d.

For every travelling chapman with a horse, passing the river or selling goods in the town................... 0. 0. 2d.

For every hawker that comes to the town to sell goods.. 0. 0. 1d.

For every load of salmon, herring or other fish brought to the town for sale............................... 0. 0. 2d.

For every bulk of mutton.................................... 0. 0. ½d.

It was enacted that all burgesses and inhabitants who bore Scot and lot[41] in the Burgh were to be exempted from the above dues, except as to the black cattle and the dues for the coal barrell and providing always that they were brought to the town upon their sea risque.

On 16th July 1756, the Magistrates having found by the Table of the Town Dues made up on 1st May 1752 that there were several goods imported to this place which had been omitted there, therefore, they ascertained the rates of the several goods which might be henceforth imposed to be as follows:-

Sterling

Each barrel of Ale, beer or porter imported, to pay   £0. 0. 3d.

Each Crate of Glass... 0. 0. 2d.

Each Gross of Bottles.. 0. 0. 2d.

Each hundred weight of sugar............................. 0. 0. 3d.

Cloths brought in for sale, each 20 shilling worth sold.. 0. 0. 1d.

Each pot brought in to be sold............................. 0. 0. ½d.

---

41 Scot and Lot: An old legal phrase embracing all parochial assessments for the poor, the church, lighting, cleansing and watching.

This Table of the Petty Customs and Anchorage was important, because it served as a standard of reference for basic and increased charges in the future.

It was only to be expected that the ferry service would be modified by the impending changes. One of the first intimations of change was the summons of removing directed against William McGibbon, Tide Waiter [42] and Donald McNiccoll, ferrier in 1746. The atmosphere of uncertainty was apparent in 1749, when the Magistrates and Town Council sett the ferryboat, house and garden to William McGibbon, providing always that in case the Duke of Argyll and his successors might at any time think it proper to demolish and take down the house and garden, then the tack would become void and null. That it was becoming less rewarding to provide a ferry service was evident in 1758 when the Magistrates and Town Council did not press William McGibbon for eight punds, Scots, of arrears in consideration of losses sustained by the new road made from this place to the Low Country.

The removal of the Burgh to a new site and the erection of a new inn (now the Argyll Arms) made the Provost, Magistrates and Town Council acutely aware of the unsatisfactory state of the roads. In 1752, they petitioned the Justices of the Peace for the Shire of Argyle, representing that the present road from the Burgh of Inveraray leading to Lorn, was very inconvenient to travellers and often impassable and required to be changed, and proposed that a new road should proceed from the New Inn of Inveraray on the south and west side of the Wintertown and by the west side of Carlunnan Mill till it joined the old road at the next ford on the River Aray.

The building of the new town necessitated a new water supply. The well which served the old town was remote from the new centre of population and other arrangements required to be made. On 26th March, 1774, the Magistrates and Town Council considered that the Burgh was not properly supplied with water and that the water lately introduced by pipes was not only insufficient in time of drought, but of bad quality. Accordingly, they resolved to bring water from the spring well of Bealach an fhuarain by pipes into the Main Street of the New Town, in so far as pipes had not already been laid by the orders of the Duke of Argyll.

---

42   An officer who waits the arrival of vessels to secure the payment of duties.

They resolved further to erect a leaden cistern to contain such a quantity of water as might at all times supply the small run of water issuing from the said spring. The water was made available at the public well of the Burgh, where the servant lasses assembled with their stoups, discoursing the news of the hour. Clothes and linen were tramped and washed at the well and spread beside it to dry. The burgesses paid a water rate known as "well money" which was collected by the Town Officer. To provide this water supply, the Magistrates and Council applied to the collegiate Kirk Session of Glenaray and Inveraray for the loan of a sum not exceeding £100 stg.

The status of a Royal Burgh, the erection of a new quay, the introduction of piped water, all cost money and the Town Council was frequently embarrassed by the lack of it. On 23rd January, 1758, the Provost received a letter from Mr. Campbell of Succoth, the Duke of Argyll's doer, mentioning that in 1755 there was fifty years feu duty due to the Crown by the Burgh amounting to £35.14s. It was thought that Lord Milton, the Lord Justice Clerk who had a long association with Inveraray, could get the Officers of Exchequer to abate their fees and that the whole might be paid with £30 stg. out of the £20 mortified by the Duke of Argyll at the rate of £10 yearly. This was agreed.

There was more grievous vexation in December, 1772, when the Provost received a letter from David Stewart Moncrieff, Esq., covering a Horning at the instance of the Receiver General against the Magistrates of Inveraray for the feu duty payable to the Crown for five years preceding Whit Sunday 1772 which amounted in all with fines and forfeiture to £25 stg. The Horning being already denounced and registrate, the Sheriff by the foresaid letter was directed to levy payment of the foresaid sums.

The Magistrates and Town Council considering the great hardships which the neglect of non-payment of the trifling feu duty brought upon the Burgh and being resolved to avoid any such scrapes in time coming, authorised their treasurer yearly at Whitsunday to pay the said feu duty of ten merks, Scots. And with respect to by-gones, they immediately applied to Mr. James Ferrier, w.s., to prefer a petition in their name to the Rt. Hon. the Barons of Exchequer, offering payment of the five years feu duty and craving that their Honours would remit the foresaid forfeiture, as punctual payment would be made in future.

In 1774, the financial position was becoming increasingly difficult. Year by year, the Magistrates and Town Council sett the ferry, the ferry house and garden, the petty customs and anchorage; they collected the rents of certain houses; they received the fines of newly elected burgesses; they counted, not in vain, upon the Duke's free annuity. But in 1774, the Corporation decided that the public income must be augmented. The Magistrates and Town Council took into their consideration that the annual public revenues of the Burgh would be insufficient to answer necessary expenses incurred. They resolved in terms of an Act of the Parliament of James VI in 1592 and ordained that the whole inhabitants of the Burgh should be assessed, stented and taxed in such sums yearly as the Magistrates and Town Council should judge adequate. These assessments were not to exceed 10s. stg., money for each person of the highest class, nor under 6d. money for every person of the lowest class. Lists were to be made up and given to the Town Officer to collect and levy the respective sums. This official had powers to carry out the distress and sale of the first and readiest goods and effects of those who did not pay. In 1777, the stent masters who implemented this unpopular measure were Duncan Campbell, merchant and David Hutcheson, writer; the Town Officer who enforced it was Duncan MacCall, changekeeper.

The new situation of the Burgh involved the re-erection of the Mercat Cross. But unfortunately, as with the Broadstone [43] in Inverness, the Mercat Cross was lost, although not demolished, as was generally believed. In August, 1776, the Magistrates and Town Council, considering that by the removal of the old town, the Market Cross of the Burgh had been demolished (sic) sometime past and that the site of it now made a part of the Duke of Argyll's policy, and considering it to be necessary that some public place in the New Town should be declared to be the Cross for the purpose of executing legal diligence thereat, and for all other purposes whatsoever, did, therefore, enact that the pillars which supported the front of the Court House should be as they were thereby declared to be the Market Cross of the Burgh accordingly, in all time coming.

The system of transporting goods by horse haulage was practised in the New Town, as in the Old Town, and the horsemen were

---

43   The stone which marked the boundary of the Burgh of Inverness.

allowed to graze their horses on the Muir of Auchenbreck at the rate of 2sh. per head. These men with their horses and conveyances were known as carmen, a car being a cart or waggon, sometimes without wheels, for bringing in peats or hay.

Despite the sincere efforts of the Magistrates and Town Council in 1723 and at other times to keep the old town clean, the general attitude of the inhabitants seems to have been "the clartier the cosier". In 1783, when elected to look after the affairs of the New Town, the Corporation made a resolute effort to enforce sanitation and good order. The Magistrates and Town Council being convened to consider different matters concerning the police of the Burgh and taking into consideration the comfort and benefit accruing to its inhabitants by cleanliness in their habitations and the streets, resolved that the following regulations should take effect:-

Primo: That all and each of the inhabitants shall keep a space of four yards at least in front of their houses and entry to their houses clear of any filth or nastiness whatever; and under no pretence, empty from the ground floors or upper apartments of their houses, dirty water or water pots to the streets or backcourts.

Secundo: That proper midden steads shall be designed and condescended upon in commodious bye-places within the Burgh and announced by public advertisement by the Town Bell; to be open for depositing all dung and cinders between the hours of 7 and 9 o'clock in the morning or after sunset in the evening, and to be carried away by carts for manure.

Tertio: That the indecent practice of trampling and washing clothes and linen at the public well be discharged.

Quarto: That no person or persons other than the Town Officer, Church Officer or School Claviger (keybearer or custodian) or others employed by them, on no pretence whatever, presume to toll or ring the bell at any hour without authority from one or other of the Magistrates.

Quinto: That no householder, servant or other inhabitant of the Burgh presume in future to draw or carry water from the Town Well or other places to their dwellings upon the Lord's Day, especially during the ordinances of divine worship, except a can-or tea-kettle-full between the meetings for worship.

Any person contravening these regulations on conviction for the first offence required to pay 1/6d. for the use of the poor, and for subsequent convictions such sums as the Magistrates might award. If the delinquents were unable to pay, they would be liable to imprisonment for six hours.

This Act like so many other Acts of the Council, was difficult to enforce. Those who did their washing at the Town Well, removed to the cistern and washed their linens there. In 1787, the Magistrates and Town Council took into consideration the small supply of water afforded from Bealach an fhuarain and that the practice of washing linens at the cistern was a great nuisance. They discharged the inhabitants of the Burgh from using the water from the cistern in washing and bleaching their linens and from laying their linens to be bleached in the neighbourhood of the cistern. The Town Officer was authorised to seize upon any such linens.

In 1795, the Act of 1783 required to be renewed. Fever appeared in the Burgh and neighbourhood and the Magistrates considering the means to prevent it from spreading still farther, were of the opinion that the herring fishers, salters and those employed by them in gutting and curing fish did, by neglecting to throw all the rubbish and refuse from their boats within the flood-mark, occasion a stink and putrefaction in the air which was very injurious to the health of the inhabitants and therefore, they renewed the Act of Council of 8th January, 1783.

During the eighteenth century, the Provost, Magistrates and Town Council frequently gave the freedom of the Burgh to various people. For instance, at Inveraray, the fourth day of July 1757, William Douglas, younger in Inveraray, was by the unanimous advice and consent of the Provost, Bailies, Dean of Guild and Common Council of the Burgh of Inveraray received, created and admitted Burgess, Freeman and Guild Brother thereof with power to him to bruik and enjoy the Privileges, Liberties and Immunities belonging to a Burgess, Freeman and Guild Brother of the same, and for the love, favour and affection the said Magistrates and Council have for and bear to the said William Douglas, who gave his burgess oath as use is. All sorts of people received this honour: packmen, travelling chapmen, soldiers, master mariners, the cashier to the Thistle Bank in Glasgow,[44] a merchant in Venice,

---

44   The Thistle Bank founded in 1761, with the Glasgow and Ship Bank going back to 1750, was acquired by the Glasgow Union Banking Company 1836-1849. As a result of mergers, this company became the Union Bank of Scotland, which in its turn was acquired by the Bank of Scotland in 1952. (The Third Statistical Account: The City of Glasgow, p. 394).

Senators of the College of Justice, Simon Fraser, Master of Lovat; Lord Lovat's eldest son was made a burgess in 1750, the year in which he received a full and free pardon from the Government. In 1758, John Wilkes, of whose part in the obscene orgies of the "Medmenham Monks", the people of Inveraray would know nothing, was elected, and in 1766, seven years before the famous Tour, it was the turn of James Boswell, yr. of Auchenleck, Esq., Advocate. These and many other men, equally interesting but too numerous to distinguish, became freemen of the Burgh.

Such occasions were expensive for the Magistrates and Town Council. While the Burgess fine was 8/4d. stg., the account of liquors furnished by the vintner and paid by the Burgh Treasurer from 1st September 1750 to Michaelmas 1750 at making a number of burgesses was £17.10.5d. stg.

The Corporation had powers to regulate the quality and sale of bread. These regulations were conceived in the interests of the bread consumers and were intended to secure fair dealing on the part of bread vendors. The price of bread was determined by adding a certain sum to the price of every quarter of flour, to cover the baker's expenses and profit; and for the sum so arrived at, the tradesmen were required to bake and sell their loaves. The Magistrates of Inveraray used the Assize of Bread at Glasgow as their norm. On 30th January, 1783, the Assize of Bread at Glasgow determined the price of the Quartern Loaf Wheaten weighing 1 lib. 5 oz. 8 drs. to be 8¾d. On 3rd February 1783, the Assize of Bread for Inveraray fixed the price of the Quartern Loaf Wheaten of 1 lib. 5 oz. 8 drs. at 10̄d. The Magistrates appointed the bakers within the Burgh to make their bread agreeable to the last assize and a reasonable allowance was considered as having been made for the risk and expense of bringing the flour to Inveraray. Any complaint against the bakers in quantity and quality was said to be inexcusable. An extract of the assize was given to each baker. The Assize was carried out at intervals of four months, the system continuing till 1836.

In the latter part of the eighteenth century, the health of the inhabitants was cared for by Mr. Alexander Stewart, Surgeon of the Burgh. Without doubt, there were gardeners who knew the qualities of physic herbs and women who were sage in plant lore. Midwifery was practised entirely by women. But Mr. Alexander Stewart was Surgeon of the Burgh. The degree of his skill and whether he had studied under one of the Gregorys in King's College, Aberdeen, is not known. The Magistrates and Town Council did not remunerate him out of the burghal revenues, but they permitted him as a freeman of the burgh to practise within the bounds. At length, in February, 1786, Mr. Stewart wrote to the Provost, demitting his charge on account of his valetudinary state of health.

Mr. Robert Ochiltree, surgeon of the late 71st Regiment of Foot [45] being present in the Town Council, represented that he and Mr. Alexander Campbell, surgeon, had joined in company and offered their united services to the Burgh as surgeons. The Magistrates approved, provided His Grace gave his approbation. The appointments were confirmed.

Towards the end of the eighteenth century, there began to blow winds of change which were to increase in force during the next fifty years. In 1785 the Provost received a letter from James Hunter Blair, Preses of the Committee of the Convention of Burghs signifying that there was an application intended to be made to Parliament by certain discontented people in different Burghs in Scotland to bring about a total alteration of the constitution of the Royal Burghs in Scotland, and requesting that the Magistrates and Council of the Burgh of Inveraray should write their Member of Parliament for opposing any bill presented for the above purpose. The Magistrates and Town Council being of the opinion that any such attempt would be attended with bad consequences, wrote to Sir Archibald Edmonstone, their present member, in these terms. Three years later, in 1788, the Magistrates and Town Council gave further consideration to a copy of a bill intituled "A Bill for regulating the Internal Government of the Royal Burghs in Scotland", along with a letter from the Preses of the Convention of Royal Burghs. They were satisfied that the Bill would not only be subversive of the ancient constitution of the Royal Burghs in Scotland, but would also open a wide field to venality and dissipation and be productive of universal anarchy and confusion in the election of Magistrates and Council, as well as in the internal government of the Royal Burghs in Scotland and they were deeply impressed with a sense of the evil and dangerous

---

45   The 71st (Highland) Regiment of Foot, 1775-1783; also Fraser's Highlanders (Chiefly engaged in the American Rebellion and afterwards disbanded). (Farmer: Regimental Records)

consequences of this measure.

Admidst these forebodings, the Magistrates and Town Council publicly demonstrated their loyalty to those in authority, both local and national. In 1786, '87 and '88, they bought candles to illuminate the Town House on Lord Lorne's birth night and purchased fuel for a bonfire. In 1788 they celebrated a temporary recovery in King George's health, which was deteriorating rapidly, by giving a ball and hiring a musician to play for the occasion. In 1792, the corporation having considered His Majesty's proclamation issued for the prevention of riots and the suppression of seditious writings, sent an address of loyalty to His Majesty via the Honourable Col. Chas. Stewart, their representative in Parliament. In 1795 the Magistrates and Town Council presented an address to His Majesty by Mr. John Campbell, M.P. for the Burgh, expressing their horror and just indignation at the late most daring insult - an atrocious and violent outrage - offered to His Majesty's sacred person.[46]

War and rumours of war with the French aroused the patriotism of the burgesses. In 1793, the Magistrates and Town Council considering that H.M. service required a speedy supply of seamen to man the Fleet, offered a reward of two guineas over and above H.M. Bounty to every able seaman, and one guinea to every ordinary seaman belonging to the Port or Parish of Inveraray, who should appear in the Council Chamber of Inveraray and voluntarily enter himself to serve in the Royal Navy. This offer was advertised in the Edinburgh Courant, the Caledonian Mercury and the Glasgow Courier and Advertiser.

Two years later, it was the turn of the Army. In 1795, the Magistrates and Town Council from their desire of promoting H.M. service and from their particular attachment to Colonel Henry Mordaunt Clavering, commanding the 2nd Battalion of the Argylshire Regiment of Fencibles, offered a bounty of two guineas over and above all other bounties, to each of the first twenty

46 Stones were thrown at His Majesty's carriage, breaking one of the door glasses, as the carriage was going to the House of Lords with His Majesty in it. A number of people were hissing and hooting and frequently repeating the words "No war! Down with George!" (The Glasgow Courier, 5th November, 1795)

47 The First Battalion was raised by the Duke of Argyll in 1793. The Second Battalion was embodied in 1795.

men, natives of Argyleshire, who should enlist with the 2nd Battalion of the Argyleshire Fencibles. This offer was intimated in the same papers as in 1793.

In 1796, having considered the Act for raising a certain number of men in Royal Burghs for H.M.'s Navy and Army, the Magistrates and Town Council appointed a committee for assessing the heritors and inhabitants within the Burgh of Inveraray in the sum of £75 stg., for the bounty to be paid to three men assessed on this Burgh.

Next year, 1797, the difficult question of billeting had to be considered, since the Argyleshire Regiment of Fencibles and the Argyleshire Volunteers were to be quartered in Inveraray.[48] The Magistrates and Town Council declared that persons first liable to the burden of quartering soldiers were innkeepers, vintners and changekeepers; and after these had been exhausted, distillers, brewers, butchers, bakers, grocers, hucksters; and after these were exhausted, the inhabitants at large. With a fine sense of duty and equality of sacrifice, the Magistrates exempted themselves for the time being and authorized the Billetmaster to quarter soldiers in the Burgh accordingly.

In these disquieting circumstances, the eighteenth century drew to a close. There was a feeling that the old landmarks were being removed; that there was a spirit of unrest abroad; there were wars and rumours of wars; and those who were old were not altogether sorry that they were coming to the end of their natural span, because none could tell what alarming changes the new century might bring.

The Nineteenth Century

The men and women of the late eighteenth and early nineteenth centuries lived in troubled times, and it could not be but that burghal administration would be affected by the Napoleonic Wars. The effects of this great conflict were felt in small everyday occurrences. In 1804, James Stewart, Burgh Treasurer, resigned because he had lately received a commission in the Army and was ordered to join his regiment. During the latter part of the French Wars, that is from 1808 to 1815, local militia were raised by ballot

48 The Correspondence of Lieutenant General Campbell of Kintarbert, 1762-1837. The Kintyre Antiquarian Society.

and served as a defensive force. Some companies of the 1st Regiment of the Argyllshire Local Militia were Stationed at Inveraray and the Treasurer of the Burgh, Duncan Munro required to make various payments into and out of the Burgh funds on that account. Between 1st March and 29th September, 1813, he received £39.3s. in billet money for the 1st A.L.M. and in the same period he paid board at the rate of 1s. per man to the 1st. A.L.M. in lieu of billet money; 10s. to one Duncan Campbell for laying straw in the barrack beds and mess rooms; and £4.5s. for the use of cooking vessels for the regiment. At length the wars came to an end and men and women gave their undivided attention to the more constructive works of peace.

Partly because the old world had passed away and a new age had been born, the nineteenth century became a time of reform and reconstruction. The happy-go-lucky administration of the burghs was regularised and standardised by Acts of Parliament, and old civic buildings were replaced by more adequate structures.

One of the first public buildings to be in need of attention was the Town House. In 1757, there was built for the Burgh a new Tolbooth in line with the Great Inn on the water front. Scarcely fifty years had passed before dissatisfaction was felt with these premises. In March 1805, the Magistrates and Council took into their consideration the "unsufficient state of the Tolbooth of Inveraray". The usual prison for the confinement of persons for civil debts was a small apartment on the ground floor of the Town House; there was no accommodation for female prisoners; attempts to rescue prisoners were made by their friends, particularly in the case of one notorious prisoner Archibald Gray, accused of house-breaking; prisoners did escape from the Tolbooth, and rewards had to be advertised and paid for their recapture.

In 1805, the Town Council appointed the Magistrates as a committee to prepare a memorial for the next general meeting of the Commissioners of Supply of the County. The Committee represented the insufficient state of the prison and prayed the meeting to take the same into consideration. For some years, the Town House continued to prove inadequate for the courts, inconvenient for the judges and insecure for the prisoners. At length, as a result of the activities of the Commissioners of Supply, an Act of Parliament (54 George III c. 102) was passed for providing a new jail and court house in the Burgh of Inveraray, and the construction of a new court house began in 1816.

On 17th February, 1819, the Town Council assessed the citizens of the Burgh for the purpose of defraying the new gaol and county house. Stentmasters were appointed, who imposed an assessment as rateably as possible with reference to the circumstances of the inhabitants. The sum of £39 was gathered by the collectors.

In 1820, the old Tolbooth beside the Great Inn was transferred to His Grace and the damp unhealthy cells were swept away. The new Court House with its back to the sea, facing the Parish Church in Church Square, was opened and more adequate provision was made for the High Court on circuit, the Sheriff Court, the Justice of the Peace Assizes, the Town Council and the Town Clerk's office. There was erected also a two storey gaol, which offered more suitable accommodation than the old Tolbooth in 1816, but still left much to be desired.

When the great storm of the Napoleonic Wars blew itself out at length, it left behind, as all such wars do, a ground swell which took long to subside. The spirit of unrest noted by the Magistrates of Inveraray in 1785 and 1788 was become much more vociferous. 1820 was the critical year. Placards posted in the cities summoned all labourers and artisans to desist from work on and after the 1st of April, till they were put in possession of the rights that "distinguish the freeman from the slave". The spirit of defiance and disloyalty was made more acute when H.M. George IV induced his ministers to set on foot divorce proceedings in which Queen Caroline would be tried for adultery. In Inveraray, as in many other towns, the Provost, Magistrates and Councillors espoused the cause of the King, while the artisans and labourers were enthusiastic in support of the Queen. On 10th November, 1820, the Bill designed to incriminate the Queen was dropped. This was a triumph for the supporters of the Princess and there was great excitement and unrest.

Ill-omened placards appeared in various parts of the Burgh of Inveraray and there was reason to fear that there might be a disloyal demonstration. The Provost, John Campbell, convened a meeting of the Magistrates and Town Council and produced some copies of the advertisements which had been displayed. The Council resolved to use their utmost endeavours to protect the inhabitants in their persons and properties and decided that a proclamation of the following tenor be posted up in different parts of the Burgh and read by the Town Crier to the inhabitants:-

"Some idle and evil disposed persons having posted up placards in various parts of the Burgh, desiring the inhabitants to illuminate their houses this evening, and the Magistrates being apprehensive that the attempt thus made, if not prevented, may be attended with the same mischievous effects which have lately been produced in other places by similar attempts, do hereby caution and require the well-disposed inhabitants not only to refrain from encouraging these ill-disposed persons or complying with the above requisition, but also to give the public authorities all the aid in their power to preserve the peace and quietness within the Burgh which is thus attempted to be disturbed and to protect the property of the inhabitants from injury. The practice of going about with drums and fifes is strictly prohibited.

"Parents and Masters and Mistresses of families are particularly required to keep their children and servants within doors and the Magistrates and Sheriff are resolved to inflict exemplary punishment on all who are found transgressing this requisition and proclamation".

Having issued this notice, the councillors made every exertion individually to maintain order. Thirty constables were appointed, sworn in and posted in various parts of the Town to preserve the peace of the Burgh. The drums which had been used on various occasions without authority, and by which the inhabitants had been alarmed and encouragement given to assemblies of idle ill-disposed persons, were ordered in and locked up in the Town House or Jail. Sergeant Donald Munro, a veteran of the Peninsular War, was appointed one of the ordinary Town Officers, and having taken the oath de fidele, he was put in charge of the forces of law and order. The situation was kept under control, but strong undercurrents of discontent had been revealed and this wide spread feeling would require to be appeased in the future.

Undoubtedly, there was need for reform both in the system of parliamentary election and in the method of burghal elections. At national level the royal burgh of Inveraray, along with four other royal burghs, Ayr, Irvine, Rothesay and Campbelltown formed a district and that district had the right of returning one of fifteen members of parliament who represented the burghs of Scotland.

When an election was due, the Magistrates and Town Council chose a delegate, usually the Provost, who met with delegates from the other royal burghs of the district, and these delegates chose a member of parliament. Such an election did not represent the choice of the burgesses and was the occasion of much discontent, although in 1830, the member for the Ayr Burghs, the Rt. Hon. Thomas Francis Kennedy of Dunure was an admirable man and was himself in favour of electoral reform.

As a result of public opinion which had been growing for forty years but was let during the French Revolution and the French Wars, the Scottish Reform Bill received the royal assent on July 17, 1832. The right to vote in the election of a member of parliament was given to the £10 householders in royal burghs. At this time, there were 63 persons resident within the parliamentary bounds of the Burgh of Inveraray, whose rents in property of tenantry amounted to £10 or upwards, of whom 31 were burgesses and 32 were not. This parliamentary reform, although not so far-reaching as the Whigs had hoped for, was never-the-less a great improvement on the election of a member of parliament by the voices of five delegates from as many royal burghs.

At local level also, there was clamant need for reform. According to an Act in the reign of James III, in which reign Inveraray had been erected to be a Burgh of Barony, the retiring Town Council had power to elect its successor; "which in practice meant that they all elected themselves".[49]

This system deprived the burgesses of the right of electing their representatives in the Town Council. This was the procedure in Inveraray until 1833: the old council annually chose the new council. The number of councillors ranged from 10 to 13 and was composed almost invariably of the same individuals.[50] This state of affairs caused discontent and contributed to contemporary unrest. In 1833, the Royal Burghs (Scotland) Act gave to burgesses the right of electing their own Town Council. This measure, long desired in Inveraray as in other burghs, quickened a sense of civic responsibility and obviated the possibility of municipal abuse.

These two reforms, the Burgh Reform Act and the extension of the Parliamentary franchise brought the Burgh of Inveraray

49   Lord-Cockburn: Memorials of His Time, Edinburgh 1946, p. 192.

50   Local Reports on Municipal Corporations in Scotland: Inveraray, 1836.

more closely into contact with the House of Commons and caused its membership of the Convention of Burghs to be less important than before.[51]

In the same year, 1833, another important bill, having far-reaching consequences for royal burghs such as Inveraray, became law. The statute intituled an Act to establish a System of Police[52] permitted the inhabitants of royal burghs to adopt a "police system" (covering watching, lighting, paving, cleansing and water supply), and so set up "police burghs." In consequence, authority was entrusted to police magistrates and police commissioners, who might or might not be the same as the bailies and councillors, and the possibility of dual administration existed.

The Magistrates and Town Council adopted the provisions of this statute, in so far as they concerned the water supply, thereby incurring an expense of fifteen shillings,[53] but in other matters they continued to act under the general powers conferred on them by the charter of erection.

There were three results of this decision: one was that the water supply of the burgh was renovated; the second was that the records of the Burgh of Inveraray were described as the Minute Books of the Police Commissioners; the third was that the Parliamentary Municipal and Police Burgh Boundary was more restricted than the boundary of the Royal Burgh.

The renovation of the Burgh water supply was long overdue: the supply had been unsatisfactory for many years. In 1803, the cistern within the Burgh from which the inhabitants were supplied was in a bad state. A public well, cistern and water pipe were constructed at a cost to the Burgh of £14.[54] In 1808, the well and cistern were repaired and new water pipes were laid at a cost of £51. In 1818, there was an outbreak of typhoid in Inveraray. After the Act of 1833, it was resolved unanimously at a public meeting to bring water into the Burgh for the general use of the inhabitants. In November, 1833, all tenants, occupiers and possessors of property within the bounds, valued at two pounds sterling or upwards

51 R.C.B.S., Vol. V.

52 (3 and 4, Will. IV, C.46).

53 Parliamentary Papers, Session 1847, Vol. lvii, p. 393.

54 Municipal Corporations in Scotland, Inveraray, 1836.

of yearly rent, were assessed in the sum of one shilling in the pound of all such premises to be immediately collected and continued annually.

In December, 1833, the Provost received letters from H.G. the Duke of Argyll on the subject of bringing in water from the valley of Eas a chosain Glen to the Burgh, of which scheme, His Grace approved and granted his concurrence.

The construction of the new water supply went on during 1834; it was finished in 1835; and in November of that year Robert Napier undertook to keep the pipes and cistern of the Burgh Water Works in a proper clean state, that the wells may be always pure, for the sum of four pounds yearly.[55]

In December, 1835, John Reid, architect at Roseneath, went with the Provost and Commissioners of Police to the fountain head at Eas a chosain. He stated that the pipes were satisfactory, but that the public wells at the Newton, Crosshouse and at the end of the Main Street appeared to be a good deal out of order.[56]

At this time, some citizens had pipes by which the water was led into their premises. They were warned that the water would be cut off, if they failed to pay their assessment. While the heavy initial outlay of constructing the water supply was met by loans which had to be repaid out of income, the annual cost of keeping the wells and waterpipes in repair was defrayed from the proceeds of the burgh manure.

In 1840, the supply of water for Bealach an fhuarain well was somewhat diminished, when heavy blasting took place in the quarries in the vicinity.

Meanwhile, the two storey gaol which had been erected in 1820 was becoming an embarrassment. There was a Debtors' Gaol and a Criminal Gaol. The Debtors' Gaol consisted of five apartments, in which on 27th September, 1833, there were eight individuals confined for debts, varying in amount from £2.10s. to £300. The Criminal Gaol consisted of eight cells, besides a large room or hall. In 1833, four cells were occupied by ten prisoners, three of whom had been sentenced for crimes to different periods of imprisonment, and seven of whom had been sentenced for offences against the excise laws. The prisoners were locked up in the

55   Minute Book, Police Commissioners, No. 1, 1833-1949.

56   Ibid.

cells during the night, but through the day the cells were left open and the prisoners assembled in the hall.

There were also five lunatics in confinement, one of whom had been a constant inmate since 1826. They occupied four cells. Night and day their cries disturbed the inhabitants of the Burgh in the vicinity of the gaol and it was impossible to give these poor creatures the attention which humanity demanded.

The expenses involved in this institution posed very serious financial problems, for the Magistrates and Town Council were under an obligation to aliment the prisoners. The sum of £65 was estimated as the gross average annual cost for alimenting prisoners after conviction. Of this amount, the Burgh paid an average of £16.8s. and the remainder was paid by the County. But at this time (1833), the County was not under a legal obligation to make this payment and might refuse to do so. The Burgh was also exposed to a constant contingent liability of indefinite amount in case of the escape of persons imprisoned for debt. As debtors did attempt to escape from time to time, the Magistrates were far from easy about the situation and were well aware that the funds of the community would be insufficient to meet possible expenses.[57]

The Town Council was in part relieved of its responsibility for the prison by the Prisons (Scotland) Act, 1839 on the authority of which a Board for the County of Argyll was set up, which managed the prison of Inveraray.

A more cheerful note was introduced into the life of the Burgh, when Queen Victoria visited Inveraray for the first time in 1847. The fishing boats were neatly and newly painted alike and each bore a little pink ensign. Addresses were presented from the County and from Inveraray, as well as the Freedom of the Burgh, in a massive chased silver box, through Earl Grey to Prince Albert. The Queen was evidently highly gratified with her reception.[58]

In the eighteenth century, there had been surgeons to the Burgh of Inveraray and by the middle of the nineteenth century, this service was defined by statute. The Poor Law (Scotland) Act, 1845 made poor law medical services a matter of statutory obligation. The local authority (at that time the Parochial Board) was

57 Parliamentary Papers: Reports, Commissioners (2), Corporation (Scotland) 1836 Inveraray, p. 183.

58 The Illustrated London News, 28.8.1847, p. 133.

required to provide for "medicines, medical attendance, nutritious diet, cordials and clothing for the poor" in addition to appointing a medical man. It was made a condition of the participation of a parish in the annual Parliamentary grant in aid of medical relief in Scotland that a medical officer should "punctually attend upon and prescribe for all poor persons requiring medical or surgical assistance within the parish".

In 1853, Doctor F. R. MacDonald was appointed Medical Officer for the Burgh of Inveraray and Poor Law Officer for the Parish.[59] The Town Council also paid for the services of a nurse. As a result of an outbreak of Typhus Fever in Inveraray, the Council paid the travelling expenses and lodgings of Mrs. MacRae, nurse, when she came to help during the epidemic.

An advance in medical services was made when the Lunacy (Scotland) Act, the lunatics' Magna Charta in Scotland, was passed in August 1857. For the purpose of providing asylums for the care of pauper lunatics, Scotland was divided into districts: the district in which Inveraray was located extended to the banks of the Water of Leven and included at that time the Isle of Arran. For this area a District Board was appointed. In 1862-63, there was erected in Lochgilphead a lunatic asylum two storeys high and containing upwards of one hundred apartments. The lunatics confined in the Inveraray gaol were transferred to this asylum and it became easier to give them the medical care which their condition required. Thereafter, a yearly assessment was laid on the inhabitants of the Burgh of Inveraray to assist in maintaining the asylum at Lochgilphead.

The position of the Burgh with regard to the Prison in Inveraray was not quite so satisfactory. In 1860 under the Prisons (Scotland) Act, the General Board of Directors of Prisons in Scotland, along with the County Board, was abolished and there was uncertainty as to what body was responsible for the supervision of Inveraray Prison. But whatever body was responsible, the prison must be maintained and so an assessment was laid on the inhabitants of the Burgh of Inveraray for the support of the general and

---

59 Eventually he became private secretary to George, eighth Duke of Argyll and private medical adviser to the Castle. Doctor MacDonald, a direct descendant of the MacIans of Glencoe, spent more than forty years ministering to Clan Campbell. He died at Inveraray in 1904 and was buried in Cilmalieu.

local prisons at the rate of one halfpenny per pound on the annual rental of property.

The Act of 1833 setting up police burghs continued to have far-reaching effects. One result was that general laws as to sanitation were introduced into burghal areas. Authority was given for the removal of nuisances and there was an Inspector of Nuisances in Inveraray. In 1866, this official reported that a number of parties kept pigs in the backyards of the Burgh. In September of the same year, he reported further that the parties keeping pigs had refused to remove them although required to do so. The Town Council attempted to take legal measures against these recalcitrant pig-keepers, but abandoned its action on the advice of Sheriff Graham.

Another provision of the Burgh Police Act gave the commissioners within Royal Burghs powers in regard to lighting. There had been public lighting in Inveraray since 1754, when the Town Council required of the Town Officer that he duly and orderly light the lamps when necessary. But now the arrangement became part of a general practice in all Scottish Burghs. In Inveraray there was an enterprise known as the Inveraray Gas Light Company whose premises were between the Cross Houses and the Newton and whose activities were directed by a Committee of Management. This was a private company and its service was not always infallible. In December, 1866, the Burgh of Inveraray was thrown into total darkness by a failure in the gas supply, the stock of coals at the gaswork having been allowed to run out. In November, 1867, an agreement was reached between the Committee of Management of the Inveraray Gas Light Company and the Council of the Burgh. It was agreed that as regards the Town and Quay lamps, the Town Council should pay to the Gas Company £2 for each Quay Lamp and 10 shillings for each street lamp, for the year. The Quay Lamps were to be lighted all the year round from sunset to sunrise, and the street lamps were to be lighted for nine months, from 1st August to 1st May, and that from sunset to eleven o'clock at night, except that for nine nights each month during moonlight, they should not be lighted at all. The Provost and Councillors directed the Town Officer to light the lamps at the following places through the town: the porch at the Argyll Hotel; the corner of the Chamber-

60   Town Council Records, 1865-1881.

lain's House; the Post Office; the Ferry House; Mr. Crombie's Land; the Church Corner; the Temperance Hotel; Ark Lane; the Dyke between the Smithy and the Newton; and several other places.

Despite these business-like arrangements, the lighting of the Burgh was not always dependable and on many a winter night the citizens had to make their way home in the darkness, splashing through puddles, stumbling over the gas tobies which projected above the level of the street, and anathematizing the Gas Light Company. The Company, however, continued to shed a kindly, if uncertain, light on the town for a long time to come, holding its Annual General Meeting in the month of June, and in some years, as in 1876, declaring a dividend at the rate of five per cent.

The Magistrates and Town Council sought to ensure not only that the Burgh be lighted in winter but also that the proprieties be observed in summer. As visitors became more numerous, some of them followed the new fashion of sea-bathing and disported themselves in the loch between the Town and the River Aray. In June 1866, in view of the opening of a new season, the Town Council instructed its clerk to put up notices requesting parties not to bathe in the bay between the Argyll Hotel and the New Bridge, and to intimate to the police constable that he should prevent any parties he might see from doing so and also to send the Bell through the Town with intimation to that effect.[61]

Two problems which were with the Magistrates and Councillors from generation to generation were the pier with the breast wall and the prison.

Of the pier, Doctor Paul Fraser had written unkindly in 1792, "the quay scarcely deserves that name". In 1798, the General Convention of Royal Burghs granted £200 stg. to the Burgh of Inveraray for heightening and repairing the quay. The Provost wrote to the Duke of Hamilton requesting liberty to quarry stones in the quarries opened in the Isle of Arran by the Crinan Canal Company. The Duke of Argyll offered the sum of £100 stg. The committee appointed by the Town Council sought subscriptions in seaports of the neighbourhood and among fishermen. The Magistrates and Councillors imposed a freedom fine of three guineas

---

61   This fashion spread to the neighbouring village of Furnace, where some caustic remarks from the ferryman about square sterns, clipper bows and keel bottoms effectually discouraged the offenders.

upon unfree persons setting up in the mercantile line of business. They also petitioned the Commissioners of Supply for assistance. Mr. John Campbell, M.P. for the Burgh, gave £50. In 1805, the Magistrates remitted £681 to the Ship Bank in Glasgow, but the work was to cost £900. The mason who undertook to build the pier was William Johns[62] He obtained stones in the old flag quarry in the Innkeeper Park, from the quarry at Bealach an fhuarain and from the quarry at Dalchenna. The work went on slowly and the money was raised with difficulty.

In 1836, it was the breast wall which was in ruins. In 1864, men were building and extending the breast wall at the Cross Houses and in 1866 the breast wall was being extended from opposite the Cross Houses to the Gaol. In November 1866, the Duke of Argyll, aware of the difficulties and expenses, gave a donation of £100 for the completion of the work.

The breast wall having been extended, the pier received much needed attention. Not only was it in need of repair because of damage wrought by winter gales, but it was inadequate on account of the increasingly large steamers of deep draft used in the tourist trade. Action became necessary when it was reported that a new steamer to be named ''The Lord of the Isles'' was being built by Messrs. D. & W. Henderson, Partick, and that she was to occupy the Inveraray Station.

In January, 1877, the Town Council approved plans for an extension to the pier. The new part was to be 60 feet out from the end of the stone pier; it was to be T-shaped, the cross part of the T was to be 80 feet long by 26 feet wide, and there would be 19 feet of water even at low tide. The work was begun in March 1877 and the new pier was formally opened on 5th June. On Saturday, 30th June, ''the Lord of the Isles'' having on board a large number of the Glasgow shareholders and friends, arrived at Inveraray and made fast to the pier.

The other perennial pre-occupation of the Magistrates and Town Council was the prison. The General Board of Directors of Prisons in Scotland, and the Board for the County of Argyll, set up in 1839, was abolished in 1860, and there was uncertainty as to what body was responsible for the supervision of Inveraray Prison.

62   Tradition relates that his son was serving aboard the British frigate Shannon during her historic engagement with the American frigate Chesapeake on 1st June, 1813.

In 1877, there was accommodation for 12 male criminals and 9 female criminals in the ordinary cells at Inveraray. There were sleeping cells and day rooms for 3 debtors. The total ordinary expenditure of the prison, including the salaries of all the officers for the year 1876 was £280.2s.5d. The average annual cost of a prisoner without allowing for the earnings of his labour was £46.13s.8d. in 1876. The average annual net profit on each prisoner's labour was £1.16s.8d. The average annual cost per prisoner, after deducting the net profit on his earnings was £44.17s. The average weekly cost of his food was 2/3½d. The gaolers were veterans of the Crimean War and of the Indian Mutiny.

In 1877, the Prisons (Scotland) Act introduced new methods of looking after local prisons. The Secretary of State directed the Commissioners of Supply of the County of Argyll to appoint Visiting Committees for the Prisons of Inveraray, Campbelltown and Tobermory, and on 4th May 1878 a Visiting Committee of six gentlemen with Sir George Home, Bart., Sheriff-substitute as chairman, was appointed to look after and report upon the prison at Inveraray. On Monday 13th May, 1878 the members of the Committee inspected the prison and found everything to their entire satisfaction. Whether everything was to the entire satisfaction of the prisoners, we shall never know.

An amenity for which the Council of the Burgh accepted responsibility was the Washing Green. The women used to wash the clothes in stone troughs,[63] in a wash house near Crombie's Land. There was usually a big summer washing when all the best of the sheets and napery, what had been used in the course of the winter, were washed. The wives of the burgesses sent a servant girl along with the town washerwoman. They started work before the break of day and having washed the clothes, carried them through a gate in the wall at the Cross Houses and spread them out on the washing green[64] The women worked till evening when they gathered up the clothes and took them home. In August 1865, a wire fence was put round the washing green at a cost of £11.

The Burgh Water supply was in need of attention in 1876. New pipes were laid between the main tank and the fountain-head

63   c.f. Homer: Iliad, XXII p. 153 "wide and beautiful stand the troughs of stone..." etc.

64   Where the Argyll Court Houses now stand.

at Eas a chosain and when the water was turned on in February 1877, all the connections were found to be water-tight. The water supply was augmented in 1893, when the Town Council authorised the Clerk of Works to lay a pipe from the source of the Allt an Aluinn water supply to the Town.

The year 1877 was made memorable by a disastrous event at the Castle. At 4 a.m. on 12th October, a fisherman saw that Inveraray Castle was on fire.[65] Immediate assistance was rendered by the inhabitants of the Burgh who turned out en masse. There was no loss of life. but 200 flint lock muskets arranged in the Hall, which had been the weapons of the Argyllshire Fencibles at the Battle of Culloden, were consumed, as were the well-worn colours of the 91st Highlanders, in the custody of the Duke of Argyll.

Following upon the renovation of the water supply, provision was made for the more efficient removal and disposal of sewage. On 3rd March, 1878, the Town Council decided to make a main drain and to lay sewage pipes along the Front Street from the Fisherland Burn to below low water mark, all the way to the pier. An offer to do the work for £164.10s. was accepted and the operation was completed before the Tourist Season began.

Toward the end of the nineteenth century, the weights and measures used in Inveraray, as in all other burghs, were regularised and standardised. Until 1878, old local and customary denominations of weights and measures were still found to be in use, although in some cases their use had been prohibited by law. Inveraray Town Council possessed an Imperial Standard Bushel, Argyllshire; an Imperial Standard Half Bushel, Argyllshire; and an Imperial Standard Peck, Argyllshire. These measures which were cylindrical in shape, were made by Bate, London before 1824, after which date the peck measure ceased to have legal sanction. Between 1878 and 1893, several Weights and Measures Acts were passed which defined the position. The Magistrates and Town Council, Inveraray, appointed an inspector who verified the weights and measures in use for trade. But even after these Acts were in force, local usages died hard, so powerful was custom with the people.

The Provost, Magistrates and Councillors were required to

65   A hundred' years later, on 5th November, 1975, a fire gutted two floors of Inveraray Castle. Estimates put the damage at £2m - two of the 150 paintings destroyed were worth £800,000.

represent the Burgh on those melancholy occasions from which no family, however distinguished, is exempt. On Saturday 8th June, 1878, the Magistrates of Inveraray and 60 men of the 2nd Argyll-shire Highland Rifle Volunteers attended the funeral at Kilmun of Elizabeth Georgina, Duchess of Argyll, wife of George Douglas, 8th Duke of Argyll. Among the mourners was the Rt. Hon. William Ewart Gladstone.

To preside over the Burgh Court was one of the principal duties of the Magistrates. When the Town became a Royal Burgh in 1648, the Provost and Bailies were given the power of holding burgh courts, of appointing their own court days, clerks, officers and other necessary members of court, and this obligation they faithfully discharged in each generation. After the Reform Bill, 1832, the Magistrates were the Provost and two bailies; they acted as Magistrates on alternate days and possessed both civil and criminal jurisdiction. For example, at the Burgh Court on 10th January 1879, Provost Macfarlan and Bailie Rose were on the Bench. John Macguillan, a hawker, and three others were placed at the Bar on a charge of a breach of the public peace. Macguillan pleaded guilty and was fined ten shillings with the alternative of five days imprisonment. The others were discharged.

During the greater part of the nineteenth century, Inveraray along with Ayr, Irvine, Campbelltown and Oban (in 1861) was represented in Parliament by the Member for the Western Burghs. In 1877, the Member for Ayr and the West Highland Burghs was Sir William Cunninghame, Bart., Conservative, who visited and addressed his constituents each year in January or February. The member met with the electors and inhabitants of the Burgh of Inveraray in the Court Room. In 1878, Sir William informed the electors that he was serving on the Commission on Trawling, and said that he was anxious to know if there was any dissatisfaction among the electors as to the manner in which the Commission on Trawling was conducted. In 1879, Sir William addressed his constituents; the Provost occupied the chair, half a dozen electors were present.

Some six years later, November 1884 - February 1885, a Redistribution Act re-arranged the parliamentary areas for the most part according to population. Burghs with a population of less than 15,000 merged in the county areas. The County of Argyll was divided in two: the Burghs of Oban and Inveraray were merged with the northern division of the County; Campbelltown was in the southern division. After this date, those who had the right to vote in Inveraray cast their vote for a member for the County and not as formerly for a member for the Western Burghs.

During the last decade of the nineteenth century, the Town Council owned and managed its own steam ferry. The Burgh had the exclusive right of ferrying passengers and cattle from Inveraray to the opposite shore of Loch Fyne, but the ferry was of little consequence as a source of revenue. For a number of years previous to 1893, the service was maintained by the Inveraray Steam Ferry Company Ltd., but in that year the Company went into liquidation, leaving to posterity some interesting records. The members of the Town Council resolved to provide a new steamer for the ferry, themselves. The paddle steamer was to be 65 feet long by 13 feet by 6 feet 6 inches. She was to cost £1,380 and was to be called "The Fairy". A man to navigate the steamer and the ferry boats was to receive a salary of £70 per annum. To assist the enterprise, the Duke of Argyll let to the Town Council the right of ferry from St. Catherine's for the annual rent of one shilling stg. The Town Council gave a subscription of £5 toward the improvement of St. Catherine's Pier.

The new ferry steamer was launched on 16th June 1893 and at her trials on 10th July, her speed was 8¾ statute miles per hour. She went into service immediately and in August pleasure sails were arranged to Strachur and Loch Finehead on Thursdays and Saturdays, the fare being sixpence per head. On the morning of 7th September, the day of the Games, the Fairy sailed to Crarae, calling at Strachur and Furnace, and she made the same trip in the afternoon. The return fare from Crarae and Furnace was 1/6d. and from Strachur 1/-.

Throughout the nineteenth century, the Magistrates and Town Council of the Burgh of Inveraray continued to function as in former times, while conforming to the Burgh Police Act of 1833. The position of the Council was at length clarified by the Burgh Police (Scotland) Act of 1892 and the Town Councils (Scotland) Act of 1900. By these Acts the traditional pattern of provost, bailies and town council was recognised along with a uniform system of elections, in which these officials were chosen by the votes of all the adult males in the burgh. The boundaries of the Police Burgh remained narrower, however, than the boundaries of the Royal

Burgh, so exactly delimited in 1648. The close of the nineteenth century was thus marked by a clearer definition of the status of the Town Council and the removal of certain anomalies in its position.

The Twentieth Century

The Third Statistical Account speaks of the gradual diminution of the Town's importance. This is certainly true in so far as the powers of the Burgh were concerned. While it is to be remembered that in some matters there was advance and improvement, in many ways there was recession.

The century began with the death of Queen Victoria on 22nd January, 1901. This was an event of profound significance, and the Provost was authorised to offer on behalf of the Magistrates and Council of the Burgh of Inveraray and of the whole community an expression of their great sorrow on hearing of the death of their beloved Sovereign the Queen. To these men and women, the death of Queen Victoria seemed to mark the end of a great period and the melancholy course of the twentieth century has shown that they were not mistaken.

Against this national background, the Magistrates and Councillors continued to struggle, as their predecessors had done with their own local and peculiar difficulties. One of these was the unceasing battle with the restless waves. The wharf was in need of repair, the breast wall was fallen down in the vicinity of the Coffee House, and the pier at St. Catherine's, to which the ferry ran from Inveraray, was sometimes so broken by the winter storms that the ferryman could scarcely come alongside, and passengers embarked and disembarked at considerable risk. In 1902, a lady claimed £50 damages for alleged injuries received by her in attempting to go on board the steamer Fairy at St. Catherine's Pier. In 1908, Inveraray Town Council contributed £100 towards improvements at that pier.

The steamer Fairy, worked by four deck hands who were issued with trousers, jersey, cap and boots was regarded with much affection. She provided a valuable service and in 1907 earned profits which contributed £170 to the Common Good Fund. But the annual over-haul and bill for repairs was expensive and in 1908 she was sold at a nominal price of £70.

The ferry rights were let to Mr. John Dewar, Inveraray. A subsidy of £30 was paid by the Town Council; there was a subsidy from the Post Master General for the conveyance of mails from St. Catherine's; and there was an income derived from the traffic in banking business. But the ferry as a profitable concern was in decline. Significant of the new forms of transport encroaching upon the service were complaints to the road surveyor of the nuisance caused by dust from passing motor cars, and an application for a licence in 1908 to keep petrol in premises in the Burgh. In 1912, the ferrier wished to give up his tenancy but was induced to carry on by an increased subsidy from the Town Council. In 1913, the ferryman terminated his agreement. It seemed as if the ferry would consist of a sailing boat and the Town Council felt that great loss and injury would be done to the prestige and trade of the Town, if only a sailing boat were employed on the ferry. The misfortune was averted when Mr. Robert L. Greig, Partick offered to run the ferry with a steam launch called Kate.

There were difficulties about the Ferry House. The Town Council was of the opinion that the Ferry House and the Ferry were one subject. The Ferry House (Tigh an aiseig) had bar premises and was granted a licence by the Magistrates. The rent of the Ferry House assisted the Council to subsidise the Ferry. In 1905, the proprietrix was Mrs. Cameron and the house was much patronised by farmers at the market, by fishermen and by passengers on the ferry. In 1909, Mrs. Cameron intimated that she had decided to terminate her tenancy at Whit-Sunday. The Town Council published the following advertisement: "Licensed Business in the Country. The Ferry Inn, Inveraray, belonging to the Town Council will be let to a suitable tenant on a five year lease from Whit-Sunday. This is the only public house in the Burgh and does a large and profitable trade". The lease was taken by a tenant from Perth at a rent of £199 per annum. He held the lease for two years and after him there was a succession of tenants. In 1917, the Mid Argyll Licensing Bench refused the renewal or transfer of the Ferry House licence.

The state of the fishing was causing grave concern to a burgh whose armorial bearings contained the motto: "May the herring always hang from thy nets". In 1905, the views of the fishermen at Inveraray were sent to the Herring Fishery Conference which was being held in the town and the Town Council suggested that drastic measures should be adopted to prevent the absolute failure of the herring fishing as an industry. They recommended that trawling should be prohibited, or alternatively that the enactments as to close time and daylight fishing be strictly enforced.

The prison at Inveraray had declined in importance since 1833 when the Debtors' Gaol confined eight individuals and the Criminal Gaol was occupied by ten prisoners. In 1905, the Secretary for Scotland (an office revived in 1885) legalised the Prison of Inveraray for a period not exceeding three days.

In 1908, the High Court met in the Burgh for the second last time. The Judges of the High Court had held sessions in Inveraray for centuries, and these occasions were attended with pomp and ceremony. In the twentieth century, the High Court met in the town only on two occasions, in 1908 and 1934. A description of what took place in 1908 may be inserted here, the procedure in 1934 being similar.

On 24th and 25th August, 1908, two cases were set down for trial: one man for murder, and another man for shooting with intent to murder. Lord Johnston, the Lord Commissioner of Justiciary, upon his arrival on Friday 21st August was met at the foot of Croit a'bhile[66] Brae by the Provost, the Bailies and the members of the Council, with two halberdiers in uniform, who saw His Lordship safely into his residence, the Town Bell being kept ringing from his first appearance till he was housed.

On Sunday the 23rd, His Lordship attended the English service in the Parish Church, occupying at his own desire the Magistrates' pew, the Provost and a bailie accompanying him. The Reception on Monday morning in the Argyll Arms Hotel was attended by His Grace, the Duke of Argyll, the Lord Lieutenant of the County, a number of the citizens (summoned by the Provost), the members of the Town Council, and the Counsel, Agents and medical witnesses concerned in the trial, all of whom His Lordship invited to dinner in the evening.

The programme of the customary procession on the first day had been prepared and adjusted by and between the Provost and the Clerk of Justiciary and approved by the Lord Commissioner. It was as follows:

66   Croit a' bhile, Croit a' mhile - the Croft of Honey.

Body of Police

Halberdier   Halberdier

Provost and Magistrates

Dean of Guild, Treasurer and other Councillors

Town Clerk, Town Chamberlain

The Minister: the Rev. P.N. MacKichan

Local Bar

Counsel

Sheriffs - Substitute

The Sheriff

The Lord Lieutenant

Trumpeters

Mace-Bearer

The Judge

File of Police

The procession was flanked on both sides by a military escort, a guard of 'A' Company, the 8th Battalion, the Argyll and Sutherland Highlanders. In this procession as well as when meeting the Judge, the members of the Town Council wore silk hats, white ties and white cloth gloves. The trumpeters were engaged by His Lordship who summoned them from Edinburgh. The macer used the ancient mace belonging to the Burgh.

The procession, having been duly marshalled, wended its way to the Court House. The Court was Opened with prayer by the Reverend P. N. MacKichan, who had been invited by the Magistrates to do so. The Burgh Halberdiers sat beside the panels on the first day of the trial. The Magistrates and Town Clerk sat in Court throughout the entire proceedings. At the close of the day's proceedings, the procession was reformed and led the Judge back to his residence.

The second day's proceedings were of an informal nature, the Provost and the police escort alone accompanying the Judge to and from the Court. The Town Council provided luncheon in the side rooms for the Judge, the Counsel, the medical witnesses and the principal officials of the Court. They also provided dinner and tea for the military escort.

At the close, His Lordship thanked the Magistrates for the arrangements they had made and for the manner in which they discharged their duties within the bounds of their jurisdiction.

In the early years of the twentieth century, the Town Council was relieved in part of responsibility for the roads and streets in the Burgh. Previously, the management and maintenance of the streets had been vested in the Magistrates and Town Council and provision was made for maintenance by petty or through customs, levied on animals passing through the Royalty. The Roads and Bridges Act 1878 made it possible for the Burgh of Inveraray to transfer the administration and management of the roads to the County authority. The roads assessment in the Burgh increased year by year and in 1906 the Magistrates were instructed to treat with the County Council for an arrangement for the maintenance of the roads. Two years later, it was agreed that the Mid-Argyll District Committee of the County Council should manage and maintain the highways and bridges, including breast walls in so far as these were road retaining walls, while the Burgh made a contribution of £90 per annum. This seemed to be a good arrangement, but it did not always work harmoniously. By the end of the year, the Town Council made representation to the District Committee about the unsatisfactory condition of the Burgh roads, and in 1910 they complained of the growth of grass in the streets. Ten years later, the agreement was discontinued.

It was an indication of the declining status of Inveraray as the first Royal Burgh in Argyll that in 1909 it was proposed and that not for the first time, that the counting of votes and declaration of poll in Parliamentary elections for the County of Argyll should take place elsewhere and not in Inveraray. The Town Council took strenuous action. They humbly petitioned Alexander L. MacLure, Esq., K.C., Sheriff of Argyll, and Messrs. Ainsworth and Younger, Members of Parliament, shewing that without interval ever since parliamentary elections had taken place in Argyllshire, Inveraray had been the Burgh where the votes were counted and the result of poll declared. The petition was successful on this occasion and the unwelcome change was postponed for the time being.

In December, 1910, the street lamps were fitted with incandescent burners. In April 1912, the Inveraray Gas Light Company was wound up. The Duke of Argyll came to the rescue however; he purchased the Gas Company and gas continued to be supplied to the Town as before.

But the trend of events was not one of recession at all points. One improvement was the modernisation of the Fever Hospital. An Infectious Diseases Hospital had been put up in 1893, in the vicinity of the Garron Bridge. This building was a portable sectional iron structure consisting of two wards with two beds in each and provided with kitchen, scullery and other conveniences. Unfortunately, this erection did not meet with the unqualified approval of the Local Government Board or of the Medical Officer of Health for the Burgh. In response to a communication from the Local Government Board in 1900, the Town Council strongly objected to patients suffering from infectious diseases being sent to the Hospital from the Mid-Argyll District, as they must pass through the town on the way. The Council added that the Hospital had been put up for the use of the Town only. In 1901, the Medical Officer called attention to a serious smallpox epidemic in Glasgow. He advised that the Isolation Hospital be put in a state of temporary residence and that a wheeled ambulance and an ordinary stretcher be provided. The Town Council complied with this advice and appointed a caretaker for the establishment. In view of extensions which required to be made, the Duke of Argyll gave to the Town Council a lease of the necessary ground at a nominal rent. In course of time, the Council purchased from Speirs and Company, Glasgow, a house of wood and iron to provide accommodation for a nurse and servant on the premises. The ward capacity of the hospital was enlarged; a road was constructed from the main road to the site and the Local Government Board agreed to sanction the occupation of the Hospital.

The dignity of the office of Provost was enhanced in 1904, when Mr. Donald Fisher, Solicitor, Glasgow, presented a gold badge and chain to the Burgh for the use of the Provost. Mr. Fisher, a native of Inveraray, belonged to a family which had been associated with the Burgh for centuries. The Fishers engaged in business in the Old Town of Inveraray and also in the New Town, and some members of the family acted as provosts. In acknowledgement of his gift, the Town Council conferred the Freedom of the Burgh on Mr. Fisher.

For a number of years the people of Inveraray had been aware of the literary fame of one of her sons and in 1909, it was unanimously agreed to confer the Freedom of the Burgh upon Neil Munro, LL.D., in recognition of his personal worth and of the fame and honour which he had brought to the place of his birth by his achievements as an author.

At this time the Town Council was enabled to relieve the aged as they had not been able to do in former generations. In 1908 the Old Age Pensions Act made old age pensions available for the first time, the maximum rate of pension being 5/- per week. This provision went far to promote the welfare of old people and to free them from the stigma of being on the Poor Roll. The whole membership of the Town Council of Inveraray for the time being were appointed as a Pension Committee, with three as a quorum.

Inveraray enjoyed some of its former glory as a Royal Burgh when George V was proclaimed King on Wednesday 11th May, 1910 at 12.30 p.m. from the Cross, the Local Clergy, the Pipe Band, a detachment of the Territorials and the Halberdiers being in attendance.

In these various ways the life of the Burgh continued peacefully: developing in some respects, declining in others. But a catastrophe was approaching which was to accelerate all the processes of change already at work.

On 4th August, 1914, the First World War broke out and for the next five years the Records of the Burgh deal almost solely with issues raised by that cataclysm. Practically all the available men of the Burgh and District went to the Services, prominent among them being Captain Alastair MacArthur, one of the bailies. The Town Council carried out the National Registration Act. The election of Town Councillors was postponed. Captain MacArthur was continued as a Bailie for a further period of three years. The

Provost and two other officials were appointed to be a War Recruiting Tribunal. A Serbian Flag Day realised £12. Many of the Town and Pier lamps were not lighted, a restriction which proved inconvenient and dangerous. Several men belonging to the Burgh, serving in the 1/8 Bn. the Argyll and Sutherland Highlanders were awarded the Military Medal and presentations were made to them by their home town. At the end of 1916, the death of the Senior Bailie, Captain Alastair MacArthur of A. and S.H. was reported from France. In 1917, the Duke of Argyll gave the lease of a suitable and accessible field for the growth of potatoes and vegetables. 31 people took advantage of the concession and the Town Council paid out of the Common Good for the ploughing of the ground and the manure required. One citizen received permission to keep pigs in a stye at the top of his garden.

As submarine warfare intensified and food supplies dwindled, the Duke of Argyll not only gave land for allotments free of rent, but also supplied firewood gratis and directed the sale within the Burgh at nominal prices of salmon, venison and rabbits. His Grace provided a health visitor, medical, surgical and midwifery nurse for the district.

On 11th November, 1918 an Armistice was signed. In Inveraray it was decided to place on record the heart-felt gratitude of the Council, as representing the community, at the glorious victories achieved by the Armies and Navies of Britain and her Allies and a suitable memorial was proposed to fallen heroes and to all who had served in the War.

Eight captured German guns were forwarded by boat to Inveraray and placed on the Cross Green and a German machine gun was received from Scottish Command.

Tuesday, 5th August, 1919 was fixed for Peace Celebrations. The Duke of Argyll gave a Ball in the Jubilee Hall, a display of fireworks and a bonfire at Duniquaich. Lord Weir provided illuminations. Flags and Bunting were flown in the Burgh and at night the town's folk set lights in their windows.

Thereafter it was the concern of the Council to resume the services and amenities of peace time. The Town Council sought and received assurances that a daily steam boat service would be provided shortly. An election of councillors to serve on the Town Council was uncontested. Only four members were nominated and declared to be elected, leaving three vacancies still to be filled.

More satisfactory arrangements were made for the Ferry. In September, 1919, Mr. James Douglas, Newton, Strachur agreed to carry on the ferry service. He was given a subsidy of £52 per annum by the Town Council. He made a journey in the morning and afternoon and charged 2/- (a double charge) for passengers carried at other times. The Ferry House was repaired and altered for his use. Six months later, Mr. Douglas asked the Council to sanction an increase in the rates for the carriage of passengers and goods, because the rates in use had been fixed in April 1887 and working expenses had risen greatly since the War. The following charges and freights on goods were fixed: passengers travelling on the ordinary mail run between Inveraray and St. Catherine's, 1/- each way; goods and livestock - Horse 3/-; Cow 2/-; Sheep 3/- per dozen; bicycle 1/6; Hay and straw 1/- per bale; beer, oil, grease and tar 1/6 per barrel.

The consideration of ferrying charges raised the question of the Anchorage, Petty Customs and Weighing Machine Dues. These were doubled. The dues on the daily passenger steamer were increased to £1 per day or £100 for the season; luggage steamers running two or three times weekly paid £1.11.6d. One penny was payable on passengers landing and embarking at the pier and two turn stiles were installed. The new dues yielded a free surplus for the season of about £80.

A great war had had the usual economic consequences of increasing prices, of increasing the amount of money in circulation and diminishing its value.

The influx of summer visitors was becoming increasingly important in the economic life of the Town and it was necessary to encourage them to come. It was agreed by the Town Council to keep a register of persons who let apartments to summer visitors. To provide bathing facilities, a track was cleared at Cromallt Bay and two bathing boxes were erected on the beach, the cost being defrayed from the Common Good. Other amenities made available were a Bowling Green and Tennis Court for which the Town Council gave a grant of £500 from the Common Good.

It was necessary also to give every facility to the summer steamers and omnibuses which brought visitors. Unfortunately, in August 1922, the Queen Alexandra, belonging to John Williamson & Co., grounded when turning to approach the pier. The Harbour Committee considered the need for deepening and extending the pier. John Williamson & Co. were consulted: they said that the proposed extension was desirable, but even with the proposed addition the pier would be only 110 feet long, whereas the Queen Alexandra was 270 feet long. To carry out the extension, the Town Council granted a bond in security, assigning the whole rates and income of the Burgh to the National Bank of Scotland. The captain of the Queen Alexandra asked that a buoy or mark be put at the sand bank off the pier.

But in the early 1920s there were various portents that a day would come when there would not be any summer steamers calling at the pier. The Town Council was now granting eight licences instead of one to store petrol in the Burgh; they asked the Automobile Association to erect a sign: "School - Drive Slowly"; they drew the attention of the Chief Constable to the noise caused by motor bicycles and motor cars without silencers, passing through the Burgh; and they made arrangements for the parking of motor vehicles in summer.

In the midst of these developments the long agony of the War was not forgotten. A sum of more than five hundred pounds was subscribed for the erection of a War Memorial. It was decided that the Memorial was to be built in front of the Green, and the breast wall was repaired. On Sunday 20th August, 1922 all was ready for the unveiling ceremony. The Town Council attended; the Provost and halberdiers appeared in their official dress; there was a procession from the Drill Hall, which had been the point of departure for so many men during the war. His Grace, the Duke of Argyll, unveiled the Memorial. The care of the Memorial with a sum of money for its upkeep was handed over to the Town Council by the Committee of the War Memorial. Subsequently, in order to have the Coat of Arms of the Burgh engraved on the National War Memorial in Edinburgh Castle, the Coat of Arms was registered according to Act of Parliament, and a fee of £20 was paid.

The Town Council continued to promote the good works of peace. In 1920, a new Medical Officer of Health for the Burgh was appointed and the Duke of Argyll offered the house Fern Point as an official residence for the doctor, rent free. The Parish Council and the Town Council each decided to increase their subsidy from £45 to £60 towards the salary of the Medical Officer. A new broom sweeps clean and the new Medical Officer was not long in office before he drew attention to the disrepair of the Hospital. He reported that a dozen houses in the Burgh required immediate repair in the interests of the health of the occupants. He stated that it was necessary to lime wash the houses and the closes. And in 1925, his successor made strictures on the housing and inadequate sanitary accommodation in Inveraray.

The Town Council was meeting with discouragement in other ways. In 1923, a suggestion was made by a Government Department to shut up the Court House. In the same year, the Provost made a determined effort to secure the restoration of Inveraray as the place for holding parliamentary elections, a distinction which had been taken away. But the Secretary for Scotland replied that he did not feel justified in substituting Inveraray for Dunoon as the place of nomination and counting of votes at parliamentary elections. In municipal elections also, there were signs that the importance of the Burgh was not what it had been. From time to time the election of councillors was uncontested, an insufficient number being proposed and elected, and to fill up the remaining vacancies in the Council, other people had to be appointed ad interim.

In 1928, it looked as if the Burgh and parish would be deprived of the services of a district nurse. After long and faithful service the District Nurse resigned, and it was intimated that H.R.H. Princess Louise did not intend to maintain a nurse in the district any longer. Through the generosity of Lady Elspeth Campbell, a district nurse was placed in the Burgh, and the monetary provision made left only a small sum to be raised by voluntary effort.

In 1928, it was proposed to allocate to the County Council some of the local government functions fulfilled by the Burgh of Inveraray. The Town was to be classified as one of the "small burghs" and was given powers over housing, water supply, sewerage and certain minor duties (lighting, cleansing and public buildings). Education, poor relief, public health and responsibility for the police were committed to the County and provision was made for the representation of Inveraray and other small burghs on the County Council.

These proposals roused the fighting spirit of the Town. In August, 1928, the Town Council strongly disapproved the Government's proposals and resolved strenuously to oppose them. In December, the Council decided loyally to support the other Burghs in their opposition to the Local Government Bill. But next year the Local Government (Scotland) Bill became law and the Town Council of Inveraray, having considered a letter received from the Convention of Burghs, agreed to take no further action in the way of opposition.

This measure, the Local Government (Scotland) Act 1929, became the basic statute in the sphere of local government during the next forty years. One of the good consequences of this reorganisation was that the Burgh of Inveraray received an Exchequer Grant towards the cost of local services. The population of the Burgh was steadily declining; in December 1931, the number was 445 and the rateable value was £2854. After 1929, financial assistance based primarily on population was given by Parliament, instalments of £59 or of £60 in lieu of rates being received from the Exchequer several times in the year.

The Town Council thought to take advantage of this new state of affairs in order to relieve them of some of their worries. In 1930, the Burgh Council asked the County Council to pay the Burgh £100 as the value of the Infectious Diseases Hospital; to pay the Burgh £50 as the present value of their interest in St. Catherine's Pier, ferry boat and rowing boat; and to relieve the Burgh of payment of £60 made annually to the ferrier. In reply, the County Council asked the Town on what grounds they founded their claim for a capital sum in respect of the Hospital, and expressed doubt whether the rights of the Ferry had been transferred from the Burgh to the County Council. The following year the Hospital Building and its contents were transferred to the County by virtue of the Local Government Act, but responsibility for the ferry remained as before.

The nineteen thirties were years of financial difficulty. Each year a requisition was made by the County Council upon the Town Council and each year the requisition was heavier. When the demand reached the sum of £1,363, strong representation was made by the Burgh to the County that the sum of the requisition be reduced and the hope was expressed that the burdens falling on the rate payers might be lightened. Despite this protest, the requisition in the following year was £1,535. Too often one reads in the Minutes that the Town Council have no money at their disposal for what has been proposed. In 1930, there was only one offer for the Anchorage Dues. Although Petty Customs had been abolished by the Burgh Customs (Scotland) Act, 1870, offers for the Petty Customs were still invited. The volume of steamer traffic was diminishing, on account of which the Clyde Cargo Steamers asked for a substantial reduction in the steamer dues. For two years, the Town had been without the church clock facing south, because the clock had fallen during the winter storms. But when the Town Council was in a position to replace the clock, the Kirk Session of the Church of Scotland, which was having its own financial troubles, was unable to repair the fabric to receive it.

Apart from the scarcity of money, the dignity of the Burgh suffered minor curtailments. For hundreds of years, the Town Council had appointed an elder of the church as commissioner to represent them in the General Assembly of the Church of Scotland. But in March 1930, the Council was informed by the Clerk to the Assembly that no representative elder could be elected by the Burgh in all time coming.

In 1931, it looked as if the Town Council would be ousted from the Court House, in which they considered they were entitled to accommodation for meetings and for holding courts. In January, the Town Council learned to their surprise that the County Council, without consulting the Burgh, had let a portion of the Court House for the purpose of a post office. In April, the Town Council intimated to the County Council that they would accept the Jury Room as a suitable place for meeting, if it were put in order and sufficient gas supplied. In May, the County Council replied that provision of accommodation was being made, without any admission of a right on the part of Inveraray Town Council to demand it. The Town Council made a dignified protest, which was not acknowledged.

Feeling this trend of events, the Town Council of Inveraray was just in the mood to consider a letter from the Town Council of Linlithgow stating that the forthcoming Convention of Royal Burghs in 1933 should appoint a committee to safeguard the smaller burghs against further curtailment of their rights.

In the decade 1930 to 1939, the Town Council was preoccupied with three concerns of local importance: housing, the ferry service and the water supply. There were also events of national and international significance, the proclamation of a new sovereign and the growing threat of a world war which required appropriate action.

In the twenties, two successive medical officers had criticized the state of some of the houses in the Burgh. In 1933, members of the Town Council Housing Committee visited the houses which had required attention formerly. All had been repaired; sinks had been put in houses which had none; sanitary conveniences were adequate; and the Town Council was of the opinion that no new houses were required in Inveraray. But under the Housing (Scotland) Act 1935 and previous acts, the Town Council was under an obligation to provide new houses and to have defective houses repaired. The Department of Health urged immediate action with regard to the demolition or closing or reconditioning of some 10 houses occupied by 41 persons in the Burgh, and the Town Council as Local Authority issued an order that these houses be vacated and demolished. The Duke of Argyll indicated that he was willing to feu to the Town Council a portion of the Barn Park for building purposes; the Town Council acquired an acre of ground; and planned to build 12 houses.

There were difficulties to be overcome. Some of the houses to be built would be near the immense beech trees which formed an important feature of the Avenue and there were objections on historical and environmental grounds to felling. The cost of building the houses in stone was found to be prohibitive; it was agreed that they be built of brick. The roofs were to be covered with Ballachulish slates, but owing to delays in delivery, slates from Cullipool were substituted. It was resolved to borrow £6,000 from the Public Works Loan Commissioners for this work. The rents of the twelve new dwelling houses were fixed. Tenants of houses presently condemned and overcrowded were interviewed and all wished to become occupiers of the new buildings. It was decided to call the blocks of new houses Barn Park, and to erect three lamps in the vicinity.

Meanwhile, events in the outside world were marching on. A cloud no bigger than a man's hand was beginning to appear on the horizon. In September 1935, a memorandum anent Air Raid Precautions was submitted to the Town Council and allowed to lie on the table. This was succeeded by a communication early in 1936, which was noted.

A touch of pomp and ceremony appeared in the Burgh at the Proclamation of the new King, Edward VIII on 24th January, 1936 at 12 noon. A procession was arranged by the Town Council and His Grace, the Duke of Argyll was invited to be present. The order of the procession consisted of the Police and the Pipe Band; the

Lord Lieutenant and the Sheriff; the Chief Constable with two halberdiers; the Provost, the Magistrates and the Councillors; the Town Clerk and the Sheriff Clerk; the Burgh Chamberlain and the Burgh Fiscal; the Clergy; the Justices of the Peace; the ex-Service men; the Girl Guides; the Headmaster and the schoolchildren.

The following year, George VI was proclaimed King and the Provost received an invitation by command of H.M. the King to be present at the Coronation of Their Majesties in the Abbey Church of Westminster on 12th May 1937.

In 1936, the problem of local importance which demanded attention was the water supply. This problem was aggravated by the large influx of summer visitors. The population of the Burgh in winter was 450; in summer there were 600 residents and many daily visitors, so that the maximum demand for water rose to 40,000 gallons each day. The source was at Eas a' chosain, from which the water was conveyed to service tanks at Bealach an Fhuarain. The Burgh was supplied by a cast-iron pipe which had been laid along the streets more than a century before. There was also a supply from Allt an Aluinn, east of the Dubh Loch, by means of a pipe, fifty years old, which passed through Inveraray to the Newton end of the Burgh. To make matters more difficult, there was leakage from the Bealach an Fhuarain tank at the rate of 40,000 gallons per day. A firm of civil engineers advised that an additional source of supply was to be found in Loch Righeachan. But a World War was to take place before this became available to the Burgh. The Town's water supply was at length renewed in 1937 and was paid for by a special water rate spread over ten years.

The other problem which obtruded itself on the attention of the Town Council was that of the Ferry Service. Toward the end of 1935, Mr. James Douglas, ferryman, gave two months' notice that he would terminate the contract for the service. Application was made to the Ministry of Transport for assistance, but the Ministry declined to make any grant, because the ferry was not available free of charge to all classes of road traffic. The County Road Board, however, recommended a grant of £25 per annum. Having been persuaded to carry on, Mr. Douglas finally tendered his resignation in the Autumn of 1937. This decision was accepted with regret. Mr. John Neil MacArthur, Arkland, offered to maintain the service, in return for a grant from the Town Council of £27 and

77

from the County Council of £25 and to provide a suitable boat. The Town Council stipulated that the boat was to be not less than 25 feet long; and that two runs were to be made each weekday at 8 a.m. and 2.25 p.m. The ordinary fare was to be 1/- per passenger; the fare for a special run was to be 4/-; the Town Clerk was to be conveyed, free of charge. The ferrier was not required to cross, if the weather were too stormy.

As time passed, the cloud no bigger than a man's hand was spreading. In April, 1938, the Provost reported that he had taken steps to carry out what was required for Air Raid Precautions; in September, there was a special enrolment campaign for A.R.P.; in October, preliminary arrangements were made and in February 1939, the evacuation of the civilian population was considered.

Two slights were offered at this time to the amour propre of the Burgh. In September 1938, the Herring Industry Board imposed a ban on Inveraray as a landing station. This was the more grievous to bear in that Inveraray at one time had been the headquarters of the Loch Fyne fishing industry. The Town Council protested against such a ban in the strongest terms to the Herring Industry Board, to the Board of Agriculture and Fisheries and to the Member of Parliament for the County. At length, the Herring Industry Board, Clyde Area Committee, intimated that arrangements had been made to permit the delivery of herring at Inveraray, provided these were sold through a salesman at Gourock, the principal port of landing.

A second development caused the Town Council to feel that the Burgh was not being treated with sufficient consideration. The Burgh Medical Officer resigned; there was a possibility that the medical services of Furnace and Inveraray might be linked together; and that the Town might be left without a resident doctor. The Council emphasized the absolute necessity of a doctor being appointed to Inveraray.

In July 1939, the cloud which had been no bigger than a man's hand darkened the whole sky. It was appreciated that preparations were urgently necessary, in view of a possible war. Wardens and Billeting Officers were appointed; accommodation was provided for the safe-keeping of food supplies; the local Fire Brigade was inspected.

In September 1939, the Provost asked the fact to be minuted that "not withstanding the unparalleled efforts made by the Prime

Minister to maintain a just peace, this country ... had on Sunday 3rd inst. declared war against Germany ...".

On the day on which war broke out, four hundred and twenty-four women and children evacuated to Inveraray were welcomed upon their arrival by steam boat during a severe thunderstorm. Viscountess Weir of Eastwood gave £50 for their benefit.

A Billeting Tribunal was set up; air raid wardens and special constables were enrolled; huts were erected at the Barn Park; lamp-posts were painted with white rings on account of the blackout; local government elections were suspended and the Provost and Bailies were continued in office till hostilities were over.

In the absence of air raids, the evacuees gradually returned to the cities. A new scheme of Government evacuation was intimated, in which 75 evacuees were assigned to the Burgh. A census of householders was carried out and it was found that only 3 householders were willing to receive evacuee children again.

In May and June 1940, the war news became much more threatening. All road direction signs and milestones were removed. Blankets were stored in the Gaelic Church and 50 camp beds for use in the event of evacuation were delivered. A military camp was constructed just outside the Burgh; plans were made to bring a supply of water from Loch Righeachan; a military canteen was built by the Navy, Army and Air Force Institute (N.A.A.F.I.); the pier was taken over for naval and military purposes, but provision was made for the herring fishing industry and the ferry service.

On 27th June 1941, the Prime Minister, the Right Honourable Winston Churchill, visited Inveraray and inspected Naval and Military units. He asked that his personal thanks be conveyed to the Town Council. His concluding words were "Carry on Provost. By our united efforts, victory is sure."

To assist the War Effort, a County War Weapons or Warship Week was held in Inveraray and District and the sum of £20,755 was raised.

In December 1941, a decision was made which was to cause controversy for many years to come. The Town Clock and Town Bell were removed from the Parish Church and the steeple was demolished.

By 1942, conscription was beginning to affect local services: the calling up of the Town Officer was followed by the call up of the ferryman.

Amid so many events which were tragic and ominous, there were touches of comic relief. The Town Council asked a citizen to apologise for his unwarranted and utterly wrong action in entering the Town Refuse Dump and burying a cow and calf there. He apologised. The Council was annoyed also by some tenants of the Barn Park houses, who kept poultry and more than one dog, in violation of the conditions of tenancy. Despite notices to quit, these tenants did not amend their ways.

As the war dragged on, its inconveniences were felt increasingly. Naval craft, moored for long periods at the pier, shook and damaged the structure, so that the crossbeams and piles were loose and almost afloat. There were difficulties of water supply, sanitation and sewage. Accumulating refuse caused a plague of rats. Some service personnel behaved in a disorderly way in the streets during the evenings. A great volume of heavy vehicular traffic passed through the Arches and the road was damaged by army tanks which careered and turned in the vicinity of the Pier and at Church Square.

But the end was foreseeable. On 6th June, 1944, the Provost rose in the Council and made mention of the momentous news flashed over the radio that the great invasion for the liberation of the Continent of Europe had begun early that day, when 4,000 ships with smaller craft, supported by 11,000 aircraft had left our shores. The meeting engaged in two minutes silent prayer.

After another winter of baffle walls, minimum lighting and erratic water supply, the Provost referred on 5th June, 1945 to the victorious conclusion of the European War. And on 14th August, V.J. Day,[67] celebrations took place. A Church parade was held; a wreath was laid on the War Memorial; the Bells were rung for fifteen minutes; and sports were held on the Cross Green in the afternoon.

The period after the war was occupied with the clearing up of war damage; the building of new houses; the augmentation of the water supply; the introduction of electricity; with the renovation of the New Town, now somewhat the worse of wear; and at length with the termination of the Town's status as a Royal Burgh.

There was the question of war damage. For six years the Town Council with deepening dismay had observed the condition

67   Victory over Japan in the Far East.

of the pier deteriorating because heavy boats were moored for lengthy periods, lorries traversed the wooden wharf, causing the under structure to become insecure, and thousands of tons of water were used for servicing naval craft. The Admiralty had promised to pay an annual rate for the pier, and a further payment for water supplied. In course of time, the pier was released and the rent paid up to January, 1946, but the Admiralty continued to use the pier, subsequently. The Town Council agreed to let naval craft use the pier, but insisted on charging a rent.

Two years after the conclusion of hostilities, the military camps in the area were not yet closed, War Department huts still stood on the Barn Park housing site and water was in short supply in the Burgh, the Army having broken forty clay water pipes. In 1949, childrens' ration books were still in use and gifts of food-stuffs were being received from Australia. The Town Council was pressing that the Inveraray Highland Games, which were yet in abeyance, might be restarted in 1950, when it was hoped that the Stable Park would be put in order to serve as a site.

One post-war problem which Inverary shared with the country at large was the provision of housing. It had been evident for a long time that new houses would require to be built for the Burgh. In 1944, the Town Council had forecast the building of thirty new houses after the War. But in 1947, the ground at Barn Park was still requisitioned and nothing could be done till the ground was cleared and reinstated. Meanwhile, the Council was dismayed by rising costs. They instructed their commissioner and assessor to the Convention of Burghs to protest about increased costs in house building and the inadequacy of government subsidies. The coun-cillors felt that they could not proceed with the erection of houses, because an increase of one penny in the rates produced only £15. In 1950, the Housing Committee of the Burgh accepted an alloca-tion of ten houses for 1952, but asked the Department of Health for Scotland to increase the allocation to twenty-eight houses, because no houses had been built within the bounds since before the War. More than three acres at Barn Park were feued and the question of access was examined. The Department of Health increased the allocation of houses to the Burgh and larger subsidies for new houses were announced. In 1953, the Town Council borrowed £53,500 from the Public Works Loan Board to meet the cost of erecting the first development of twenty houses at the Barn Park site. In the end, thirty-four families were accommodated; the over-crowding which had existed previously was relieved, and young married couples were no longer obliged to share houses with their parents or with other families.

The water supply continued to demand attention. It had been heavily overdrawn during the War and the return of peace had not solved the problems. In 1948, it was agreed that the Town Council take over the Loch Righeachan Water Supply when it was no longer required by the War Department. This was made more urgent when the Fire Master, Western Area Fire Brigade, report-ed that the water supply might be sufficient for domestic needs within the Burgh, but that it was not adequate for fire fighting purposes, in addition. The Trustees of the 10th Duke of Argyll intimated that they were prepared to sell to the Council, the water pipes from the Righeachan Dam to Inveraray and a figure was agreed upon.

Times had changed, however, since the days when servant girls gathered with their stoups at the Town Well and the water was drawn up by a windlass. The Department of Health now asked to be furnished with reports of chemical analyses and bacteriol-ogical examination of samples of water from the Righeachan Water Supply and from Eas a chosain together with comments from the Medical Officer of Health for the County. The samples were submitted, tested and approved and the water was turned on.

For generations, the people of Inveraray had tholed not only an erratic flow of water, but also vagaries in the gas supply. Now there was a prospect that the darkness would be lightened. For a number of years gas had been supplied to the Burgh by the Vale of Leven Gas Company. There were many complaints: it was alleged that there were impurities in the gas; that there was need for improvement in the quality of gas; that the supply was poor; that the pressure was low; that the gas was cut off daily from 1.30 p.m. till 4 p.m.; that the price of gas in Inveraray was higher than else-where. In 1947, the Town Council asked the Grampian Electricity Supply Company whether they were in a position to supply elec-tricity. In 1949, the Area Manager of the North of Scotland Hydro Electric Board said that he hoped to give a supply of electricity to Inveraray in the autumn. But there were to be long and vexatious delays. At length in 1951, the electricity was switched on; the old gas lamps were disposed of and the gas pipes were sealed. There were one or two people who voiced a nostalgic regret for old ways. But what was lost in picturesqueness was more than compensated by efficiency.

In 1957, there began the rehabilitation of the Town, a development which involved the Town Council in new and heavy responsibilities. Changing times, rising costs and heavy death duties on the Argyll Estates had all taken their toll of the original design of the Town of Inveraray. Most of the houses fell below the requirements of modern living standards and many of them were in a state of disrepair. The Trustees of the 10th Duke of Argyll desired to remedy this state of affairs, but were unable to carry out a costly renovation without financial assistance. They sought aid therefore, from outside sources. As a result, an arrangement was reached which involved the purchase of Town properties by the Ministry of Works, who in turn handed them over to the Town Council, while retaining the feu superiorities.

The Burgh as a whole was considered to be such an outstanding example of eighteenth century architecture and town planning that the Ministry of Works, on the recommendation of the Historic Buildings Council for Scotland, made capital grants towards the restoration of the Burgh, that it might be carefully preserved in accordance with the original design.

The Town Council was invited to participate in the scheme and before accepting gave careful consideration to its implications. It was considered that the proposed renovation was a unique opportunity for the Town, and that suggestions of local representatives might be helpful. It was realised that a work of this kind, involving the movement of people from their homes, could not be carried out without inconvenience and that the Government Departments promoting and providing the funds, lacked the local knowledge which the Town Council could supply.

Capital grants of £26,000 together with an annual grant of £500 for twenty years were made by the Ministry of Works in conjunction with the Historic Buildings Council for Scotland, for the restoration work. Improvement grants which amounted to £75,000 were made by the Department of Health. In addition to these sums, the Trustees of the 10th Duke of Agyll made a contribution to the scheme of thousands of pounds representing the balance remaining to them after paying death duties on the houses which were the subject of sale. A portion of the cost was paid by the Town Council.

The Town Council appointed Ian G. Lindsay, Edinburgh, as architect for the scheme. In co-operation with other interested parties, and with careful regard to the original work, he prepared plans for most of the houses, including the provision of modern bathrooms and kitchens and considerable renovation to the fabric. The properties affected were all those not privately owned within the Burgh between Maitland's House and Cross Houses. It was necessary that during the period of rebuilding each block, families should be moved into what ever accommodation was available at the time. The tenants were co-operative and the Town Council made money available to cover reasonable expenses. Work on the first four houses began in the middle of 1958 and by 1963, all the houses were completed and old and worn pavements were renewed. The exteriors of some sixty-four houses were restored and the interiors were modernised. The Ministry of Works handed over the property to the Town Council, and the Council accepted responsibility for maintaining the restoration. Inveraray became once more one of Scotland's beauty spots and the white town front reflected in the tranquil waters of the loch, attracts the interest of people from all over the world.

But concurrent with this notable advance, there were signs of recession. After the war, it was ruled that, in view of the duties performed by the Burgh Officer, he was not, in fact, a Burgh Officer, but a general utility worker, and he was issued with two suits of dungarees, a sad change from the days when he carried a halberd and wore crimson breeches, white worsted stockings and shoes with silver buckles.

The functions of the Old Age Pensions Committee, a committee composed of the Provost, Bailies and Councillors, who knew intimately the circumstances of every pensioner, were transferred to the National Assistance Board.

It was minuted also that there was no resident doctor in Inveraray.

The summer steamers, bringing visitors on which the shops and tearooms depended, were calling, despite repeated requests to the Marine Superintendent, on two days per week only. In 1952, the Clyde Shipping Services intimated that it would not be possible to give a service to Inveraray at all. This decision was amended and one steamer called once a week on Tuesdays, but the time for passengers to be ashore was severely curtailed. It was a melancholy contrast with the times when the Lord of the Isles and the King Edward ran in opposition every day on the Loch Fyne route. On the other hand, it was necessary now to reserve parking space for four service buses belonging to David MacBrayne.

In 1950, there was no Burgh Prosecutor and no response to an advertisement of this part-time post. The Chief Constable consented to allow the police sergeant in Inveraray to act as interim Burgh Prosecutor.

A letter to the Provost from the Lord Justice General in 1953, stated that owing to difficulties of access and inadequacy of accommodation, the use of Inveraray as a Circuit Town in the County of Argyll for the purposes of trials before the High Court of Justiciary, had for a considerable time been discontinued and that under the changed circumstances a revival of Inveraray Circuits was virtually impossible. He stated that he had in view to propose to his colleagues, an Act of Adjournal, having as its object the discontinuance of Inveraray and the substitution of Oban as the Centre for Circuit Courts falling to be held in this area. A copy of the Act of Adjournal was received at the end of the year.

In 1954, an order was made to cease holding Sheriff Courts at Inveraray. Thereafter, the Inveraray Court House was used only for Police Courts and Courts of Justices of the Peace. Four years later, the Court House was vacated altogether because it was in a state of disrepair. In 1962, the Argyll County Council sold the Court House and it was decided next year that Quarter Session Meetings of County Justices of the Peace, formerly held in the Burgh of Inveraray, should take place in Lochgilphead.

There was a decline in community life. In 1953, it was noted that the Inveraray Choral Union, the Inveraray Dramatic Society and the Inveraray Golf Club had all ceased to function and that it would be necessary for the Town Council to consider what should be done with the balance of funds.

The Ferry Service was meeting with many difficulties. After the call-up of Mr. John N. MacArthur in 1942, there was a succession of ferrymen, each one resigning after a short time. In 1950, there was no ferry service between the months of March and May and in September it was resolved that the ferry service be abandoned. Immediately, there was a chorus of disapproval. The Cowal

District Council protested strongly. In December, the Harbour and Ferry Committee of the Burgh made an effort to put the ferry service in operation again. The Burgh undertook to give £52 per annum and the County Council conceded a subsidy of £130 each year, to be reviewed annually. Mr. Hope MacArthur undertook to operate the ferry. But the service was fighting a losing battle. The ferry no longer carried the mails; the business of the bank went by road; a 'bus service in connection with the ferry from St. Catherine's to Dunoon was withdrawn; and the ferryman resigned in 1962. At once the ferry service was discovered to be invaluable: it served the tourist traffic; it was useful to hikers travelling between Youth Hostels at Loch Eck and Inveraray; it was used by school children at weekends, attending Dunoon Grammar School. Another man attempted to continue to run the ferry, but after a year, he also resigned. When the County Council intimated that the subsidy payable by them for maintenance of the ferry was terminated permanently, the service which had a history of more than five hundred years, came to an end.

A notable landmark was removed when the Beech Avenue, which had been planted by the Marquess of Argyll in 1649, was felled in 1956.

There was the problem of the Muir Farm or the Muir of Auchnabreck. Originally, the privilege of the use of this land had been granted to the burgesses that they might graze their cattle, sheep and horses. But the day was long past when the Town Herd drove the cattle from the Burgh to the Muir in the mornings to the sound of his horn. The Muir of Auchnabreck had become the Muir Farm and the rent paid by the tenant was treated as part of the Burgh income. The expenses of fencing, of repairs and other items were such that the Burgh derived little financial benefit from the arrangement. At length, the Trustees of the Tenth Duke of Argyll offered an ex gratia payment for the farm and lands of the Muir of Auchnabreck, and on 5th November, 1963 the Town Clerk was authorised to hand over the keys of the Muir Farm and give entry to the Chamberlain on behalf of the Trustees of the Tenth Duke of Argyll. Behind this simple act lay two hundred years of local history. Alas, when all expenses were paid and liabilities discharged, little if any benefit accrued to the Common Good Fund of the Burgh.

There was the question of what was to be done about the pier.

By 1965, the pier was in a bad state of repair. The stone work required grouting; the Burgh workman, treading unwarily, went through the decking; several of the main bearers were badly rotted; the outside fender was cracked; the wooden wharf had been damaged. The probable cost of carrying out necessary repairs amounted to £8,000, and as Navy Department vessels used the pier regularly and frequently, the Ministry of Defence made an offer of a 50% grant towards the total cost of renewal. But where was the other four thousand pounds to come from? In May 1966, the Town Council informed the Ministry of Defence that unless immediate repairs were carried out, the pier would require to be closed to all users as a safety measure. In 1967, it was stated that the Ministry of Defence Lands Office was interested in acquiring the pier, and it was agreed that it would be a "Red Ensign" pier, which meant that the Town Council would still have access to it. After further negotiation, the pier was sold to the Ministry of Defence for £100, as at 1st July, 1968.

In common with all other Town Councils, Inveraray faced the difficulty of rising costs. Every year a letter was submitted from the National Joint Industrial Councils for Local Authority Services (Scotland) concerning wage increases. This was not a cause but a symptom of inflation. Wages were no longer keeping pace with the cost of living. In 1965, it was noted in the Budget of the Burgh that all items continued to show increased costs in keeping with the general rise in the cost of living.

The End of the Burgh

After 1929, the Burgh of Inveraray had been administered under the Local Government (Scotland) Act of that year. Forty years later this arrangement was terminated by Olympian powers which did not act however without consulting Burghal authorities. In 1966, a letter was received from the Royal Commission investigating the re-organisation of Local Government, asking for the opinions of the Town Council. Next year, three members of the Town Council attended a conference on Local Government Re-organisation. In 1969, the Wheatley Commission drew up plans which replaced the old authorities by a two tier system of local government and the Town Council sent representatives to a meeting which was held for joint discussion of the Wheatley Report. In 1973 the Local

Government (Scotland) Act took effect. In 1974, a few die-hards, but none from Inveraray, attempted to make a last stand against innovations. They were informed by the Scottish Development Department that Local Government Re-organisation was too far advanced to be halted now.

Under this reorganisation, local government administration of that part of Argyll in which Inveraray is situated became the responsibility of the Strathclyde Regional Council and of the Argyll and Bute District Council. Strathclyde Regional Council has taken over the water supply and sewerage services and Argyll and Bute District Council has taken over the housing, scavenging and some other functions of the Town Council.

This caused drastic changes in Inveraray. The Town Council, which had made the arrangements for the celebration of the Quincentenary of the Burgh on 15th October, 1974, held their final meetings on 6th May, 1975. Provost Helen Buntain, who had been elected first Lady Provost of Inveraray on 8th May, 1970, used the gavel for the last time. The Magistrates relinquished their judicial functions: they became Justices of the Peace in their own right but not ex-officio as heretofore. The Councillors reached the end of their term of office. The Town House became a Local Office of Argyll and Bute District Council and to this body the records of the Town Council were handed over. It was noted that there was no Common Good Fund. It was proposed to turn the Court House into a museum in which old uniforms, bushel measures, a hand-mill, the Provost's Chain and other articles might be kept. In the meantime, the Council asked His Grace the Duke of Argyll to accept the Royal Charter and other articles of historic interest and to display them in the Castle.

This reorganisation brought to an end the picturesque ceremony and service of the Kirking of Inveraray Town Council. It involved also the dissolution of the Convention of the Royal Burghs of Scotland. The Annual Convention met in the Council Chamber in the City Chambers of Edinburgh on the first Tuesday of April, 1974. The Lord Provost of Edinburgh was appointed Preses and among the four hundred representatives of the Burghs was the Provost of Inveraray as commissioner and the Town Clerk as assessor. On the second day, the Convention of Royal Burghs which had a history of more than eight hundred years, and in which Inveraray had been represented for three hundred years, adjourned to meet in November, for the last time.

On 15th May 1975, Inveraray ceased to be a Royal Burgh and on that day the breast wall, so often mentioned previously was still broken by the unquiet sea.

SELECTED REFERENCES

The Register of the Great Seal (R.M.S.G.S.)

The Register of the Privy Council of Scotland (R.P.C.S.)

Minutes of the Kirk Session of the Highland Congregation, Glenaray

Minutes of the English Congregation, Inveraray

The Records of Inveraray Town Council

Manuscript Notebook of Archibald Campbell, Postmaster at Inveraray, 1734

Records of the Convention of Royal Burghs (R.C.R.B.)

MacIntyre, Peter: Ancient Records of Inveraray, Glasgow, 1904

Innes, Cosmo: Sketches of Early Scotch History and Social Progress (Innes: S.E.S.H.)

MacTavish, Duncan C: Inveraray Papers, Oban, 1939

The Illustrated London News, 28.8.1847

The Rehabilitation of the Old Town, John Campbell, Provost, 1959

The Clan Campbell Abstracts

The Old Statistical Account

The New Statistical Account

The Third Statistical Account

Mackechnie, Donald: 'Inveraray - The Beginnings', The Kist, No. 9, 1975

Local Reports on Municipal Corporations in Scotland, Inveraray, 1836

Parliamentary Papers, Session 1847, Vol. lvii

Pryde, George S. The Burghs of Scotland: A Critical List, London, 1965

Pryde, George S.: Burghal Administration

Rait, Robert S: The Parliaments of Scotland, Glasgow, 1924

Turner: History of Local Taxation in Scotland, 1908

A Source Book and History of Administrative Law in Scotland, London, 1956

Burrell, L.: The Standards of Scotland, 1961

Lipson, E.: The Economic History of England

2

THE OLD TOWN

The first township of Inveraray was made up of a few fishermen's huts at the mouth of the River Aray. They were wattle houses built by setting up substantial uprights and connecting them with interlacing branches and twigs in basket-making fashion. At a short distance within this outer wall, an inner wall of the same kind was made and the space between was filled up with turf or clay. A fairly substantial wall was created and when the structure was roofed with thatch, there was a dwelling-place. Such buildings required to be renewed every few years and might be allowed to fall into decay, leaving no trace. Alternatively, the dwellings were all of "faile" or turf.[1]

Adjoining these huts were cultivated patches of ground, middens and refuse heaps.

In the neighbourhood of the township were the church and the mill, although much grinding was done by means of hand querns, when the mill could not grind on account of frost or drought.

The inhabitants of such a township inevitably suffered from arthritis, rheumatics and tuberculosis. Their teeth, however, were better than those of people at the present time. A high rate of infant mortality, an uncertain and inadequate food supply and tribal warfare limited the growth of population.

In the fifteenth century (1432) the Castle or Manor of Inveraray was built or rebuilt by Sir Colin Campbell, first laird of Glen Urchy, tutor to his nephew, the Earl of Argyle. "He built the town and house of Inveraray... the Tower called the Large Tower of Inveraray (as there was another tower called the Little Tower) which Large Tower had then a battlement..."[2]

Inveraray became a residence of the Lords of Lochawe and one of their two principal messuages or dwelling houses, including

1   Innes: S.E.S.H., pp. 433, 436.

2   Highland Papers, Vol. ii, Scottish History Society, Second Series, Vol. xii, pp. 95-96 (later H.P. Vol. ii, S.H.S.)

out-buildings, orchards, courtyards and gardens. In 1470, Colin, Earl of Argyll was dating his charters at his manor of Inveraray.

When the castle or manor became the residence of the Earls of Argyll after 1457, it was a momentous development for Inveraray and for Mid-Argyll. The Earls of Argyll were consistently important members of the Councils of the Realm. They were frequently included among the great Officers of State; their talents were held in high respect by the Crown. Colin the first Earl was appointed, with Lord Boyd, Justiciary of Scotland and he eventually became Lord-High-Chancellor of Scotland. The Earls followed a clear and consistent policy in Mid-Argyll. Their aim was to gather their scattered lands together into one concentration of land in and around Inveraray, Loch Awe and Loch Fyne. Therefore, they sought to exchange the good lands of Menstrie for the inferior lands of Glassary held by the Scrimgeours. They exchanged rich lands in Kinross and Fife for the Lordship of Lorne. They built up their estates by exchange, by purchase and by marriage with heiresses. As a result of this policy, Inveraray became an important centre of administration, surrounded by lands, the superiority of which belonged to the Earls. For lesser breeds without the Law, it was a far cry to Lochow.

In 1474, Inveraray was erected into a burgh of barony. There was a weekly market on Saturdays and there were fairs, one at the Feast of Michael the Archangel in September, the other on the Feast of St. Brandan in May, these dates being determined by the agricultural seasons of the year. Shops were opened and crafts were followed. Among the commodities bought and sold were herring, furs and weapons. The MacNabs, noted armourers and workers in metal, came from Barr a' Chaistealan (near the modern Dalmally) to sell their wares, such as sharp-pointed knives or gear skin (gearr sgian) of a great length. In the midst was the Mercat Cross, an outward and visible sign of the status and authority of the Burgh in matters of trade. In the neighbourhood of the cross was a well. There were houses about the cross and there were houses by the shore. There was a bridge over the river; there was a booth for collecting tolls; and there was a gibbet on the Gallows Green or Gallows Knowe, on the other side of the river from the Castle. There was a ferry across Loch Fyne in 1482. It did not run

3   Origines Parochiales Scotiae, Vol. ii, Part 1, p. 85 (later O.P.S.).

between Inveraray and St. Catherine's but at Cragane or Creggans, which crossing was shorter by half a mile and was directly opposite the track by Loch Eck to Dunoon. With this ferry was a half merkland, part of the lands of Kilbride.[4]

The sixteenth century was remarkable for two royal visits, among other events. It was the policy of James V to maintain the royal authority by keeping a close correspondence with the different chiefs and by visiting the West Highlands, as often as he could. To this end, James resided in Inveraray at least from the seventh day of September 1533 until the eighth day of October.[5] While he was in Inveraray, the King was in regular communication with the Lord Treasurer and Secretary in Glasgow and messengers passed between the episcopal burgh on the Molendinar Burn and Inveraray. Sometimes they travelled with writings to the King's grace, which required an answer; sometimes with musical instruments, such as a lute bought in Glasgow, with the case and a dozen strings, sent with Troilus, who was presumably a royal minstrel.

The visit of James V in 1533 was followed thirty years later by the visit of his daughter, Mary Queen of Scots. At Easter 1563, Mary proposed to make a progress through Argyle.[6] There were many reasons for such a journey. The "gentil-mennes places" where she stayed were held of the Queen and the hospitality which she received was a form of rent. Also the Countess of Argyll was the Queen's half-sister and the fifth Earl of Argyll was under Mary's influence, politically. Mary herself wished to confirm the allegiance not only of Catholic nobles, but also of a Protestant noble such as Argyll, and this she held until the fatal field of Langside, on which Argyll was made prisoner but was purposely suffered to escape.[7]

For these various reasons, Mary proposed in 1563 to visit the West. Leaving Edinburgh on the 29th June, she was in Inveraray

4   O.P.S.

5   Accounts of the Lord High Treasurer of Scotland, Vol. vi, 1531-1538, H.M. General Register House.

6   Calendar of State Papers, Foreign Series of the Reign of Elizabeth, 1563, H.M.S.O. 1966.

7   Patrick Fraser Tytler, History of Scotland, 3rd Edition Vol. vi, p. 43.

on 23rd July. On her journey she wore Highland apparel.[8] At Inveraray there was a meeting of the Privy Council, and there was granted a precept of remission to John MacPhatrick MacFarlane in Gorten for theft and the reset of stolen goods, provided that he made satisfaction to those who had suffered loss. Which precept, was recorded in the Register of the Privy Seal.[9] On the 24th and 26th she wrote royal letters.[10] On the 26th of July, the Queen of Scots left Inveraray and rode to Creggans, whence she was ferried to Strachur.

While these events were taking place at the highest social level, the ordinary occupations of life were being pursued.

The fishing was of great importance. In 1555, the western burghs such as Irvine, Ayr, Dumbarton and Glasgow stated in the Scots Parliament that in all times by gone they had resorted to the fishing of Loch Fyne for making of herring and other fishes.[11] In 1561, part of the rent of Kilbride was a yearly payment of six barrels of good and sufficient herring of Loch Fyne, of which one was to be a large barrel containing 1000 red herrings[12] (that is herrings smoked hard and red and tasty). This postulates a considerable fish-curing industry with coopers and coopering. There were also the fishings of the water of Aray "as weill high as laigh"; the fishings between Auchinbreck (later the Muir Farm) and the water called Garron; and the salmon fishing of Portinstonich, near the Kirk of Kilmalew,[13] where it is still carried on at the present day.

In 1573, there was a smith in Glenaray called Michael the Smith: he obtained fuel for his trade from land (terrarum carboniarum) within the messuage of the mains of Inveraray.[14]

There was a brewster and a maltster in the service of the Earl,

8   Calendar of State Papers.

9   R.P.C.S. Vol. v.

10   D. H. Fleming, Mary Queen of Scots, London 1898.

11   Duncan C. MacTavish: Inveraray Papers, p.87

12   O.P.S.

13   Ibid.

14   Ibid

a chamberlain, a gardener and a keeper of the Forest of Ben Bhuidhe.[15] Secretarial work was done by a sharp boy that could write and read.[16] There were orchards which produced pears and plums.

Travellers, then as now, visited the Burgh and sought for lodgings. In September 1591, these lodgings were kept by a man who was a stranger to the district, and the meal was served by the man's wife. For dinner there was meat, ale, wine, aqua vitae or whisky and fruit sent in by the gardener. Outside in the street waited the poor, expecting alms, an awmous, which amounted to 28 pence. Since there were no roads, the journey from Inveraray to Dunderave was by ferry boat, navigated by more than one ferryman.[17]

By the end of the century (1595), the environs of the Burgh bore some of the names by which they were known in recent times: there was the fisherland, the brewsterland, the maltland and the peatland.[18]

According to local tradition it was in the sixteenth century that the Munros settled in and around Inveraray. It was said that they called themselves McNorvaich. Later their name appeared as McNorevick or Munro.

In the early decades of the seventeenth century (perhaps about 1630) Walter MacFarlane wrote an attractive account of the "frie litle burgh" of Inveraray.[19] The ferry of Loch Fyne which was called Kilmaglash continued to run to Portchregan (Creggans) which was three miles from the Burgh.[20] Inveraray was the Earl of Argyll's principal dwelling house in the Highlands of Scotland, and there he had built a very fair and pleasant palace and yards (or

15 Ibid.

16 Innes: S.E.S.H., Appendix A, p. 513.

17 Innes: S.E.S.H., Appendix, p. 523.

18 O.P.S.

19 Geographical Collections relating to Scotland, made by Walter MacFarlane, Scottish History Society, Vol. lii, 1907, Vol. ii, p. 145.

20 In the vicinity was French Farland or Rudha nam Frangach, a French trading Post.

gardens). In some of the zeairds (or gardens) there were divers kind of herbs growing, and other yards were planted with sundry fruit trees very prettily set. There were fair greens to walk upon with a wall of stone and lime lately built about the green.

The lands of the township were fertile of corn, and the town had liberty and full power to buy all kinds of merchandise and wares. These wares were of country stuff, butter and cheese from Glen Shira and wares out of other countries.

Land reclamation had taken place in Glen Shira. Despite the damage wrought by the River Shira, which was very strong and ran swiftly through the country in time of spates and vehement tempest and stormy weather, taking away and destroying many lands and houses, nevertheless, there were biggings builded with stone and lime and zairds or orchards and gardens, with innumerable fruit trees planted therein and sundry other corn lands on every side of the river, and in the place where the country men were wont to slay the salmon fish before in the river, corn did grow thereon.

The fishing was of great importance. Inveraray lying at the sea coast and at the mouth of the Water of Aray was very profitable for the abundance of herrings which was taken there. In Loch Fyne, there was abundance of herring and several other fishes slain. There was a little freshwater loch (the Dhuloch in Glen Shira) and there was abundance of salmon fish slain yearly in that loch. It was not far from Inveraray for the Earl of Argyll[21] used oftimes to come to this loch to behold and see the salmon fish slain.[22]

At this time there is a clear picture of the education, apparel and way of life of the grandson of the Earl who used to watch the salmon fish being slain. When Archibald who was to become 9th Earl was a child, being four years of age in 1633, he was naturally an object of great care to his grandfather, the Earl and to his father and mother Lord and Lady Lorne. Arrangements were made to provide him with a sufficient man who had both Irish (Gaelic) and English, who would have a care not only to attend him, but sometimes likewise to learn him. The child was given a psalm book, a New Testament and later an English Bible. After some years, the boy began to weary of the Gaelic language, and his mother Lady

21   That is the 7th Earl, if this account were written in 1630.

22   End of notes from MacFarlane's Geographical Collections.

97

Lorne gave instructions that he was to be made to speak it, because since he had bestowed so much time and pains in learning it, she would be sorry if he lost it, with laziness in not speaking it. The boy was a resplendent figure when he came from Glen Urchy, where he was fostered by the accomplished Sir Colin Campbell of Glenurchy, to visit his mother Lady Lorne in Inveraray during the summer. He had a scarlet coat with red silk buttons, red stockings and green satin head gear, called after the German fashion, a mutch. His pedagogue or teacher wore a plaid of many colours, and his page, Duncan Campbell, had a stand of clothes of grey cloth. As he became older, he wore a gold ring set with a turquoise stone; he carried a small Spanish pistol; and for pocket money he was given an angel of gold, an old English coin bearing the figure of an angel, worth £6.13s.4d., Scots. When his grandfather, the 7th Earl, died in 1638, the boy was dressed in a stand of duilueid (what was known later in Scotland as "a stan' o' black") for mourning.[23]

Alas, for the mutability of human affairs.[24] The pleasant summer visits of the young heir were succeeded in December 1644 by visits of a very different kind. In that year, the Town of Inveraray was laid waste by Montrose and MacColkitto. The houses and dwellings were burned by the Irish.[25] The kirk was not completely destroyed and the castle was not captured, since the enemy had no siege-train. The people, however, were in a state of great necessity through the burning of the parish, being left very poor and indigent.[26] The situation was partly relieved by a voluntary contribution "for our distressed brethern in Argyll" organised throughout Scotland by the Commission of the General Assembly of the Church, during the course of the rebellion.

Inveraray was just beginning to recover from the visitation of MacColkitto when she or it received a visit from MacColkitto's enemies. On 21st May, 1647, General David Leslie arrived in the town with two regiments of Highland soldiers and several troops of horse. One of the regiments was commanded by the Marquess of

23   Innes: S.E.H.S., pp. 369-374.

24   Nulla sors longa est. L. Annaeus Seneca.

25   Minutes of the Synod of Argyll, 1639-1651.

26   Fasti Eccl. Scot., Vol. viii, 313 Col. 1 (later F.E.S.).

Argyll, of which regiment Mr. John Nevay or Nevoy, of equivocal memory, was chaplain. The little army rested on the 22nd and on Sunday 23rd May marched for Kintyre.

The army was followed by the pestilence. The first symptom was a blinding headache and a high fever; then came a swelling of the throat and glands and a quick delirium. The dead were buried in pest graves on which stones were heaped[27] and if one of these graves were accidentally opened in after years, the contacts were confined to their houses till further enquiry, and the treasurer of the Kirk gave them a merk every day till there was ground to release them.

Five years later, the long-suffering town had to admit the soldiers of the Commonwealth. On 19th July, 1652, Colonel Reid, one of Cromwell's officers, came with his men to Inveraray. The Marquess of Argyll hastened into his own country to receive these invaders as guests. The Parliament of the Commonwealth undertook to respect the person of the Marquess, his property and rank, and to abstain from placing a garrison at Inveraray except upon extraordinary necessity. There was an English garrison in the town, however, in 1656.[28]

But the Burgh and country were required to pay cess. The officer in charge said that he was willing to accept such things as the country did produce. He offered 26s. or 28s. for each cow that the Marquess should send, provided that the cows were fat, and 4s. for each tree which was between 20 and 24 feet long and about 12 or 14 inches square, to be delivered at a convenient place where the English ships might load them in safety.[29]

Despite these military occupations, unfriendly, friendly and neutral, the spirit of the citizens of Inveraray remained unbroken. After the departure of Montrose and MacColkitto, the reconstruction of the town began. The houses in the neighbourhood of the Mercat Cross were rebuilt and were known as the High Gate or Main Street; the houses by the shore were raised again, as were those at the Bridgend of the Town, called the Old Kirk. According to local tradition, it was after the visitation of 1644 that Baron

27 Minutes of the Kirk Session of Inveraray Church, 15.5.1651 (later K.S.M.)

28 K.S.M.

29 Scotland and the Commonwealth, S.H.S., Vol. xviii, p. 204.

MacCorquodale, his home on Loch Tromlee in the Parish of Kilchrenan, having been destroyed by the invaders, he erected a house in the Town of Inveraray and caused a pot and pan to be built into the dyke, which marks were to be traced until recently. Beside the Burgh was the town kiln, a stone erection having a lower chamber with walls four feet thick for the fire and an upper chamber with thinner walls, in which the grain dried on a latticed floor.

The better type of houses were built of stone and had a slate roof. The door was known as the yeatt and could be locked. Overhead, was the peat loft. At the gable end or at the door was the deas, a seat of turf or stone on which people sat in the evening sunshine after a hard day's work in the fields, or on a Sabbath day in the merry month of May.[30]

The gear and plenishing of the houses varied according to the wealth and social status of the tenants. In the home of a burgess, there was a table, a feather bed, under which was a bag or pock (poke), one or more chests in which things were laid up and keeped, a little coffer, an ambrie or cupboard for victuals, a barrel full of salted beef, a kebbuck of cheese, a quart of butter. The gear consisted of shears (or scissors), an axe, a graip, a spade, a scythe, some herring nets. Wooden vessels, cogs or cogies, were used for eating and drinking. Most houses contained one or more weapons; a dirk, a sword, a sword belt, a pistol, a gun, a powder horn. The houses were lit by candles set on the table. In country houses the floors were earthen. The yards or gardens were planted with green kail.

In Glen Aray there were sheall houses, such as the sheiling of Tulloch. These were huts or rude shelters of stones or sods (failes) built for the accommodation of shepherds and dairymaids, during the summer grazing of sheep and cattle.

The shops of the Burgh, which kept open long after dark, might be equipped with an ell wand or measure (with which in a moment of provocation the shopkeeper might strike a difficult customer); a balk with brods and weights (a beam with scales); a little coffer full of silks and ribbons; two rolls of tobacco; and £44.13s.4d. of money.

The 8th Earl and Marquess of Argyll beautified the environs of the reconstructed town with trees. He planted a great beech

30 K.S.M.

avenue in the Fisherland and a beech avenue, which still stands, leading into Glen Shira.

Within the Burgh, the pulse of life beat strongly. As always, the fishing was of paramount importance. God was pleased to send the fish of the sea as a help to His people's necessity,[31] and the people were not backward in taking advantage of this provision. There was a tax on herring, and the "assize herring" were declared to be one of the inalienable revenues of the Crown.[32] There appears to have been a closed season: fishing time drew near in the month of June. Boats came from Ayr and busses from Holland. There was the fear that the town might be filled with vagabonds and rascals. The fishing community dwelt in the Fisherland, a formidable community which might make common cause against anyone who offended them. Sometimes they cast their nets on Saturday and lifted them on the Sabbath, or let their nets lie on the Sabbath. There were good years and bad. In 1658, both in the east and in the west, there was a great disappointment of the herring fishing. Occasionally, fishing boats and busses met with disaster in the unchancy waters of the Loch. In 1651, the Kirk Session must needs help poor ship-broken men of Aire. In 1653, shipbroken Dutchmen were given assistance.[33]

In 1659, four "ship-wreckit" men were lodged one night in Inveraray.[34]

The other important industry was agriculture and this also was subject to fluctuations. In September, 1658, there was universal and constant stormy and unnatural rainy weather, the like whereof had been rarely seen in any former time, whereby it came

---

31 K.S.M., Sept. 1658.

32 MacTavish: Inveraray Papers, p. 87.

33 This was magnanimous when one remembers that relations between the Commonwealth and Holland were very bad in 1652-53; and also that the decline of the local fishing industry in the seventeenth century was due to the effective competition of the Dutch, who having evolved a special method of preparing herring for salting, had gained for themselves the leadership of the industry. (The Story of the Herring)

34 K.S.M. 1651, '53, '79, '80 passim.

to pass that there was little expectation of a harvest, so that both great penury and dearth was threatened and much to be feared. [35] The produce of the country which was sold at market was great oats, small oats, groats (the grain of oats deprived of the husks), salt beef, butter, wool, candles and tallow. The wealth of the people consisted in their cattle: Kyloes (small highland cattle, having shaggy hair and long curving horns), horses, sheep, goats and pigs and in these was brisk trade. Drovers were present, with sums of nine or ten pounds sterling, mostly consisting of forty shilling pieces, carried in a belt round their middle.[36]

The people subsisted, as might be deduced from the articles for sale at the market, on meal and fish, on goat's milk, cows' milk and mutton. Brewing took place in houses in the Autumn, and at that time some people were always fou', being both in drink and somewhat distracted.

The clothing worn by men was a cloth coat, sometimes spoken of as a cassog, a pair of breeches, a pair of trews, a pair of hose, a bonnet, a belted plaid and a pair of shoes. The garments most often mentioned as being worn by women were plaids and red shag petticoats, that is petticoats made of cloth with a rough nap. Both men and women were given to idle vageing or going for walks on the Sabbath day.[37]

The lives of the poor make sad reading. Some gathered shellfish in the month of September. One woman sought shelter in a wast or deserted house where no person lived, without light of fire, candle or food for her entertainment. Another poor and indigent woman came to a field where people were sowing corn, to seek alms and charity and obtain some small quantity from some of the people sowing which she would keep in a little poke or apron about her, this being the only means of her subsistence to preserve life.

35   Ibid.

36   The terms used to describe the beasts on these occasions may be worth recording, as the words and their meanings are now forgotten. A brandit cow was brindled or striped across the back. A tydie cow was·a cow which had not been in calf. A keir horse was dark coloured. One which was ringle-eyed had a great deal of white in the eye. A lyart horse was dappled; a belled horse was one having a bell, a blaze or white mark on its face. A stoned horse was an entire horse. Horses were marked by cutting off their lugs.

37   K.S.M.

In the speech of the people there were picturesque phrases, instinct with the natural poetry of an earlier age and reminiscent of Scripture and of Homer. They spoke of midnight as "the dead hour of the night"; of dawn as "very early in the morning about the sun-rising"; of evening as "the sunsetting".

An important feature of life in the Old Town was the fairs. Markets and fairs were held at Inveraray by charter of James III and of Charles I. The Fairs took place, as was customary, in other burghs, on Saints' days: on 16th May, St. Brandane's Day and on 16th September. Among the commodities sold at Inveraray were aqua vitae or whiskey, rolls of tobacco, plaiding and tartan cloths. Irish cattle and victual were imported, until this traffic was prevented by laws, which were enforced in 1676.

Well-known figures at these fairs were packmen, who had got to the town at no small risk. They might be stopped on their journey and have money extorted from them for liberty and safe passage by way of blackmail, being forced to come under the protection of robbers. There were packmen, chapmen, pedlars and hawkers, the meanings of which terms shaded-off into one another. Packmen carried small goods in a bundle or pack. Pedlars bore a small leathern bag or paidle, which contained the smaller articles of trade. Chapmen spoke of their customers as chaps. Hawkers cried their wares aloud.[38]

A packman at the fair in Inveraray at this period carried two plaids, a dirk, a bonnet, an eln of linen, shears or scissors, elshoe irons, indigo, a belt, alum, pepper and aconite, strings of blackbeads, some prins or pins, three combs and five or six shillings sterling of money in his pockets.

The currency which circulated on these occasions in the Burgh was of various origins. In 1651, there were shillings, sterling, good money current with the merchants. Less satisfactory were pieces of broken silver, pieces cut in halves or quarters to make smaller

38 Scots packmen ranged far and wide over Europe. Sir George Skene (1569) met a vast multitude of his fellow countrymen in that condition at Cracow. Poor Scots swarmed into East Prussia and Poland. They suffered great privations and dangers and often died of hunger. A Scots pedlar's pack in Poland became a proverbial expression. It usually consisted of cloths, some kind of woollen goods called "Scottish", and linen handkerchiefs. They sold tinware and ironware, such as scissors and knives. A mandate was issued against Jews, Scots and other vagabonds. (Papers relating to the Scots in Poland, 1576-1793: S.H.S.)

denominations. Scots pounds by gradual debasement of the coinage had declined in value to a twelfth of the English pound. The merk was a silver coin having the value of 13/4d. Scots and was used in payment of wages. The groat was an English coin long current in Scotland; ten groats bought clothing for a poor girl in 1677. There were legg or liege dollars and four merk pieces.

It was necessary that guards be present on Fairdays because these events caused a great resorting of poor idle persons from other parochs; there was pyking and stealing and many other abuses scandalouslie committed.[39] The fairs at Inveraray were not only markets but pleasure fairs. In 1661, there was a horse race for the prize of a saddle, and a foot race, the winner being given a pair of tartan trews.

There were other occasions of communal festivity, enjoyable but not altogether respectable. These were the penny brydells, so called because each neighbour contributed one penny, Scots. It was considered that great abuses were made by the too great confluence of people at penny brydells[40] and in 1661 it was appointed that the number at such weddings in Inveraray should not exceed thirty-two persons.

From another point of view, the Burgh of Inveraray was regarded with apprehension because the Justice Court of Argyll was held in the Tolbooth. This was the court for the whole Shire and for the Western Isles, with the exceptions of portions of Arran belonging to the Duke of Hamilton. Trials took place in the Court House and the persons of Assize removed furth of the Court to the Kirk next door to reason and vote upon the points of the dittay. The Court consisted of the Hereditary Justice General, the Justice-Deputes and Justice Substitutes. The jury numbered fifteen. The crownar arrested the person of the offender. The accused usually awaited trial in the Tolbooth but when that building was in a state of greater disrepair and insecurity than usual, they were committed to the Castle. The verdict was pronounced by the Dempster or common hangman. In early centuries, the gallows stood on the Gallows Green, on the other side of the river from the Castle; in later centuries, it was situated at Gallows Foreland, where the town now stands; by 1691, it was erected beyond the Gallowgate or

39   K.S.M.

40   K.S.M.

Newton at North Cromalt, where there are said to be holes in the rock for the upright posts. Sometimes the gibbet was set up at the place where the murder was committed.

Punishments were severe: two young boys were scourged publicly at the market cross for their stealing and killing of three goats; a merchant was unlawed and amerciat in the sum of fifty pounds, Scots money, for striking a customer; a man who stole and killed a cow and salted the beef was taken and scourged by the hand of the common hangman through the town (the offender was probably starving); for persistent theft, men and women were brought to the cross of the Burgh and by the hand of the hangman stigmatized with a hot iron upon the palms of their hands.

For murder the penalty was death. After sentence the condemned person might be kept for two days, he might be kept for a week; or he might be hanged next day. The guilty person was hanged on a gibbet to the death. The usual time of execution was two o'clock on Saturday, but it might take place between eleven and twelve o'clock on a Monday or on a Wednesday. One man who committed murder under trust was hanged and his right hand was put upon an iron pike on the gallows, there to continue till it evanished away. The Assize were most reluctant to hang women, but for the crime of child murder no mercy was shown.

There was one hanging, the course and consequences of which were so unusual that it is remembered to this day. According to local tradition, Archibald M'Phune at Drieppe was hanged for sheepstealing. According to the Justiciary Records of Argyll, Archibald M'Phune of Driep, his house being the ordinary Inns, gave to Duncan Campbell in Kinlochlean, one deadly wound whereby he died immediately.[42] At any rate, M'Phun was taken to the Crags and hanged. His relatives came over from Strachur by boat to collect the remains and on laying him down between the thwarts of the small craft, it was noticed that life was not extinct. A nursing mother in the party managed to get him to swallow some of her milk and Archibald M'Phun recovered and lived to a ripe old

---

41   Justiciary Records of Argyll and the Isles, passim.
       (As one reads these sad records, one is reminded of the Ballade of Villon:-
       "Hommes, ici n'a point de moquerie;
       Mais priez Dieu que tous nous veuille absoudre!")

42   Justiciary Records, vol. 1, pp. 131-133

age. The law having had its way, he was left to end his days in peace, but his head was twisted to one side, and he was known thereafter as "Half Hung Archie".[43]

As the seventeenth century wore on, the Town of Inveraray became more and more throng. There was the sheriff in the person of Mr. Alexander Duncanson in 1681; there was a notar Mr. Duncan ffisher and a writer; there were two ministers of religion and a chyrurgeon; there was a poet, Duncan MacIntyre in Braleckan (circa 1652-1683) who wrote an elegy Cumha Teaghlaich a Mhain, mourning for a family called MacKellar who held the farms of Maam and Kilblaan in Glen Shira.[44] There was an officer home from the wars (of whom there always have been two or three in Inveraray in every generation), in this case he was Major John Campbell of Clonary;[45] there was a poor soldier lately come out of the Barbadoes. There was the schoolmaster, the usher, several poor scholars and the landladies who kept the scholars. There was the miller and the miller's knave. There were merchants expecting the arrival of lowland boats loadned with merchand ware. There were shopkeepers, change-keepers, brewers and malt men. There were tradesmen a-plenty: slaters, locksmiths, glovers, weavers, tailors, cordiners or shoemakers, joiners, saddlers, wrights. There were gaein'-abootbodies: hawkers, tinclars, sorners, vagabonds and wandering pipers who would play for a dram in any house. Of more substance were the coupers, dealers in cattle and horses and the drovers. There were some who magnified their office; the beddal, bedral or beadle, the messenger, the public crier who affixed his proclamation to the most patent yeatts of the house. There were those who worked on the estate, the gardener and the forester. There were those who went down to the sea in ships, skippers, ferriers and fishermen; and those who awaited their return, the fish-curers, the gutters and the packers.

There were the poor: a leper, an old man with a lunatick oy or grandson, relicts of former citizens who supplicated the Kirk Session for some supplies.

There were the strangers who did not have the Gaelic, who

43   I.C. Douglas: A History of Strachur and District.

44   The Clan Sept MacKellar, pp. 10,11. The Celtic Monthly, 1908.

45   F.E.S., iv, p. 9.

might have more money but who were regarded as poor menial servants, who had no relations; and there were the people of Glenaray, the old and only parish. There were also Highland families, who had settled in the surrounding country and had become completely identified with the life of the town: the ancient family of Bell, who came from Glen Shira; and the Sinclairs, known as Mac na Cearda, M'Nocaird and M'Nokaird, of whom one was Duncan M'Nokaird in Coulfockan, beside the Boshang Gate.

The 9th Earl like his father the Marquess was keen on planting trees. He enclosed gardens, planted trees and laid out walks. He planted large numbers of laburnums, planes, firs, oaks and elms.[46]

The setting of Inveraray was beautiful: the town itself was a great and famous burgh. There was always something happening; there was fresh news every day.

But to this busy little town there came the threat of destruction. In 1681, the ninth Earl of Argyll, having subscribed the Test Act with an explanatory declaration, was forced by royal displeasure to escape to Friesland. He was sentenced to death on evidence which would not hang a dog and his titles and estates were declared forfeit. The titles and estates were restored to his son Lord Lorne but his heritable jurisdictions were distributed by Charles II among the friends of the Court, during pleasure.

In 1684, there was the possibility of a rising in the Campbell country. On 2nd May, 1685, Argyll sailed from Holland with three ships to invade Scotland. And on 4th May, the Marquiss of Atholl received letters of gift and tack bestowing on him the office of Lieutenant and Justiciar of the Shires of Argyll and Tarbert.[47] He marched into Argyllshire with one thousand men from Mar, Weem and Sleat, all armed and boddin in feir of weir. On 27th May, Argyll required all his vassals everywhere to go to arms and to join him. About 37 men from the parish of Glenaray from such townships as Craleckan, Braleckan, Auchindrain, Kilian, Auchnagoul, Pennymore, Kilbride and Achnabreck[48] came out. The Marquis of Atholl did not hesitate to make full and even ruthless use of the

---

46   Willcock, J: A Scots Earl in Covenanting Times, pp. 152-153.

47   R.P.C.S., Vol. xi, p. 32.

48   MacTavish, Duncan C: The Commons of Argyll.

wide powers committed to him by the Privy Council. He destroyed and made useless all buildings which might be of service to the invaders and by his authority, Stewart of Ballechin seized Inveraray Castle.

The rising was a failure: the Earl of Argyll was captured at Inchinnan on the banks of the River Cart and was executed at Edinburgh on 30th June. Open proclamation in the royal name and authority was made at the Mercat Cross of Inveraray that all good and loving subjects were to use their utmost endeavours for apprehending rebels and traitors and were prohibited from entertaining any persons whatsoever unless they had a pass.[49]

From the Marquis of Atholl, Stewart of Ballechin or Ballequhan received commission to hold courts in Inveraray and was given indemnity for all executions and any other deeds what so ever done by him. Many were tried on a charge of rebellion and of refusing to take the Test Oath. Several gentlemen of the name of Campbell were put to death on a gallows on Gallows Foreland.[50] The Atholl men "harassed and plundered the whole country for thirty miles round about Inveraray which belonged to the Earl (of Argyll) and his friends.... All this did not satisfy but parties were afterwards sent to pull down houses, break mill-stones and burn the woods. In this last, their spite was remarkable, the upper part of the timber was cut down and disposed of and fire set to the under part and the very roots burned: this was done both to barren and fruit trees. Great barbarities were exercised towards the poor women who came to look after their husbands' goods and the whole shire of Argyll was dreadfully depopulated. And when Providence was pleased to send a relief to the starving people, by a remarkable take of herring ... and the poor people were making some shift to support themselves, the Marquis of Atholl's men came down upon them and broke their boats and burnt their nets."[51] The grounds at Inveraray Castle were stripped bare and no fewer than 34,400

49 Wodrow, Robert: The History of the Sufferings of the Church of Scotland, Book III, Chapter IX, section X, footnote.

50 The obelisk marking the site of the gallows is in the garden of the Bank of Scotland, Inveraray.

51 Woodrow: History.

trees, some sixteen years of age, among which were six hundred beeches, valued at six hundred pounds, Scots, were carried off.[52]

At length the Privy Council sent an express, ordering restraint to be exercised and the Marquis of Atholl was replaced in the lieutenancy by General Drummond.

One result of the Rising of 1685 was the compilation of a "Booke of Valuation of Argyleshire" to be the rule and standard of exacting and uplifting all public dues and other burthens within the said Shire and Isles in all times coming. The work was undertaken by William, Viscount of Strathallan and completed by Sir John Drummond of Machonie. The returns for most of Mid-Argyll have been lost, but a note of the rent to be paid for Stuckagoy in Glen Shira is still extant. It was calculated at 83 pounds, Scots: 8 lib[53] of silver feu duty and the balance in meal, bear, marts, present wedders, butter, a kayn wedder and meal. The summa was 83 lib.[54] How the Privy Council of 1688 expected to raise such sums from a shire robbed and despoiled as Argyll had been, perhaps only Strathallan and Machonie knew.

It is little wonder that when his Highness William Henry, by the grace of God Prince of Orange, appeared in arms to restore the laws and liberties of the ancient kingdom of Scotland, the event was hailed as "the glorious and never to be forgotten Revolution".

The fines and forfeitures pronounced against many Campbells, MacArthurs and other persons in and around Inveraray were rescinded in 1688 and the case of the Earle of Argyle and of all other sufferers for repairing their damnadges was remitted to the Lords of their Majesties' Privy Counsell.[55]

But the evil consequences of these unhappy years could not be easily remedied, particularly as the question of reparations was not yet settled in 1693. The destruction of property, the plundering of goods, the great loss of cattle and horses, where in the chief wealth of the heritors consisted[56] were not made good. The people

52 Anderson: Mark L: A History of Scottish Forestry Vol. 1, p. 377.

53 Lib - a pound, Scots.

54 MacTavish: Inveraray Papers, pp. 81-83.

55 Acts of the Parliament of Scotland, Vol. ix, Appendix, p. 92.

56 R.P.C.S., Vol. xi, p. 32.

were robbed and impoverished and the burgesses and inhabitants of Inveraray faced the eighteenth century debilitated and exhausted.

The eighteenth century saw the end of the Old Town of Inveraray. But at the beginning of the century it was by no means apparent that this was going to take place. As happens so often, it seemed as if things would go on as they had always done.

The Old Town was built on the west bank of the River Aray and was dominated by the old Castle. The Castle consisted of the large old High Tower and the Little Tower. Before the Castle was the court and the office houses, the stable and the coach-house. At a considerable distance behind the Castle and encircled by a bend of the river were the Upper Garden and the Lower Garden.

The river which like the River Ness has since been straightened and canalized was spanned by a bridge. This bridge was approached by an avenue of trees and over the bridge there passed droves of cattle from southward to northward; horses; oxen for labouring; scores of sheep and goats. The houses beside the bridge were known as Bridgend.

The bridge led into the market place at the centre of which was the Mercat Cross. To the left of the Mercat Cross, as one looked up at Duniquaich, was the Tolbooth, with some of its windows heavily barred. Adjoining the Tolbooth was the Church and beside the Church was the School. Contiguous with the Tolbooth was a tenement. This was the High Street where the Provost, the Sheriff Clerk and other important people dwelt. Tacksmen such as Braleckan had tenements or town houses in this part, just as Simon Lord Lovat had his town house near the Old High Church, Inverness. These houses were slated and some had crow-stepped gables. They were furnished with office houses, and gardens. Betwixt the Cross and the Tolbooth in 1721 there was a great midden. But what of that? What could one expect when the Cross was the focus of weekly markets and annual fairs? Was there not a dung heap at the Dardanian Gate of Ilium [57] and another such heap at the gate of Odysseus' Palace in Ithaca? [58] In Inveraray, the place was eventually made clean and redd and spread with sand or gravel.

57   Homer: Iliad, XXII, p. 414.

58   Odyssey, XVII, p. 297.

Below this part of the Burgh which was known as the Brae-head, there was the Laigh Street. This street ran approximately from west to east; people spoke of the houses on the east side of the Laigh Street. These houses were smaller and lower and were thatched. Many of them also had office houses and gardens.

Round the bay to the south was the Fisherland where the fishing community dwelt in their thatched houses, with their poles and nets by the shore. Alongside was the house of the boat carpenter. At the end of the tapering point of land or corran was Gallows Farland or Foreland and far beyond that was the Gallowgate (later called the Newton) leading to the place of execution at the Crags.

Within the Old Town, there was plenty to do. The business of the day began with the ringing of the Town Bell at six of the clock in the morning and closed when the bell was rung at ten at night.

The magistrates and Council convened within the Tolbooth; they enacted measures which were written down by the Clerk of Court; extracts of their acts were given to the Town Officer to be proclaimed through the Burgh and the proclamation was affixed to the Cross.

The fishing was good at the beginning of the eighteenth century. In 1703, tenants on Lochfyneside paid part of their rent in herring, five hundred sufficient herring with white fish and shell fish.[59]

In addition to the occupations noted in the seventeenth century, there was Archibald McVicar, cady or messenger; William McGibbon, ferrier, navigated the ferry boat which was the property of the Town Council, not between West and East Creggans, but between Inveraray and St. Catherine's and occupied the Ferry House, a tied house. He was also tide-waiter, awaiting the arrival of vessels to secure the payment of duties. Patrick Campbell was Riding Officer of the Customs, checking the export of wool and the import of uncustomed goods; Alexander Fullerton was the Officer who collected excise. There was also the waterman who plied his boat for hire; the post or runner who carried the packet between Inveraray and Dumbarton; a sempstress, a watch-maker, a wig-maker, a butcher, the Town-herd. By the middle of the century there were ten workmen, ten fishermen and four weavers. There were chapmen who paid a freedom fine and had the right as bur-

59 The Black Book of Taymouth, XXXII, p. 428.

gesses, to trade freely and there were unfree tradesmen on whom a fine was imposed.

One noteable figure in the streets of Inveraray in the early part of the century, was Rob Roy MacGregor Campbell. Having failed in business as a cattle drover and having suffered the diligence of the law, he received shelter, wood and water from the Duke of Argyll.[60] He resided in Glen Shira, occupying a house, the ruins of which may still be seen on the south slopes of Ben Bhuidhe. According to local tradition, he was a well-known figure in the Burgh and a popular person at marriages and funerals, despite the fact that an advertisement for his apprehension appeared in June 1712 and was several times repeated.[61] When the Rebellion of 1715 broke out, he left Inveraray to join the forces of the Earl of Mar, although his patron, the Duke of Argyll, was at the head of the army opposed to the Highland insurgents.

The by-name Rob Roy or Red Robert was not the only nickname in a town where many men bore the same surname. There was one change-keeper who had the unfortunate name of Guinach or the venomous; another man was known as Cruit or hunchback.

There were many publick change houses and victualing houses, at which it is said Rob Roy was a regular visitor. Some of these pot houses were kept by widows, such as Widow Murray in 1721. In these premises strangers and passengers were furnished with meat, drink and lodgings at reasonable prices. A the house of Archibald Campbell, vintner, (Circa 1730-1740) one might call for a bottle of rum, a bowl of punch, a chopin of brandy, a bottle of ale, of claret or of white wine. The masons took "their morning" there, and in the evening the guests played "at the cards" by candlelight. The horses were kept in straw in the night, given bread, fitted with girths and buckles, watered and shod for the journey. Archibald Campbell was post master, keeping a note of letters sent to and from Inveraray in 1736. He sold flour, raisins, currants, vinegar, pepper, veal, lamb, mutton, eggs, tobacco. He would arrange to have shoes made and shirts mended. He loaned money and sometimes required to borrow.[62]

In terms of the charter of 1648, the Burgh had the power and liberty of enjoying traffic and trade as well within the kingdom as

60   Scott, Sir Walter: Rob Roy, Introduction.

61   MacIntyre, Peter: Ancient Records of Inveraray.

62   Accompt Book belonging to Arch. Campbell, Inveraray, 1733.

in others beyond the same, and the merchants in Inveraray were not slack in taking advantage of this privilege. Among the vessels anchored off the town were the Endeavour of Dumfries (1750), the Stanhope, Brigantine of Liverpool (1750), the good ship the Agnes of Irvine (1753), the good ship the Cecilia of North Queensferry (1757). Gabbarts carried coals to the mouth of the river and the coals were sold by the barrel.

Ships of the Royal Navy called from time to time. In 1745, the Greyhound, Man of War, came with money to pay the Militia. She was a twenty-four gunned frigate, of four hundred and fifty to five hundred tons and a hundred and sixty men. She was short-bodied, high-sterned with bluff bows, low decks and a square yard on the jib-boom. The fact that she sailed round the Oitir and through the reefs at Eilean Aoghainn was in accordance with the skilful seamanship of the Navy. She sailed away from Inveraray to take a leading part in the sea fight in Loch nan Uamh on 3rd May 1746, the last battle of the '45 Rebellion.[63] In 1750, there was a visit from the Princess Augusta, Commander John McCunn.

A glimpse of the easy-going life in the Old Town at this time has come down to us, by tradition. Some men were arrested by the Coast-guard in Loch na Cille at Keills, North Knapdale for smuggling. The Coast-guard sank their ship where she lay, cargo and all, and the men had to go and stand their trial "They were taken to Inveraray and they got three months for their misbehaviour for smuggling - and the loss of the boat. The governor of the jail was a full cousin ... they were out in the street every day having the time of their life, shooting parties and other things, fishing, all sorts of things. It was no punishment for them. They were well treated. Three months up and of course, they were allowed to go home and home they made for; so they took the hills for it, the shortest way for them, you know." But unfortunately, the Press Gang were waiting for them just inside the gate at home and the Press Gang proved to be less cousinly in their attitude.[64]

Very different was the treatment given to James of the Glens in Inveraray, when the Old Town became the scene of a cause célèbre. Between the 21st and the 25th September, 1752, from Friday morning 6 a.m. until 7 a.m. on Sunday, the English Church

63   Gibson, John S: Ships of the '45, passim.

64   The Kist, 10, Autumn, 1975.

was used as a Court House in the trial of James Stewart for the Appin murder.

In the middle of the century, Inveraray was a busy and reasonably prosperous town in which the citizens carried on trade by which they lived comfortably.[65] Yet the burgesses themselves said that they were allowing their office houses to fall into disrepair. The reason was that His Grace had expressed his intention to remove the Burgh of Inveraray, and in 1746 a summons of removal had been issued against a large number of the inhabitants, including several of the principal townsmen. This proposal affected more than 122 people. Six years later, some sixteen people had still not removed from the Old Town. In 1753, a Precept of Warning was directed against about twelve people who were reluctant to leave and in 1758 pressure was brought to bear on twenty six people who had not at that time quitted the East Side of the Laigh Street.[66]

Under John, 5th Duke of Argyll, 1723-1806, the demolition of the Old Town went on with growing momentum. "He caused throw down the large old High Tower ... and all the office houses and the Little Tower ... the Lowland Kirk, the Old Tolbooth and the Cross, the tenement contiguous to the Kirk and Tolbooth, the tenement of houses below the Brae, the Stable, Coach-house, old office and court thereof, all in the years 1771, '72, '73 and 1774. In 1775, he demolished ... Provost Campbell's, Arch. McLean's, Provost Duncansons's, Dugald Murray's and John Colquhoun's tenements and all the office houses belonging to them in 1776 ... the Old Town being mostly now demolished in 1776."[67]

So the Old Town was swept away. What Montrose and MacColkitto could not do in 1645, and what the Atholl men failed to do in 1685, took place a century later by mutual agreement between the Duke and his tacksmen. By 1785, the Old Town had disappeared and at the present time its situation is a matter for surmise and conjecture.

65   MacTavish: Inveraray Papers, p. 52

66   Ibid.

67   H.P., Vol. ii, S.H.S., p. 111.

SELECTED REFERENCES

Innes, Cosmo: Sketches of Early Scotch History (Innes: S.E.S.H.)

Highland Papers, Vol. ii, Scottish History Society, Second Series, Vol. xii. (H.P., Vol. ii, S.H.S.)

Origines Parochiales Scotiae, Vol. II, Part 1 (O.P.S.)

Accounts of the Lord High Treasurer of Scotland, Vol. vi, 1531-1538. H.M. General Register House.

Calendar of State Papers, Foreign Series of the Reign of Elizabeth, 1563. H.M.S.O. 1966

Tytler, Patrick Fraser: History of Scotland

The Register of the Privy Seal of Scot., Vol. V, H.M.S.O. 1957 (R.P.C.S.)

Fleming, D.H.: Mary Queen of Scots, London, 1898

MacTavish, Duncan C.: Inveraray Papers

Geographical Collections relating to Scotland made by Walter MacFarlane, Scottish History Society, Vol. LII, 1907

The Minutes of the Synod of Argyll, 1639-1651; 1652-1661. The Scottish History Society, Third Series, Nos. 37 and 38

Fasti Ecclesiae Scoticanae, Vol. VIII (F.E.S.)

Minutes of the Kirk Session of Inveraray Church (K.S.M.)

Scotland and the Commonwealth, Scottish History Society, Vol. XVIII

The Story of the Herring, The Herring Industry Board, 1968

Papers relating to the Scots in Poland, 1576-1793, Scot. Hist. Soc. LIX, 1915

Justiciary Records of Argyll and the Isles. The Stair Society, 1949

A History of Strachur and District by Isabella Cameron Douglas, Strachur and District, W.R.I.

The Clan Sept MacKellar. The Celtic Monthly, 1908

Willcock, J: A Scots Earl in Covenanting Times: Being the Life and Times of Archibald, 9th Earl of Argyll (1629-1685), Edinburgh 1907

MacTavish, Duncan C.: The Commons of Argyll

Register of the Privy Council of Scotland, Vol. XI (R.P.C.S.)

Wodrow, Robert: The History of the Sufferings of the Church of Scotland (Wodrow: History)

Anderson, Mark L: A History of Scottish Forestry, Two Volumes.

Acts of the Parliament of Scotland (A.P.S.)

Homer: Iliad and Odyssey

The Black Book of Taymouth

Scott, Sir Walter: Rob Roy

MacIntyre, Peter: Ancient Records of Inveraray

Accompt Book belonging to Arch. Campbell, Inveraray, 1733

The Records of Inveraray Town Council

Gibson, John S: Ships of the '45, Hutchinson, 1967

The Kist. The Magazine of the Natural History and Antiquarian Society of Mid-Argyll.

3

THE NEW TOWN

The Old Town on the Braehead above the River Aray and the New Town on the Foreland to the south over-lapped one another in time. While the Old Town was gradually being deserted and demolished, the New Town was being built and occupied.

The New Town was the conception of Archibald, 3rd Duke of Argyll, realised with the co-operation of Andrew Fletcher, Lord Milton, his adviser and representative, and a nephew of that notable Scot, Andrew Fletcher of Saltoun. The ideas of His Grace and Lord Milton were translated into substantial and suitable buildings by Robert Adam, a modest and competent architect in Edinburgh.

The first house to be built, as was not surprising, was the Chamberlain's House in 1751. It stood at what is now the corner of Main Street West and Front Street. The Provost urged the Duke's tacksmen to give in proposals about building in the New Town, and in response John Richardson, Merchant, built Fern Point in 1753. This is one of the oldest houses in the town and has a typical Scottish circular stair case. Two establishments necessary in the New Town were a Town House for administration and an inn for the refreshment of travellers. The Great Inn, now the Argyll Arms Hotel, was opened in 1755 and the Town House, with Court House, Custom House and prison was begun with masonic ceremony in 1755 and opened in 1757.

On the death of the 3rd Duke in 1761, there was an interregnum. The New Town consisted of the Great Inn, the Town House, the Chamberlain's House, Fern Point and a large house built on the front to the east of the Chamberlain's House, by the same John Richardson, Merchant. There was no green, no church, no breast wall and only a rudimentary jetty. The centre of population was still the Old Town on the banks of the Aray.

When John Campbell became 5th Duke of Argyll in 1770, the construction of the New Town was resumed in earnest. The opportunity of planning the lay-out and buildings was entrusted to Robert Mylne, the last of the long line of master masons to the Kings of Scots.[1] While the Old Town on the river came tumbling down, the tenement of Arkland was erected parallel to the Beech Avenue in 1775 and on the other side of the road the tenement of Relief Land in 1777. To the north in what is now Main Street, individuals were building houses of plain Georgian type, slated, gabled and harled, with dormer windows. These houses built in 1775 and 1780 harmonise with the planned construction of Arkland and Reliefland to the south.

In 1788, the appearance of the Town was greatly enhanced by a harled screen wall with five high arches in which there were three gates, linking the Great Inn with the Town House. This was the Avenue Screen Wall, its central gate giving access to the Beech Avenue which was more than one hundred years old, at that time. This impressive facade was extended when the Dalmally Road Screen Wall, a high arch, flanked by two lower arches set at an angle, was built in 1790.[2]

To balance these imposing buildings on the west, there were three houses on the east at the wharf. There was the large house in the centre, fitted with cellars and storerooms for exports and imports, built in 1760 and subsequently called Niel Gillies' House. On either side of this merchant house, there were two smaller houses raised in 1776: the one the home of the minister of the English congregation, Doctor Paul Fraser and his beautiful daughter, Caroline; the other the manse of the minister of Glenaray.

There remained the Church. After the churches in the Old Town were knocked down, the two congregations had, as Scripture saith, no continuing city. For some years, the people worshipped in two contiguous houses, built in 1779, which now form the George Hotel. Thereafter they moved to a house on the west of what is now Church Square.

The Parish Church of Glenaray and Inveraray was built betwen 1800 and 1805. It was constructed according to the plan of

1   Rehabilitation of Old Town, Inveraray, 1959.

2   List of Buildings of Architectural or Historic Interest.

Robert Mylne and at the expense of the 5th Duke of Argyll who closely supervised the work. An oblong Georgian building, it was designed to house separate Gaelic and English-speaking congregations under one roof, but was divided by a solid partition. The church was aligned from south to north: the entrance for the Gaelic congregation, above which was a bell, faced south between Arkland and Reliefland; the entrance for the English-speaking congregation, above which was a clock, faced north. The house in which the congregations had worshipped latterly, to the west of the church, became the Grammer School.

Mention should also be made of the Barn at the Newton. The Newton itself was a row of cottages, on the line of the former Gallowgate, built to accommodate workmen building the New Town, and affording shelter to the minister of Glenaray before a new manse was built. The barn above the Newton was a drying barn with an outside stair, constructed in the closing years of the 18th century, as part of the improved system of agriculture which was being introduced into the Argyll Estates. A landmark for nearly two hundred years, it was destroyed by fire in 1950, but it is not likely to be forgotten, since it gave its name to such places as Barn Brae and Barn Park.

Inveraray, which the representatives of the Convention of Burghs did not visit in 1690 "because of the difficulty of access," had now become more accessible. After the Jacobite Rising in 1745, a military road had been constructed from Dumbarton to Inveraray and the River Aray was spanned by a bridge.

With the building of the new Castle and the removal of the Town, Inveraray became a place to be visited by those on tour in the Highlands. Doctor Samuel Johnson and James Boswell on their way back from the Hebrides stayed at the Great Inn in October 1773. Robert Burns was a guest at the inn in June 1787, and feeling that he had not been received with sufficient ceremony, he wrote an epigram, more remarkable for sarcasm that for poetic merit. William and Dorothy Wordsworth came in August 1803 and the poet's sister wrote about the town. In 1806, the future Mrs. Grant of Laggan passed through the Burgh on her way north and recorded her impressions in her book "Letters from the Mountains". In 1818, Keats saw a play called "The Stranger" in the theatre on the first floor of the Jubilee Hall, Maltland.

While these great changes were taking place in the town at

home, many of Inveraray's younger sons were away at the wars. Some of them fell in hopeless charges against the stockade at Ticonderoga in July, 1758, and of several strange stories concerning that disastrous day one may be given here, because it concerns the environs of Inveraray. "On the very day in July 1758 on which the Battle of Ticonderoga was fought, two ladies Miss Campbell of Ederline and her sister were walking from Cilmalieu to Inveraray and had reached the new bridge over the Aray. They both of them saw in the sky what looked like a siege going on. They saw the different regiments with their colours and recognised many of their friends among the Highlanders. They saw Inverawe and his son fall and other men whom they knew. When they reached Inveraray, they told their friends of the vision they had seen. They also took down the names of those whom they had seen fall and the date of the occurrence.... Weeks after, the Gazette corroborated their statements in its account of the attempt on Ticonderoga".[3]

The French Wars continued indefinitely, claiming a quota of the youth of Inveraray in each generation. The Argyll Highlanders were raised in 1777, and the 74th (Highland) Regiment of Foot was raised in 1787.[4] Of this regiment the Rev. Paul Fraser wrote[5] that many of the natives of Inveraray have joined the 74th Highlanders. The 74th Foot eventually became the 2nd Battalion Highland Light Infantry. War was in the air and the Old Barracks in the Maltland (now a sawmill) were occupied in the 1790s by the Marquess of Lorne's Fencibles and Clavering's Regiment.

It is not surprising that disorders broke out, when so many men were quartered in close proximity. Soldiers with such names as MacDonald and Campbell, Stewart, MacGregor and Colquhoun came from the Maltland to the Town; and the streets, especially on pay days, were filled with noisy and quarrelsome men with old memories of clan feuds. One one occasion a fight began near Relief Land where an old lady called Miss Betty Balfour conducted a school for young ladies. The men struggled in the street, in the close, and at length burst into Miss Balfour's classroom where they grappled and strove with one another, until a piquet appeared

3   The Oban Times, 23.7.1932.

4   Farmer, J.S: Regimental Records.

5   Old Statistical Account.

and arrested them. The screams of the young ladies' and of their teacher were heard all over the town and Miss Balfour lodged a complaint in writing with the Provost of the Burgh.[6]

"The French have landed" was the news most feared by many people and that was the message brought by a horseman to Inveraray on 8th October 1798. The Argyllshire Fencibles raised in 1793 and 1795, fell in to the sound of the pibroch and the roll of drums and marched away to the scene of action in Kintyre. The Volunteers mustered in their turn, while the Town piper blew a rouse in the Main Street and cruisie lamps and candles shed a flickering light on the martial scene. The only serious engagement was a naval battle off the north coast of Ireland which was witnessed from the shore at Kilchenzie.[7]

A great war scatters people all over the world and causes them to be found in unlikely places. When the 71st (Highland) Regiment of Foot (later the 1st Battalion H.L.I.) captured Buenos Ayres in July 1806, a British subject named Duncan Bell from Inveraray was relieved from confinement in the Spanish city and sent on board a British ship of war.[8]

Amid these alarums and excursions the usual interests and occupations of the Burgh were proceeding as normally as possible. In 1795, the herring fishers were making good catches and the salters and those employed by them in gutting and curing the fish were kept hard at work.[9] In 1796, there were no less than 500 boats employed in the herring fishing, besides 100 busses and vessels of large size from various parts of Britain, Ireland and the Isle of Man.[10]

Sea-borne trade was brisk. The bay and harbour were frequented by vessels from different quarters, employed in importing grain, meal, coal and other articles and in exporting wool, timber, bark and other productions of this part of the country.[11]

6   MacIntyre, Peter: Ancient Records of Inveraray.

7   The Correspondence of Lieut.-General Campbell of Kintarbert, 1762-1837.

8   Ibid.

9   Minutes of the Town Council, 12.8.1795.

10   Ibid.

11   Ibid.

The Town was busy: there were grocers, tailors, shoe-makers, brogue-makers, wig-makers, watchmakers, milliners, barbers and butchers.[12] A visit to Inveraray was an exciting experience; there were many wonderful things to be bought with one's money.

There were more melancholy occasions. In May 1805, a man named MacLagan having been accused and found guilty of murder was hanged and buried at the Crags, one mile south of the Burgh. Whin and broom cast their yellow flowers over his solitary grave amid the rocks beside the Loch.

At length the lads came marching home, covered with glory from many distant fields, although in the case of others, they returned no more. Among those who did not come back were Major James Campbell, the 2nd Battalion, The Royal Scots, who fell in action at Corunna on 16th January, 1809, Captain Dougald McGibbon, the 57th Foot, (1st Battalion Middlesex Regiment) killed at Albuera, and Captain Peter McArthur of the 5/60th (Royal American) Regiment of Foot, who was killed at Waterloo.[14]

Of the many men who distinguished themselves were General Charles Turner, C.B., who resided for some years after the War at Maam in Glen Shira; General Dougald Campbell who was severely wounded in the head by a splinter from a shell at Waterloo; and Lieut.-Colonel Colin Campbell, C.B. who commanded the Royal Scots at Waterloo. He retired to live with his brothers and sister in the Paymaster's House, Main Street East, Inveraray.

The Homeric battle of Waterloo made a great impression on people in the Burgh. It is said that over 60 officers and men from Inveraray fought under the Iron Duke that day and that seven of them were killed. This event gave rise to a saying which was long current in the Town: "Waterloo was a hard day and a long day, but it came to an end." [15]

The Royal Navy was represented by Mr. Peter Brown, who

12   Stent Roll, 1791.

13   Ancient Records of Inveraray, p. 67.

14   Oman, C.W.C.:Wellington's Army, pp. 227-228, 302-303, 335.

15   Oban Times, 12.6.1937.

lived in the Three Bridges Cottage, Glenaray. He took part in the Battle of Trafalgar, being a member of the crew of the Victory.[16]

Among land soldiers prepared for sea service was Captain Alexander Campbell of the Royal Marines who lived at Pennymore with his brother, his brother's wife and family. Captain Alexander Campbell fought under Nelson at the Battle of Trafalgar. He was on duty on board H.M.S. Bellerophon when Napoleon Bonaparte came on board and surrendered to Captain Maitland, commanding the ship. Captain Campbell was in charge of the escort of Marines who acted as guard to Napoleon, while he was on board the Bellerophon.[17]

After the long strife came peace and some further building was done, giving the town the appearance which it has today. The Court House, Crown Point was built with a projecting central pavilion and classical window in 1819; the Old Jail, a prison for debtors as well as criminals was built in 1820; and the New Jail was built for male offenders in 1845.[18]

One of the shops in the Burgh was a bookshop kept by John Shaw, Bookseller in 1820. John Shaw was a descendant of Neil Shaw, Valet to the Marquess of Argyll in 1660.[19] He sold "Inveraray Ballads", a collection of about fifteen ballads, printed by Thomas Duncan in Glasgow between the years 1800 and 1810.[20] These ballads were also carried by Peter Turner, chapman, in his tours through the Highlands.

Business in the Town was expedited when a branch of the National Bank of Scotland was opened on 26th September 1830. It was located in the large house in Front Street, built by the merchant John Richardson in 1760. The branch was opened in Inveraray before there was an office of this Bank in Glasgow. Eight years later, 1838, the Glasgow Union Banking Company obtained premises in the Burgh and Mr. James M. Wright, solicitor was app-

16   Ibid. 29.7.1933.

17   Ibid. 9.7.1932.

18   List of Buildings of Architectural or Historic Interest.

19   Family tradition.

20   MacLean, Donald: Typographia Scoto-Gadelica, Edinburgh, 1915, p. 156.

ointed agent. He was succeeded in the Bank by his son Quintin Montgomery Wright who likewise carried on a flourishing legal business.

But peace has its trials no less severe than war. In 1845-46, the potato crop failed. Before this time, potato disease had been unknown, each season brought good crops and the people lived on potatoes and herring (sgadan agus buntata). In 1845, however, potato disease made its appearance. At the same time, the herring left the shores. The two main sources of food having failed, the people were brought to the verge of starvation. The Government sought to relieve the worst of the distress by shipping loads of meal to this coast and some of the old people formed a liking for Indian meal porridge during the famine and insisted on supping it long after better times had come. Young gulls and all kinds of sea birds were kippered like herring. They were smoked in the peat smoke and formed a scanty provision for the winter.[21]

This disaster led to emigration. A system of emigration to Canada was worked out, and vessels were hired to take the people across the seas. Populous little townships were deserted. The houses fell into ruins.[22] The stones of the walls were used to build sheep fanks. The wells became over-grown with green weed, and in the long shadows of dawn and sunset one may still discern the lazy beds and the old fail dykes along the edge of the fields.

Troubles never come singly. The failure of the potato crop and the herring fishing in 1845 was followed by an epidemic of cholera in October 1849.[23] The disease raged up and down the West High-

---

21 The Oban Times, 24.7.1937.

22 Some of these houses had been built with much labour. Four large stones with a smooth face were laid, one at each corner of the house. Big stones, lying perhaps in moss, were chosen. They were heated to a great heat with a peat fire. One the hot stone, cold water was dropped along a line, causing the stone to crack with a smooth face. Other great stones which obstructed the cultivation of the ground were used for the footings or foundations of the walls. These boulders were moved by gradually inserting strong poles under them to be used as levers or crowbars. If these levers were used unskilfully, the workers might so injure themselves internally, that they died. When possible, ropes, a contrivance similar to a parbuckle, were passed round the stone, and it was drawn on to a slipe or sledge. The slipe fastened to a horse's harness by ropes was dragged to the site and the stones were built into the foundations of the cottages, or placed as the boundaries of fields.

23 Minutes of Kirk Session, The United Presbyterian Church, Inveraray.

lands. The inhabitants fled the village of Kenmore and lived in tents on the Kenmore Hill.[24] Two brothers were returning from the market when one took ill upon the road. The other hoisted his brother on his back, carried him home to the croft house, filled him with whisky (illicitly distilled) and the sick man recovered.[25] Some of the victims were buried in mass graves in the vicinity of Old Port Ann. Here and there cholera graves covered with bright green grass may be clearly seen among the dark brown heather.[26]

Before and during these troubles there was a certain amount of rebuilding, some of it on account of the religious controversies of the period. In 1836, a few of the more primitive cottages in the Newton were rased to make way for a United Secession Church. This building was harled, with a slated roof and a curvilinear gable[27] In 1844, there was a further demolition to provide a site for a Free Church for the"Free Protesting Church in Inveraray".[28] This was followed four years later by the removal of more cottages to make room for the Free Church School, with gabled projection and plaque inscribed "Free Church School, 1848".[29] A house, harled, gabled, with slate roof and dormer windows had been built in the early nineteenth century and was taken over for a school master's house. A house of two storeys of the same date served later as the United Presbyterian Manse and a house with three storeys came to be used as the Episcopal Rectory. A number of one storey cottages were built in the middle of the nineteenth century; much of the old Newton was swept away and replaced by the buildings which look out across the loch at the present time. In the landward area of the parish a manse (Craig Dhu), having a panel with a relief bust of Doctor Guthrie, was provided for the Free Church minister in 1851.

In the eighteen fifties, there was growing up in the neigh-

24 Local tradition.

25 Family tradition.

26 Local tradition.

27 List of Buildings of Architectural and Historic Interest.

28 Inscription on Presentation Clock.

29 List of Buildings of Architectural and Historic Interest.

bourhood of Inveraray a boy who was to make some stir in the world. In 1848 or 1849, James Chalmers, missionary in New Guinea, lived with his parents at High Ballantyre in Glenaray, where he went to school. In his autobiography, Chalmers relates how he saved a school-fellow called John Minto from drowning: "There had been very heavy rain during the morning and until near school-closing time, when the sun came out, and we had a fine afternoon to get to our homes. There was a very big spate on, and the Aray was rushing, tumbling and roaring. The affluents were all full and rushing on to swell the Aray's volume of water. Some of us were a short distance ahead and a few were coming up behind. When at the Three Bridges which were wooden then, the old stone ones having been swept away the year before, there was a cry from a short distance up the river that Johnnie Minto was being carried away. There was a rush and in the course of it off went my jacket, and I could see the boy come rolling down. I got quickly to the down side of the bridge and stretching well out, I, as he was pasing under, seized his dress, dragged him near, and held him tightly with my left hand. I then slipped down a little, and allowed us both to be carried a little distance on, when I seized a branch, and getting near the bank was helped up with the saved boy. Why I went to the down side and acted as I did, I cannot say; but it was the only way in which he could have been saved. He was carried home and for some days did not come to school. I had the thanks of his parents and, what pleased me still more, the admiration and cheers of the master and scholars." [30]

After the dearth of 1845-46, there was a revival of the fishing industry in 1853. In that year the number of barrels of herring cured in this district was 23,739, the number of persons employed in the fishery was 4,466 and the total value of the boats, nets and lines used was £37,000. [31] That the fishing industry continued to prosper for some decades appears from the fact that the 8th Duke at his own expense built a public reading room and social centre for the town fishermen about 1880. [32] This House, Quay Close,

30   Chalmers, James: His Autobiography and Letters, London, R.T.S., 1902.

31   The Imperial Gazetteer of Scotland, Fullarton & Co., London.

32   List of Buildings of Architectural and Historic Interest.

bears a panel with the ducal coat of arms and motto; and a plaque commemorating Elizabeth, Duchess of Argyll.

It was known that there were pockets of copper in Mid-Argyll and in the nineteenth century attempts were made to exploit these natural resources. The Craigerrine Mine not far from Auchindrain was opened in 1799 and subsequently mining operations were begun at Coille Bhraghad near the Cromallt Burn, about one and a half miles south of Inveraray. The mine was begun as a copper mine by the Duke of Argyll and in 1851 the workings were found to contain nickel. For this nickeliferous ore there was ready sale. Between 1854 and 1867, nine tons of copper ore and 417 tons of nickel ore were produced. The mine was worked open cast; several small shafts were sunk; and an adit level cross cut, that is a horizontal working made from the surface to strike the mineral vein, was driven from a point about sixty yards to the south east. This adit may have served for drainage purposes, also. The remains of the old dressing floor can still be made out. The miners descended the shafts by ladders. In 1853, there were six pickmen independent of surface and other labourers. The pickmen worked by the light of an ordinary tallow dip-candle carried in the hat. The air was kept in circulation by windmills which supplied it to fans and fanners and was conveyed through the workings by air pipes. The workings were kept free from water which was continually seeping in, by pumps which operated day and night.[33] The ore was washed, weighed, packed in boxes, carted to the quay at Inveraray and shipped to Liverpool. This industry gave employment to local men, to miners from Strontian, Argyll, and to overseers and miners from Cornwall. Until 1873, the miners under their foreman Neill McGougan worked part of the week at Craignure near Auchindrain and part of the week at Coille Bhraghad. At that date, business was transacted between the Manager at Coille Bhraghad and Messrs. Watts, Blackburn & Co., Clay Merchants, Newton Abbot, Devon.

There was also a mine on the hillside, a quarter of a mile south west of Clachan Beag at the head of Loch Fyne.[34] The workings

33 Joiners and Wrights' Time Records, Inveraray, 1851-1854.

34 Memoirs of the Geological Survey of Scotland, Vol. xvii:

Lead, Zinc, Copper and Nickel Ores of Scotland, H.M.S.O., 1921.

were in the nature of a trail for argentiferous or silver-bearing mineral. There appears to have been one foot width of ore and an assay yielded lead 12 per cent; silver 2 oz. to the long ton, and traces of gold. There is a small dump of from 10 to 20 tons of ore at the mouth of the mine. Little was done and the workings were soon abandoned. Some of the local men bearing such names as McNicoll, MacArthur, MacIntyre, Dewar and Campbell may have worked in the mine for a short time.[35]

The weaving industry gave employment to a number of people. In 1774 a wool-spinning industry was begun at Factory Land in Inveraray. Two years later, this industry was removed to Claonairi and the factory was called St John's. Houses were built, machinery was installed, and a schoolmaster was appointed to Bridge of Douglas School. In 1783, there were four weavers in the Burgh itself.[36] There was likewise an extensive weaving industry at Bovuy and at Cladich, Loch Awe. Bovuy was once a populous township and in every cottage there was a spinning wheel, a warping frame and a loom. Many families by the name of MacIntyre wove tartans and garters[37] to be sold at markets in Dalmally and Inveraray.

The sixth of August, 1866, was the twenty-first anniversary of the birth of John Douglas Sutherland Campbell, Marquis of Lorne. The occasion was celebrated suitably by a County Ball at Inveraray Castle. There was a dinner for the Duke's workpeople in a building temporarily erected and decorated with heather, laurel and sweet bog myrtle in the Cherry Park. The Freedom of the Burgh was presented to his Lordship in the Court House. The burgess ticket was enclosed in a casket, made of a piece of oak, part of one of the vessels of the Spanish Armada, wrecked at Tobermory. The health of the Marquis was drunk by a large number of people at the Cross and the glasses were tossed in the air after the liquor was quaffed. H.M.S. Lion fired a salute of nineteen guns, which was answered by a salute of two pieces from the top of Duniquaich and by another gun in the Castle grounds. There was a display of fire-

35 Clachan Chapel and Graveyard.

36 Town Council Records.

37 The Oban Times, 20.5.1933.

works in front of the Castle and the whole Town of Inveraray was illuminated.[38]

In the autumn of that year, there were exciting pursuits of a different kind. In September 1866, an otter hunt took place on the Duke's Estate in which the Duke, the Marquis of Lorne and his brothers, Lords Archibald, Walter and Colin took part.[39] Early in November, "the Largie Hounds, eight couples, arrived by steamer. On the morrow, the River Douglas was tried and the hounds at once struck the trail. An otter had passed up the river shortly before. From the river mouth dogs and men in full cry hurried on, sweeping underneath the bridge at Kilbride and following the course of the river through woods and meadows. After running about a mile, the leading dog dashed into a hole formed by some large roots on the bank; behind, came the rest of the pack. In a moment, the otter darted out and made for the thickest part of the wood. 'Gone away—away' resounded above the noise. Not till he had almost reached the high road, did the leading hounds gain upon the otter. Suddenly wheeling round, he made for the river again and by rapid doubling tried to baffle his pursuers. It was in vain; just as he was about to plunge into the water he was gripped. He left his mark on several of the pack, before he was over-mastered. He was a large sized otter and had lost one of his forefeet, probably in a trap."[40]

During the sixties and the seventies strong communal life developed in the Burgh. The threat of hunger was less immediate, epidemics were less frequent and less fatal. In the early sixties, the local newspaper arrived once a month and later once a week. The journey between Inveraray and Glasgow took the greater part of a day, either by steam boat or mail coach. The result was that the Burgh to a certain degree was a world by itself. People had to provide their own amusements and to develop their own interests and activities. Consequently, there was a wide variety of organisations and a vigorous community life.[41]

38   The Oban Times, 6.8.1866.

39   Ibid, 15.9.1866.

40   Ibid. 3.11.1866.

41   The Oban Times, passim.

The Volunteer Act was passed in 1863.[42]   The Argyllshire Highland Rifles and the Argyllshire Brigade of Artillery, volunteers (of which the Marquis of Lorne was Colonel) were formed; arrangements were made in 1866 for the erection of a suitable drill hall; and drill instructors from the regular army were supplied by the Government. In August 1881, 'A' Company, Inveraray, Argyllshire Highland Rifles paraded at the Wet Review in Edinburgh. In addition to these companies, there was a corps of archers in the Town of Inveraray.[43]

There was an Inveraray Cricket Club which went to Ayr to play the Ayr Cricket Club on the Low Green, Ayr, in July, 1866. The match ended in a draw.

In winter there was curling. A match was played on the River Aray in January, 1867 between Mr. MacPherson, The Argyll Arms and Doctor Campbell, Cladich, for a load of meal for the poor. After three hours of keen competition, Doctor Campbell's rink was declared victor by eight shots.

The Inveraray Public Library founded in 1832 had been some what neglected, but at the prompting of one of the ministers a public meeting was held in the Court House in 1867; a librarian was appointed, and the books put in circulation once more.

Shinty was a sport for which the young men of this district were namely. In 1865, the Inveraray Estates Team under the captaincy of Lord Archibald Campbell played the Land of Ardkinglass Shinty Team. The match was a great shinty tussle, sixty players being engaged on each side.[44] There was a shinty match every New Year's Day. In 1878, the Vale of Leven Club sent a team of 15 men to compete with an equal number of the Inveraray Club.[45] The match was played at the Winterton Park. The result was Inveraray 12, the Vale 1. This was followed by a match on Old New Year's Day (the twelfth of January) between the Inveraray Shinty Club and the Excelsior (Furnace) Shinty Club. The fifteen players from Inveraray travelled to Furnace by the steamer Fairy.

42   Act 26 and 27, Vict. cap. 65

43   Gazetteer of Scotland.

44   The Oban Times, 3.9.1932.

45   The Oban Telegraph, 1877-1878.

The match took place at Goatfield Park and was refereed by Doctor Campbell, Brenchoille.[46] In January 1879, a game of Shinty was played under unusual conditions. The ice on Loch Fyne was from three to four inches thick and a shinty match took place on the ice between the New Bridge and Inveraray Pier.[47]

An important contribution was made to adult education when Mutual Improvement Societies were formed in rural districts such as Bunchrew, Inverness-shire and in county towns such as Inveraray, Argyll. The first meeting of this association in Inveraray was held in November, 1874, when office-bearers were elected, the majority of whom bore local names. The president gave it as his opinion that such societies were calculated to do a great amount of good, especially to young men. Debates took place on such questions as, "Are we better off with steam engines, telegraphs et cetera than we would be without them, as our forefathers were?" Papers were read on Superstitions, Emigration, Liberalism in Religion, The Rebellion of 1745.

The spectre of poverty however was never far away especially for orphans, widows, old people, and for weavers, when the trade of hand-loom weaving failed in 1870. Monthly concerts for the benefit of the deserving poor were given in the Court House and on these evenings there were large attendances. A Clothing Club which provided useful articles at a reduced price was formed under the patronage of Lady Victoria Campbell.

While it is true that charity begins at home, the people of Inveraray were ready to help the unfortunate in other burghs, such as those in the City of Glasgow. In the summer time during the seventies a number of poor workers came to Inveraray from Glasgow on the steamer Vale of Clywd. The bakers laid in an extra supply of loaves; saveloys and red herring appeared in heaps at shop windows. The Parish Church and the Duke's barns were opened to provide sleeping accommodation. The quiet town was astir to give welcome to the city toilers.

Into the Burgh they marched, two hundred or more of them, with gay flags, a big drum loudly beat, a piper blowing lustily. Everybody came to their doors to see the procession pass up the street. The children ran to meet it and accompany it to the Kirk

46 Ibid.

47 The Oban Times.

door, where those in charge arranged the future mode of procedure.

The local people did not grudge the visitors their holiday, but they made a noise and upset the place and created much excitement.

The Kirk was the rallying-point of the holidaymakers. If a child went amissing, the old bellman went slowly up and down the Main Street, ringing his bell and calling out in his quavering voice, "Volunteers wanted to search for the lost child. Meet at the Kirk.[48]

The holiday passed only too quickly and in a few days the visitors were aboard the Vale of Clywd on their way home to the tenements and foundries of Glasgow.

An important local institution was the Inveraray Pastoral and Agricultural Society. Amid its many interests and activities, this Society organised ploughing matches. On 19th January 1877, a fair number of ploughs were on the field at the Maltland. There were prizes for the Best Start and Finish; the Best Kept Harness; the Best Groomed Horses; for the Youngest Ploughman; for the longest service under one master; for the Best trimmed Horses; and for the Oldest Ploughman.[49]

Three times a year members of the Pastoral and Agricultural Society attended the Falkirk Trysts[50] which were held on the second Tuesday of August, the second Monday of September, the second Monday of October and the following days, generally for three days at a time. When the visitors from Inveraray attended the concluding tryst for the year 1878, held on the usual stance on Stenhousemuir, they could not but note that the show of sheep, estimated in round numbers at about 25,000, was the smallest exhibition that the oldest frequenter of these markets could recollect. They attributed the obvious decline to the Perth Sales and to the rapid communication between sellers and buyers. Lots at a prior time intended for such a meeting had been bought at the farms in Argyllshire and sent direct to pastures in the south. On the second day, there were 15,000 head of cattle and of horses. The

48 Saxby, Jessie M.E: Milestones and Other Stories, 1891.

49 The Oban Telegraph.

50 There were Fairs held from time immemorial under the name of the Falkirk Trysts. They used to be held on the Reddingrig-moor, then on the Bonnymoor, and after 1775 on Stenhousemoor. Imperial Gazetteer.

trade in horses however was affected by the failure of the City of Glasgow Bank.

We may suppose that the members of the Inveraray Society were too seriously minded to be interested in caravan shows, Wombwell's Menagerie, stalls, huxtery-carts, merry-go-rounds, tumblers, tricksters and fiddlers. But they may have been tempted to enter the tents where there was the treatings, which took place at all the great Scottish fairs.

In Inveraray itself the Sheep and Wool Market was held at the end of July and the Inveraray Cattle Market at the end of October. These markets gradually came to an end in the Burgh. The sheep market was held at Dalmally, because Dalmally was on the railway, transport was more convenient and means of communication quicker. The wool was sent by sea and later by road to wool brokers in Glasgow, who either sent a cheque at once and sold when they could get a good price, or who sold on commission on behalf of the crofters and farmers.

The Feeing Markets were important events in the agricultural year. There was not much feeing at Inveraray and the farmers used to go in April to Dalmally and Lochgilphead, to engage servants from one half year to another. Early in the morning of market day there was a stir as refreshment tents were erected with booths for the sale of sweets, trinkets and all other things dear to the ploughboy's heart. Soon after breakfast, the market was crowded by farmers and their wives, ploughmen and female servants. Besides these, there was a general assembly of all the idlers and ne'er do weels in the countryside: tramps, tinkers, ballad-singers, beggar women with starving babies, ship-wrecked sailors who had never been to sea, veteran soldiers who had seen no service. At one place in the open air by the end of a tent a women would be piling up a blazing fire of peat, over which a huge pot was boiling with farmers' broth. Close by, a master would be higgling with a ploughman about five shillings more or less of half-yearly wages (the wages being between £3 and £3.10s.). The bargain would end by "splitting the difference", which was followed by a dram. One shepherd who had a wife and family depending on him, not having been feed at Dalmally, walked all through the night to Lochgilphead, a distance of forty miles, to stand in the market which was held in that town on the morrow.[51]

51 Local tradition.

At this time, 1878, Mrs. MacNaught, the guid-wife in Tighna-fead beside the infant Aray on the long road from Dalmally, got a public house licence. The ale-house was called Tighnafead, "the house of the whistle", because wayfarers on the road above used to whistle through their fingers for refreshments, which were carried out to them.[52]

The planting carried out by the Marquess, the 9th Earl and the Dukes of Argyll was producing results. The hills at Inveraray were covered with plantations which extended for six miles on the way to Dalmally. There were vast extents of spruce in the shire and in the neighbourhood of the Burgh, there were Weymouth Pines, beeches, limes, oaks, chestnuts and ash trees.[53]

The people of Inveraray were highly gratified when John Douglas Sutherland Campbell, Marquess of Lorne and 9th Duke of Argyll married H.R.H. Princess Louise in 1871. One citizen of the Burgh said: "Queen Victoria will be a proud woman today".[54] For many years the Princess and the Marquis visited Inveraray Castle every autumn. Her Royal Highness owned Dalchenna and Kilcat-rine on Lochfyneside.

An event which was eagerly anticipated every year was the Christmas Tree and the Christmas Treat, said to have been estab-lished at the Castle by George 8th Duke of Argyll. This colourful occasion meant much to the citizens in the Burgh and to the work-ers on the Estate. The Oban Times of 3rd January 1885 recorded "The Duke of Argyll and the Marquis of Lorne welcomed their guests."

Another event which has taken place in the neighbourhood of the Castle for generation after generation is the Inveraray High-land Games. The origin of these field-days may be traced to the policy of each Highland chief that he might have a body of young clansmen trained in physical strength and endurance. The simple form of such games may be seen, when a few young men gather on the short grass in front of a big house on a summer evening and compete in feats of strength, in piping and dancing.

52   Local tradition.

53   Anderson, Mark L: A History of Scottish Forestry.

54   Local tradition.

When this sport was held within the park dykes of the Castle, the same games were played, but in a more organised and competitive form. Prizes were offered and competitors from the surrounding countryside were invited to take part. There was tossing the cabar, putting the stone, throwing the hammer, foot races, piping and dancing. The interest which Queen Victoria showed in Highland life and customs encouraged the promotion of these gatherings.

At the present time, the Joint Chieftains of the Games are Their Graces the Duke and Duchess of Argyll and the Hon. Life Vice-President is Mathilda, Duchess of Argyll. There are Local Events confined to natives and permanent residents in the Counties of Argyll and Bute, and there are Open Events. Some remarkable feats of strength have been performed. The 16 lb hammer has been thrown 141 feet, 2½'' and the 56 lb weight has been thrown a distance of 44 feet 4 inches.

The Games have drawn crowds from a wide area for many years. In 1893, they were held in September and the Town Council's own paddle steamer 'The Fairy' brought people from Crarae, Strachur and Furnace, making the return trip in the afternoon. Boys walked miles to the Park and after watching the contests for hours under a hot sun, they went hungry and foot sore to the fishermen's boats in the harbour and were given a dish of fresh herring which, they said, was the sweetest food they ever tasted. In the early nineteenth century, there used to be five steamers calling at Inveraray on the day of the Games. Having been interrupted only by two world wars, this Gathering continues to attract many visitors each summer.

In the last decade of the nineteenth century, Lord Archibald Campbell raised a Pipe Band in the Burgh, of which photographs are still extant, and in 1895, this Pipe Band marched through Glencoe.

At this time, increasing attention was being drawn to Inveraray by the writings of Neil Munro, the most distinguished literary son of the Burgh. Born in 1864 and brought up in Crombie's Land, he went to school in Inveraray under Henry Dunn Smith. The boy used to go with his book under his arm to the Ramparts which were about the old Tolbooth and walking round the bastions on a foot-wide ledge, he sat on the ledge reading with his legs dangling over

135

the water.[55] Leaving school, he went into the office of William Douglas, writer, as a junior clerk. He joined the staff of the Falkirk Herald and eventually became editor of the Glasgow Evening News. He made Inveraray the scene of many of his stories, building up the landscape in stately poetic prose. He was buried in Cilmalieu on Christmas Eve, 1930.

At the turn of the century, the poor had a hard struggle for life. Some gathered whelks for which they searched in the brown tangled seaweed and in the warm shallow pools left behind by the ebbing tide. The whelks were collected in tin pails, transferred to strong coarse hempen sacks and left below high water mark, that they might not lose their vitality. They were sold to a local merchant who might either pay for them in cash or give in exchange goods such as tea, sugar, meal, boots and articles of clothing. The whelks were sent to Glasgow, London and Liverpool to be sold on barrows in streets in the East End.[56] A whelk gatherer was able to earn about nine shillings per week.

The packmen were still on the roads, but the ballad-managers with their penny sheets (such as "Wha saw the Forty-Second, Wha saw them gang awa'?"), the chapmen and the pedlar poets had almost disappeared. A colporteur, however, pale and tired, dressed in seedy blacks, with his bicycle laden with books and periodicals occasionally went from house to house in summer.[57] The packman arrived at the door, bent under his load, a wooden box with a heavy carrying strap and above this a bundle wrapped in black shiny oil cloth, criss-crossed with straps. He sometimes wore a tweed greatcoat, muffler and cloth cap. The bundle contained flowery overalls and aprons, petticoats and dishtowels, pillow-slips and sheets. When the box was opened there was a series of little drawers: in the top drawer were dozens of spectacles; the next drawer held ribbons; the third drawer had laces, black or brown, leather or cotton; the last drawer was filled with beads, gold and silver, chains, bangles, hat-pins brooches, even watches.[58]

55   Munro, Neil: Gilian the Dreamer, 1899.

56   Murray, Eunice G. Scottish Homespun, Blackie, 1947. Local tradition.

57   Local tradition.

58   Sandeman, Mary: When the Years were Young, Kist, No. 9, 1975.

During and after the First World War, from 1914 to 1920, women called pedlars took the place of the men. Their stock-in-trade was wrapped up in a brown and white check plaid. On being asked into the kitchen, they took the bundle from off their shoulders, untied the opposite corners, spread it on the floor and offered prins, bobbins, pirns of thread, darning wool, handkerchiefs, sox, stockings and table covers. Having finished their troking, they tied two opposite corners tightly so that their wares could not fall out. The other two corners were not knotted so tightly and the bundle was slipped over their heads. The burden hanging round their necks, rested on their backs and they relieved the pressure on their throats by holding the knot with their hands. In the morning, they were bowed with the weight; in the evening, the bundle was smaller and they walker more uprightly.[59]

Men who lived hard lives were navvies and labourers, tramping from one job to another in the nineteen twenties and thirties. Hearing of work in Kinlochleven or Fort William, they set out to walk, sleeping under haystacks, eating swede turnips out of the fields, set upon by dogs, and thankful for even a gate to put between themselves and the night. Passing through the Burgh of Inveraray, they applied for assistance before 1929 to the Parish Council Poor Law Officer; after 1929 to the Public Assistance Officer. They spoke of this official as "the kind man" either in sarcasm or in gratitude. He might give them a shilling, or he might give them a note which entitled them to bed and breakfast for one night in a local lodging house. There used to be such a lodging house near the Court House in Inveraray.[60]

The travellers have left a reminder of their presence in and around the burgh in the place-name The Tinker's Burn. This stream flows from Loch Riochan and Coille Bhraghad and enters the River Aray near the Maltland. The people of Inveraray knew the travellers well and noticed some of their characteristics. When a horse was taken out of one of their carts, the cart was left with its shafts or trams resting on the ground, where as a farmer's cart was left with its shafts or trams almost erect in the air. The palms of the travellers used to be so hardened that without feeling pain they

59 Local tradition.

60 Local tradition. There was a similar lodging house called The Cadger's in the Back Street of the village of Lybster, Caithness.

could scoop up red hot embers in the hollow of their hands to light their pipes. They knew of a process by which red heather was changed into white heather and they sold sprigs of it at the corner of Main Street West, Inveraray, to tourists "for luck". They used to play the pipes at the Pier in summer, while one of their women with a tartan collecting bag went round the visitors, grouped around the touring omnibuses. It was observed that the fingering of pipers who are tinkers differs from the fingering which is taught in formal schools of piping. The one school of musicians plays with stiff fingers, the other with bent fingers.

Well-known in the Burgh were Betsy Williamson and her husband. They lived in a wooden hut at Bealach an fhuaran above Inveraray, cooking over a fire of wood in the open-air and drawing water from a near-by stream which at that point flowed into a natural rock basin. Betsy split sticks, made them up into bundles and sold them for firewood. She could not read; a grandson read the paper to her; he used to tell her the time and remind her of the hour when the local 'bus was due.[61] She died at an advanced age on 10th January, 1975, the matriarch of her tribe. Her funeral was attended by travellers from Lochgilphead, Campbeltown, Helensburgh, Perth, Cumbernauld, Lanark, Stirling and Inverness. The company, in which there were many children, grand-children and great grand-children distinguished by a shock of flaxen-coloured hair, was colourful. The mourners arrived in vans, dormobiles, caravans, pick-ups, lorries, trucks and saloon cars. The vehicles were of many colours and combinations of colour and the clothing of the company was as picturesque as their transport. Betsy Williamson who had never stayed in one place for any length of time was committed to her last long home in Killevin, Crarae, with the rites of the church.

In the nineteen twenties the poor in the Burgh had their own economy. Venison from Inveraray Castle was sold by the butcher in various cuts. Rabbits off the Argyll Estate were sold at 1/6d per pair, and the skins were resold to hawkers for 2/6d per pair. The rabbit's head from the stew was regarded as a tasty bite. A bowl of roast dripping could be purchased for a few pence from the Castle kitchen. This dripping was spread like butter on bread or bread was fried in it. Cooking was done on an open fire of coals and

61   Local traditions.

wood, which the children gathered from fallen trees in the Estate, by permission of the Duke. Pots and kettles were suspended from a swee over the fire. The stone hearth was whitened with pipeclay in the morning, and again in the afternoon when the mid-day meal had been cooked.

Each summer the Sunday School Trip took place to the Waterfoot or Kilbride. The children, gaily dressed and highly excited, rode in a horse-drawn wagonette. Every autumn, the minister of the Gaelic Charge started a Gaelic Class in the evenings. He began with the Lord's Prayer in Gaelic, asking those present to have the prayer prepared for the next meeting of the Class. This was too difficult, the attendance dropped off, and the Class came to an end.[62]

Familiar figures at the Games, Shinty Matches and Fairs in Inveraray were the quarrymen from Furnace and Crarae.[63] These men also lived hard lives. The work in the Quarries was so heavy that some of them, suffering from heart failure, did not live the allotted span. When the quarry men received a small rise in their wages, the price of groceries and clothing in the shops rose correspondingly. There used to be three workings in Furnace Quarry, known as Klondyke, Colorado and Bulgaria, but the ridges between these workings have now been broken down by blasting. The quarry workers paid a small sum each week for medical attention, for an ambulance, and a penny or two weekly for a lair in Killevin Cemetery and for the upkeep of the grounds. For this, they received a card marked with stark simplicity "Killevin". There was one man in the quarry known as "the Boot". He used to come round married tenants in houses owned by the Quarry Company and ask them to give lodgings to unmarried workers who were strangers to the district. If the tenant in the "tied" house refused, there was the ever-present threat of "the sack".[64] When these lodgers came in drunk the women and children were terrified.[65] The quarry men worked hard and played hard and some of them died hard.

62 Local traditions.

63 There is a painting of Crarae Quarry in the Art Galleries, Glasgow, entitled "The Streets of a Great City".

64 Loss of work and house.

65 Local traditions.

The Fishing continued to be of some importance to Inveraray in the early decades of the twentieth century. In December 1899, 1020 cwt of herring valued at £3,339 were landed at Inveraray with 8 cwts of cod, valued at £3.[66] By 1932 there were few herring in Upper Loch Fyne, but the herring fishing crews received news of large catches off the Ayrshire coast and one crew had catches of 200 baskets. Unfortunately prices were low: from 3s. to 4s. per basket was paid. In the autumn of that year, a catch of about 300 herring was got by a fisherman at Lochfynehead fishing with a short trammel net. The fish were sold at 10s. per hundred. Next year 1933 the Upper Loch Fyne Herring fleet had a season of only fair success. To make matters worse, whitings, haddock and cod abandoned the fishing grounds of Upper Loch Fyne. In 1937, the ineptitude of Thomas Henry Huxley, scientist, who visited Loch Fyne in 1863-64 was shown beyond any manner of doubt. On the advice of Huxley, fishing for herring with any kind of net had become legal in 1866. In 1937, the situation had grown so desperate that the local fishermen appealed to the Member of Parliament for Argyll to urge the importance of prohibiting as illegal the use of the trawl net in Loch Fyne. The petition of the fishermen met with no success. The upper reaches of the Loch were destitute of herring. The fishermen were compelled to lay up and sell their boats and the young men looked for other jobs. Today, from a Burgh whose motto is, "May the herring always hang from thy nets", not a single boat sails to fish for herring.

In 1939, the difficult years of the thirties were followed by the catastrophe of the Second World War. Hundreds of naval men visited Inveraray and received a welcome from Kirsty MacLachlan in the Temperance Hotel. So well known did she become that she was known as "Mother of the Fleet". Her house, where many a lonely soul spent a few pleasant hours by the fireside, used to stand at the corner of Main Street East and Front Street.

After the Inveraray Grammar School was removed in 1962 from the premises in Church Square to new buildings in the Avenue beside the Episcopal Church, the old class rooms built in 1907 were in danger of deteriorating. In 1967, the citizens of the Burgh, on account of the lack of a centre for civic activities, petitioned the Town Council to obtain the use of the Old School for the

66 The Oban Times, passim.

Town, as a Community Hall. The question having been examined, it was found that the Old School was the property of the Ministry of Works. In 1968, the Inveraray Hall Committee was encouraged by the promise of a grant from the Scottish Council of Social Service In 1970, the Solicitor to the Secretary of State for Scotland offered the Old School to the Trustees for the Community Hall at a nominal feu duty. Plans were approved and warrant was granted to the Inveraray Hall Committee to carry out alterations and extensions to the Old School for use as a Community Centre,[67] and in course of time the Centre was opened.

During the latter years of the twentieth century there has been noticeable a growing tendency both in conversation and in the written record to refer to "the Old Town". And as one met with this expression, one realised with surprise tinged with regret that the Old Town was not the Inveraray which once stood between the Braehead and the River. It was the town which was built by the Dukes of Argyll betwen the Great Beech Avenue and Loch Fyne. One became aware that what was once the New Town had become the Old Town. But the word "old" may be an expression of respect and affection and whether it be called old or new the Town of Inveraray is valued by all. It has an aura of history. Other tides may break, as Newbolt writes, on other sands of time, but it will be long before Inveraray is forsaken by students of the past and by those who can appreciate a landscape.

SELECTED REFERENCES

Rehabilitation of Old Town, Inveraray, 1959, leaflet

List of Buildings of Architectural or Historic Interest. Area Argyll, Department of Health for Scotland, 1962

The Oban Times

The Oban Telegraph

The Old Statistical Account
The New Statistical Account
The Third Statistical Account

Farmer, J.S: Regimental Records, London, 1901

67   Records of the Town Council, passim.

MacIntyre, Peter: Ancient Records of Inverary, Glasgow, 1904

The Correspondence of Lieut.-General Campbell of Kintarbert, 1762-1837

Minutes of the Town Council of Inveraray

Stent Roll, 1791

Oman, C.W.C: Wellington's Army

Family tradition
Local traditions

MacLean, Donald: Typographia Scoto-Gadelica, Edinburgh, 1915

Minutes of the Kirk Session, The United Presbyterian Church, Inveraray

Chalmers, James: His Autobiography and Letters, London, R.T.S., 1902

The Imperial Gazetteer of Scotland, Fullarton & Co., London

Joiners and Wrights' Time Records, Inveraray, 1851-1854, unpublished

Memoirs of the Geological Survey of Scotland, Vol. XVII: Lead, Zinc, Copper and Nickel Ores of Scotland, H.M.S.O., 1921

Stones, Clachan Chapel and Graveyard

Act 26 and 27, Vict. cap. 65

Saxby, Jessie M.E: Milestones and Other Stories, 1891

Anderson, Mark L: A History of Scottish Forestry, Nelson, 1967

Munro, Neil: Gilian the Dreamer, 1899

Murray, Eunice G.: Scottish Homespun, Blackie, 1947

The Kist: The Magazine of the Natural History & Antiquarian Society of Mid-Argyll.

4

THE CHURCHES

It is only to be expected that Inveraray, a plain at the mouth of the River Aray, and the natural meeting place of several roads in pre-historic and historic times, would be a centre of Christianity and missionary activity.

The Early Church

The Church stood on the left bank of the River Aray, where its site is still marked by a green mound between the stream and the present burying ground.[1]

The name of the Church in A.D. 1450 was Kilmolew.[2] In that year, Sir Duncan Campbell, Lord of Lochow, gave to the collegiate church of Kilmun in Cowal, which was poorly endowed, a grant of land of Kilmolew in the barony of Lochow.[3] The loss of income as a result of this grant would fall on the Lord of Lochow: Kilmolew would be unaffected.

At the time of the Reformation, the church was called Kilmalew; and about A.D. 1600 Kilmaliew.[4] This was a dedication to S. Moluag of Lismore "Moluag the pure and brilliant, the gracious and decorous". The name Kilmalew is equivalent to the Church of my dear little Leu.

1 O.P.S.

2 The identification of Kylmalduff with Inveraray appears to be an error. The Church of St. Malduff was in Lochaber, Argyll diocese and would appear to be Kilmallie, Kylmale or Kylwale. Scottish Supplications to Rome, 1423-1428, pp. 121n., 132, 136.

3 R.M.S.G.S. Vol. xi, A.D. 1450, 346.

4 O.P.S. p. 85.

Not only was there a church at Kilmalew but there were chapels at Kilmun, Glenaray, Kilbryde, Kilian and Achantiobairt, the cemeteries of some of which were in use in the eighteenth century.[5]

In 1529, the rector of Kilmalew was Master Niel Fischear and in 1541 the rector was Sir Niel Fischer. The fact that Kilmalieu was a rectory and not appropriated—when the priest would have been a vicar—is an indication that the endowments were low. The word "sir" was an honorific title for a parish priest at this time and indicates one who was not a graduate.

The Reformation

Inveraray was prepared for the coming of the Reformation by Archibald, fourth earl of Argyle[6] (fl. 1530-1558). He was one of the first of the Scots nobles who embraced the principles of the Reformation. He employed as his domestic chaplain Mr. John Douglas, a converted Carmelite friar.[7] "The old earl of Argyle took the maintenance of John Douglas, caused him preach publicly in his house and reformed many things according to his counsel."[8] In Inveraray, Douglas read the common prayers with the lessons of the Old and New Testaments, conform to the order of the Book of Common Prayers,[9] using doctrine, preaching and the interpretation of scriptures.

The progress of the Reformation continued to be promoted by Archibald, fifth earl of Argyle (fl. 1532-1573) who was educated under the direction of Mr. John Douglas, his father's domestic chaplain. On his accession to the title in 1558, the young Earl, find-

---

5 New Statistical Account.

6 Knox: History of the Reformation

7 Not to be confused with John Douglas, Provost of St. Mary's College, St. Andrews in 1547 and rector of the University in 1550. Kirkwood Hewat: Makers of the Scottish Church at the Reformation.

8 Op. cit.

9 Edward VI, The Second Prayer Book.

ing that Mr. Douglas was often absent, thought it necessary for the comfort of his own family, and for continuing the work of reformation among his friends and vassals, to choose another domestic chaplain. In 1560 he made choice of Mr. John Carswell, who was then priest or rector of the parish of Kilmartine, afterwards one of the five ecclesiastical superintendents and Bishops of the Isles.

In 1562, John Carswell, domestic chaplain to the Earl in Inveraray, was making use of the Service Book used by John Knox at Geneva, which book was introduced into Scotland at this time and circulated for general use in the vernacular.[10] Anxious for the propagation of the Gospel among the Gaelic-speaking people of Argyle, Carswell set to work to translate the Service Book into Gaelic. The volume was printed in Edinburgh, whose other name is Dunmony, the 24th day of April, 1567. There were then three service books which might be used for worship in Inveraray: the Second Prayer Book of Edward VI, which had been used by John Douglas; the Genevan Service Book in the vernacular, used by John Carswell; and the latter book, the Genevan Forme of Prayers, translated into Gaelic by Carswell.

While these events of historical and literary significance were taking place at the Castle, the rector of Kilmolew in 1561 and in 1563 was Nivinus Makvicar. Master John Makvicar of Stronmagachan, said to be kin to Nivinus Makvicar, became parson of Kilmolew. He was educated at Rome and entered into holy orders there. Embracing the doctrines of the Reformers, he returned and settled in his native parish, discharging its pastoral duties with prudence, charity and wisdom.[11] It is related that he preached for some time at Kilmolew under a rock in what is now the new part of the burying place, which was long known as the parson's pulpit, until a church was built for him.[12] If this tradition be correct, the mediaeval church of Kilmolew must have been in a ruinous state.

10   This book was known as the Genevan Service Book 1556; it was also known as the Genevan Forme of Prayers; after 1564, it became known as the Book of Common Order; it was also known as the Psalm Book, because a collection of fifty metrical Psalms in English was added. W.D. Maxwell: The Liturgical Portions of the Genevan Service Book, 1931.

11   F.E.S., iv, p. 8.

12   Craven: Records of Argyll, p. 15.

state. The church built for the Rev. John Makvicar was in all probability a reparation of the old church.

He is said to have baptized in either the old or the new form as people desired. When he was dealing with parishioners who adhered to the "old" religion, he would be prepared to recognise the baptism administered by midwives in cases of extreme' necessity, if it were seen that a child might die before he himself could be summoned.

But if he were dealing with people who wished the new form of baptism, it may be that he would insist that baptism should always be administered in church, and as soon as possible after the birth of the child. However, perhaps he was not so strict as to insist on the order of the Genevan Service Book—"easy-going soul", Neil Munro calls him.

For the purpose of the sacrament of baptism, there is a large stone which belonged to John Makvicar. The stone is about thirteen inches in height and two feet in diameter, cut into an octagonal form, with a font above and below.[13] This he used in the baptism of Protestants and Catholics, by turning either side for water or for holy water, according to the opinions or prejudices of his people.[14]

Without doubt John Makvicar made use of the Forms of Prayer and administration of the sacraments, turned from English into Gaelic by Mr. John Carswell. In his Sunday morning service, he began with the confession of sins, proceeded to the sermon, which being ended, he used a prayer for all estates or else prayed as the Spirit of God moved his heart. If the service were in English, two of the fifty metrical psalms, added to the Book of Common Order, were used. If the service were in Gaelic, there were no psalms; the psalms not having been translated into Gaelic or rendered into metre.

The people within and beyond the parish of Kilmolew were divided in their allegiance, some adhering to the Roman Catholic others to the Reformed Church. Protestants and Roman Catholics on the way to their respective places of worship could not refrain from hostile demonstrations against one another. In Glen Shira, which at this time was not in the parish of Kilmolew, the Roman Catholic portion of the inhabitants was made up of followers of

13   This font is now in All Saints Church, Inveraray.

14   Colin Smith: New Statistical Account, Inveraray, p. 19.

MacNaughton; the Protestants were followers of Argyll. The river alone which flowed between the two factions prevented them from coming to blows.[15]

John Makvicar was supposed to have the gift of the second sight. He foretold his own death by drowning, and being sent by the Earl of Argyll to Stirling, he stumbled from an outside stair on an alarm of fire, and fell head foremost into a dyer's hogshead, which had been put to catch rainwater. When his gillie returned, he found the parson drowned in the hogshead with his feet uppermost. His remains were brought to Inveraray, when all the inhabitants of the parish turned out and buried him at Kilmolew.[16] A stone, on which is the form of Christ on the Cross is said to mark his grave.[17]

In 1570, Archibald, fifth earl of Argyll presented Donald Makvicar to the rectory and vicarage of Kilmolew, reserving the life-rent of the same to Ninian Makvicar, apparently the same Nivinus Makvicar who was rector of Kilmolew in 1563. His signature to charters shows him as rector in 1574.[18]

The Kirk of Kilmolew appears in record in connexion with the burgh of Inveraray in 1595.[19]

The Establishment of Episcopacy

Before and during the episcopacy of James I and Charles I, the incumbent was Donald Makolvorich or M'Ilvorie. He was educated at the University of Glasgow and graduated Master of Arts in 1593. He declined a call to Aberfoyle in 1594 and became minister of the Barony Parish of Glasgow in that year. He was translated to Rothesay in the same year and was translated and admitted to

15 Craven: Records of Argyll, pp. 34-35. (The division of opinion in Glen Shira is reflected in the conversation between the two soldiers of fortune in chapter III of Neil Munro's John Splendid.)

16 F.E.S. iv, p. 9.

17 The stone is an interesting piece of sculpture, but the head has been broken off. There is no inscription on any part of the stone. In 1933, it was placed in an upright position, and set on a firm base. (The Oban Times, 25.11.1933)

18 O.P.S., p. 85.

19 Ibid.

Glenaray in 1595. He was a member of the Genral Assemblie of the Kirk of Scotland, Holden in Glasgow, the 8th of June, the year of God 1610 years, and was a member along with the Bishop of Argyll, John Makcallum parson of Cillvickocharmaig and others, of the Commission anent the Reformation of the Discipline of the Kirk.[20] In 1634, he was still serving as a member of the Commission for the Maintenance of Church Discipline.

The Marquess as Churchman

Among the members of the Glasgow Assembly in 1638 were the 8th Earl of Argyll and Donald M'Ilvorie, minister of Glenaray. During this Assembly, Alexander Henderson held meetings for prayer, and "the Marquis[21] of Argyll and several others who sometimes joined in them, dated their conversion, or a knowledge of it, from those times".[22] The Earl joined the ranks of the Covenanters; the Church in Argyll was organised on a Presbyterian basis; and a Kirk Session was formed for the Irish congregation of Glenaray.

In the regular Gaelic services which he held in the parish, Donald M'Ilvorie used John Knox's Book of Common Order translated into Gaelic by Carswell. Non-Gaelic speakers, who were not regarded with favour by the natives,[23] were being encouraged by the Marquis of Argyll to settle in Inveraray and Donald M'Ilvorie was increasingly asked to provide services in English. This part of his ministry may have been troublesome to him.[24] In English services, he used the Book of Common Order, more commonly spoken of as the Psalm Book.

When Donald M'Ilvorie had been minister of the parish of Glenaray for a considerable number of years, it was proposed that there should be a substantial addition to his cure. The parish was

---

20 Calderwood: Historie of the Kirk of Scotland, Vol. vii, p. 107.

21 Argyll was not made a Marquis till the visit of Charles I to Scotland in 1641.

22 Woodrow: Historical Fragments, p. 81.

23 The natives subsequently described the incomers as "poor menial servants". (Register of the Kirk Session of Glenaray, 22.7.1722. Cf. also Neil Munro: John Splendid, chapter 11)

24 Minutes of The Synod of Argyll, 1639-1651.

regarded as being of small extent in comparison with the parish of Lochgoilhead and Kilmorich. It was therefore thought expedient by the Provincial Assembly of Argyll on 7th October 1642 to disjoin Glen Shira from Lochgoilhead and Kilmorich and to join that district to the parish of Glenaray. By this division, the people of Glen Shira would have the occasion of a weekly preaching, whereas before they had but preaching once in the month.[25]

The closing years of Donald Makilvorich's ministry were difficult. In December 1644, Alasdair MacColkitto descended upon Inveraray. The minister was without doubt sheltered with the garrison in Inveraray Castle but Mr. Donald's parish, houses and dwellings, were burned by the Irish.[26] The kirk was not completely destroyed, however, as it was in use by the Synod of Argyll two years later.[27] Donald Makilvorich died in 1649 and on 1st May 1650 his widow Janet Campbell represented to the Synod of Argyll that she was in great necessity and that through the burning of the parish, she was disappointed of that composition which ministers' wifes get either from Ann[28] or for contentation of glebe and manse, and so was left very poor and indigent. The Synod granted to her the share of her husband from the money granted by the Estates for distressed ministers of Argyle.[29]

With the coming of the vacancy, there were re-adjustments. As had been proposed eight years before, the Commissioners of Parliament appointed for plantation of Kirks within the Province of Argyll, dismembered the lands of Glenshira from the parish of Kilmorich in 1650 and annexed the same to the Highland congregation at Inveraray.

In April 1651, it was proposed to transport Mr. Neil Cameron of Inverchaolain to the Irish (or Gaelic) congregation of Inveraray. To this proposal, Mr. Cameron was willing to accede on certain

25   Ibid.

26   F.E.S., Vol. viii, p. 313.

27   Minutes of the Synod.

28   Ann, a payment to the executors of a minister dying while he serves a cure, probably derived through Low Latin Annata, from annus, a year. (Black: Parochial Ecclesiastical Law, Third Edition, p. 218). "Ann" involved the payment of six months stipend to the widow of a minister.

29   F.E.S., Vol. viii, p. 313.

conditions, and these conditions give an idea of the state of the parish at this time.

A new kirk was to be built in the most centrical place of the parish; a sufficient manse was to be built, and a glebe designed; a sufficient maintenance for the minister was to be agreed upon with the mutuall consent of my Lord Marquis of Argyle, the Presbytery and the Parish of Inveraray; and Mr. Neil Cameron was not to be troubled with preaching to the English congregation more than any other of the ministers of the presbytery. In the end, Mr. Cameron was not transported to Inveraray. It is evident however from the conditions stipulated by him that the Gaelic Church was not in the Burgh but in the landward parts (the old church at Kilmolew) and that there was no manse or glebe.

At the end of the year, December 1651, the Commissioners of Parliament modified to the minister serving the cure of the Irish (Gaelic) congregation of Inveraray, a stipend which was about the minimum. A sufficient manse and glebe were appointed, the glebe being the church lands of Kilmolew, immediately adjoining the Castle.[30]

The Irish (or Gaelic) congregation continued to be vacant for a number of years. There was not a service every Sunday, but the pulpit was supplied from time to time when an Irish (or Gaelic-speaking) minister visited the parish.[31]

The Marquess and the English Congregation of Inveraray.

The English congregation of Inveraray owed its inception to the Marquess of Argyll. It was his policy to settle lowland tradesmen from south-west Scotland in the Burgh of Inveraray. He brought Shaws and others from Ayrshire to introduce crafts such as weaving and iron work.[32] Some of these men were Covenanters, the young Earl of Argyll having committed himself to the National

30 Cf. Appendix at the end of this chapter. (p. 191)

31 The Session Book of the English Congregation of Inveraray, 17.4.1651.

32 Neil Shaw, Achnagoul was valet to the Marquess. John Shaw, Book seller, Inveraray, 1820, was a descendant of this Neil Shaw. Tradesmen called Munn from south west Scotland were induced to settle in Argyllshire, and their descendants may still be found in the Island of Tiree and in Oban.

Covenant in 1638. Some were merchants whose industry contributed to a peacable and prosperous economy in the Burgh. These men bore such names as Loudon, Roger, Fleming, Yuill and Brown, in contrast with the Highlanders who were called Campbell, McOlvory and Cameron.[33] The incomers were not Gaelic speakers, they could not profit from the services of a Gaelic-speaking minister such as Donald McIlvorie and their religious convictions were of importance to them. It was therefore necessary that services in English should be held. The Earl invited Covenanting ministers to conduct services in Inveraray from time to time for periods of weeks or months, and the English-speaking incomers attended these services. This was however but an intermittent ministry at the best. It was necessary that a settled ministry be provided for the non-Gaelic speakers, and this provision the Marquess proceeded to make.

An English congregation was formed in the Burgh and Parish of Inveraray, distinct from the Gaelic congregation, and with a distinct Session. This charge was in the Presbytery of Inveraray and in the Provincial Assembly or Synod of Argyle.

A call was addressed to Mr. Alexander Gordon, M.A., minister of a church at Tynemouth, Northumberland to undertake the charge of the ministry in Inveraray. This call he was very unwilling to accept. So great was his disinclination to come to Inveraray, that both the Presbytery and the Provincial Assembly conferred with him that they might persuade him to acquiesce, and on 12th November 1650, Mr. Alexander Gordon was admitted minister of the English congregation in the Burgh.

It was necessary that a Kirk Session for the English congregation should be constituted and on 25th November 1650, after encalling the name of God, there was a general election of my Lord Marquess of Argyll; my Lord Lorne; George Campbell, Sheriff depute; Archibald Campbell, Master of the Household to my Lord Marquess; Donald McOlvory, provost; Donald Cameron, William Loudon, David Roger and Patrick Fleming to be elders; likewise of John Yuill, William Brown and Duncan Fisher to be deacons.

It was a formidable Kirk Session of which Alexander Gordon was moderator; it met monthly, fortnightly or weekly, according as business arose; and having been constituted it set to work at once.

33   Session Book of the English Congregation, 25.11.1650.

Money was allocated, perhaps out of the 2,000 merks set aside for the Grammar School at Inveraray, to buy clothes for poor scholars. It was ordained that Donald McKenochow the Kirk beadle receive a fee of 10 sh. for ye ringing of ye deid bell [34] and ye making of ilk grave.

The Session appointed Robert Peibles to be Session Clerk, an office for which he was paid ten pounds out of the Kirk monies or collections, and the court purchased books to be used as baptismal register, marriage register and minute book of Kirk Session.

Two of the pre-occupations of the Church courts were to ensure that the Sabbath Day was observed, and that people attended public worship unto edification.

To make sure that the Lord's Day was observed, the Session of the English Congregation passed a resolution concerning the people of the Irish language who frequented the town on that day. As it was feared that, when there was no service in the Gaelic Church, the people of the Irish language might commit abuses, it was ordained by the Session of the English Church, that none such come to the town upon such Lord's dayes whereon there is no sermon in the Irish language, or if they do, they shall repair to the English sermon.[35] On 4th May 1656, with a like purpose in mind, the Session appointed that the town people keep their houses on the Sabbath Day after public worship and that the landward peoples repair home. There had been an English garrison[36] in the town for four years, and the presence of the soldiers had an unsettling effect on the people, tempting them to wander about.

The other concern of the Session was to ensure that members of the congregation attended the services unto edification. Women came to church with plaids about their heads and wrapped round their shoulders. During divine service, they kept their heads and faces muffled in their plaids, making it possible for them to sleep through the sermon.

---

34 At funerals, the beadle or bellman walked before the light coffin, which was borne by four young men, ringing a handbell. The bell penny in some cases was paid to the poor. (Edgar: Old Church Life in Scotland, second series, p. 258) This money was sometimes used to repair the church. (Dunlop: Parochial Law, p. 12)

35 Minutes of the Kirk Session, 12.12.1650 (K.S.M.)

36 The garrison arrived under Colonel Read on 19th July 1652.

To prevent this drowsiness and sleepiness which several are given to, as if God's worship was appointed for no other use but to rock them asleep - to prevent this, the Session[37] appointed that such plaids be not used hereafter, under the pain of the beadle taking their plaids from them for the time of the service, and that intimation be made hereof in public.

Meanwhile, the Rev. Alexander Gordon was exercizing his ministry in the parish and in the courts of the Church. He was a member of the General Assembly of St. Andrews in 1651 and was one of forty Remonstrants or Protesters, mentioned in the paper, "The Nullity of the Pretended Assembly at Saint Andrews and Dundee", protesting against the policy of conciliating Charles the Second. Gordon subsequently published an Account of this General Assembly.[38] In courts of the Church nearer home, Mr. Gordon attended the Provincial Assembly or Synod of Argyll, which met regularly twice every year until 1661, and went through much business with great deliberaton.

For stipend, he received three chalders[39] of victual and 900 merks out of the revenues of the bishopricks of Lismore and of the Isles. He did not receive any part of the parish teinds.[40]

Alexander Gordon received much encouragement from his leading elder, the Marquess of Argyll. He said that the Marquess was very pious; that besides family worship and private prayer morning and evening, he still prayed with his lady morning and evening, his gentleman and her gentlewoman; that he never went abroad, though but for one night, but he took his write-book, inkstand and the English notes, the Bible and Neuman's Concordance with him.[41]

The Marquess attended the meetings of the Kirk Session when he was at home, being present at three meetings in 1652; once in 1654, in which year the elders of the Irish or Gaelic con-

37   K.S.M., 29.5.1656.

38   'Peterkin's Records' (F.E.S. Vol. iv, p. 11)

39   A chalder was equivalent to 16 bolls of corn; a boll was equivalent to 16 pecks. The chalder varied according to the locality and the commodity measured.

40   John Connell's 'Law of Scotland relating to Parishes'.

41   Wodrow: Analecta, 1, p. 22.

gregation sat with the elders of the English congregation: after a period of absence, the Marquis attended in 1657 and 1658; three times in 1659; and twice in 1660.

During this decade, Mr. David Dickson was two years with all his family at Inveraray, where the Marquess kept him. Mr. Dickson preached in the forenoon,[42] Mr. Gordon in the afternoon and Mr. Patrick Simson on Thursday, The Marquess wrote the sermon which Mr. Gordon preached.[43] The Rev. Alexander had a singular talent for lecturing.[44] He delivered discourses which were of a less formal nature than a sermon and consisted of a running commentary on a large passage of scripture, such as the exposition of a whole chapter.

In the early years of Mr. Gordon's ministry, the English Church was not yet built, and the Gaelic Church was used for services by both congregations. The old church was slated, not thatched as the school house was. There was a porch to the Kirk door. Within, there was a pulpit with pulpit doors on which were handles. The floor of the kirk was of earth or clay and was damp. Each worshipper provided his own church seat.

It was not a satisfactory arrangement that two congregations should use the same church and in 1652, in which year the Marquess was present at three meetings of the Kirk Session, material was being gathered to build a new church. Among the material were deals or pieces of timber framing, six feet or ten feet long. The new church was to be situated in the town, but the work of building went on slowly. On the one hand, money was scarce; the Marquess, although he lived very sparingly, was in straitened circumstances; a heavy cess in timber and cows required to be paid to Colonel Lilburne, representing the Commonwealth of Oliver Cromwell.[45] On the other hand, the induction of the Rev. Patrick

42 The sermons of Mr. David Dickson were written out at the desire of the Marchioness of Argyll. These sermons were afterwards published with the co-operation of the Rev. Mr. Durham under the title of "The Sum of Saving Knowledge".

43 Wodrow, Analecta, Vol. i, p. 22

44 F.E.S. iv, p. 11

45 Scotland and the Commonwealth, Scot. Hist Soc., Vol. xviii.
    "The Commonwealth - very much a misnomer in Scotland, where the extent of Cromwell's depredations have curiously tended to be forgotten".
    George Scott-Moncrieff: The Glasgow Herald, 27.10.1973.

Campbell to the Gaelic charge in 1657 made it more necessary than ever to have another church for the English congregation. By 1658, the walls and the steeple were raised. It was proposed to have a peal of bells and joists were fitted in the steeple for supporting the bells.

The kirk having been built, the Session proceeded to furnish it. In 1659, the office bearers acquired a mort cloth. This article was of the best London black cloth. It was well-mounted and trimmed with good fringes, both long and short, of black silk. It was heaped up in a black baize bag with a good soft brush for brushing the mort cloth, as required. The whole was kept sure and clean in a good clean chest by Duncan McKenochow, the beadle. It was his duty to let out the mort cloth and to make sure that it was returned to him safe, sound and clean. He received payment for its use: from each person within and belonging to the town, two shillings sterling; from each person within the Highland paroch of Glenaray and Glenshira[46] three shillings sterling; and from ilke person in any other part of the country, without the town and parish, four pounds, Scots.[47] The Kirk Session had the exclusive privilege of letting out the mort cloth to hire, for the benefit of the poor.[48]

An important piece of church furniture was the Poor Box. It was to be found in the Gaelic Church, before the English Church was set up. The monies contained in it, sometimes described as "ye poores silber (silver)" were made up of the church collections. They were augmented by penalties or fines imposed by the Kirk Session on parishioners for such misdemeanours as drunkenness. The contents of the Poor Box were administered and allocated by the Kirk Session. For example, the Session appointed the treasur-

---

46 The Kirk Session of Glenaray acquired a mort cloth on 25 Nov. 1716 (Register of the Kirk Session of Glenaray).

47 The mort cloth in Inveraray must have been in use frequently: on 17th January 1680, the accompt of the mort cloth was audited and it was found that the Session was owing Duncan McKenochow the beadle, after all his intromissions with the mort cloth, the sum of 8 pounds, 16 shillings unpaid of his fees and a dollar of drink money.

48 Dunlop: Parochial Law.

ɜr to give out 3 libs[49] 4 shillings, Scots, for paying for quarters to four shipwreckit men, who were lodged here one night in their passing through. On 16th June 1658, they appointed the treasurer to pay out four pounds for the winding sheet of a poor honest young man, Neil McDougall, school master in Kilmodan, who died in this town lately. They also allowed forty shillings to be given to Archibald McNicoll whose house was lately burnt in the Fisherland.

Such liberality invited encroachment and the Session, perceiving that many poor have come to the town, who belong not to the town itself, recommended to the bailies that they see that they settle not in the town but go forward to seek alms or else to go to the place of their abode.

Under the careful supervision of the elders, the money accumulated and it was used in a number of ways. The Session ordained the treasurer to give out eight pounds for the completing the payment of the dails (pieces of wood) for the building a porch to the Kirk door. They also acted as bankers, lending money on security and receiving an annual rent from the borrower. On 8th March 1654, the Session appointed that the most part of the money within the box be put into the hands of responsible men for good security and therefore any that has a mind to borrow the same upon good security are appointed to come against the next diet. A week later, William Browne one of the elders gave in his bond to the Session to honour three hundred merks[50] of the poor money which the Session condescended to give him. The members of the Kirk Session were likewise responsible for at least 2,000 merks which had been allocated to the Grammar School at Inveraray in 1648/49. They loaned out this school money on what they believed to be good security, in order that the interest might be used to pay the schoolmasters. The sums loaned from the principal of the school money might be 1000 merks or 500 merks, much larger than those loaned out of the poor box, and the borrowers sometimes found great difficulty in paying the interest and repaying the original sum. In some cases after twenty four years had elapsed, the borrower could not repay the money. The Session then put the

49   Pounds.

50   Merk: an old Scotch silver coin worth 13/4d. Scots or 13⅓d. sterling.

matter in the hands of the Sheriff and instructed the treasurer to raise letters of horning[51] against the unfortunate debtor.

Towards the close of the first decade (1650-1660) of the ministry of Mr. Gordon in the Lowland Congregation, the parishes of Glenaray and Inveraray were adequately supplied with religious ordinances. The Gaelic congregation, having had services irregularly for eight years, was at length settled with a minister. Patrick Campbell of Torblaren[52] became minister of Glenaray in 1657, when he was twenty four years of age. He was the second son of the Rev. Dugald Campbell of North Knapdale; his elder brother was the Rev. Duncan Campbell of Glenorchy; and he had graduated Master of Arts at Glasgow University in 1651. There were therefore a young minister in Glenaray in his first charge and an older minister, ten years his senior, in the Lowland Congregation which was his second charge. Both were men of strong character and firm convictions.

The Marquess attended the joint meetings of the Kirk Session once in 1658, three times in 1659; and twice in 1660.

The new church for the English Congregation was erected by 1661 and a new school house was built at the end of the Kirk. Duncan McKennochow the Kirk officer was appointed to lock the Kirk door. In May 1661, intimation was publicly made to the congregation that whosoever of the inhabitants desired to build seats in the Kirk should repair to the next Session, where they should have their rooms designed, or a place marked out for them in which to build. It was certified that whosoever built first, should be preferred with the best rooms.

At the end of 1660 and the beginning of 1661 the churches in

---

51 Letters of Horning: a term in Scots Law. Formerly all decrees of court for payment of money might be put in execution by letters issuing from the King's signet. These signet letters were called Letters of Horning or letters of four forms. Under them the debtor was charged four times successively to make payment, but in the fourth charge he was called on either to pay or to enter himself in a specified prison. Failing implement of the fourth charge, he was denounced rebel at the horn. The method of declaring a person a rebel was by giving three blasts on a horn and publicly proclaiming the fact; hence the expression "put to the horn". This system of execution was simplified by an act of 1837 (Personal Diligence Act) and execution is now usually by diligence. (Encyclopedia Brittanica, 14th edition)

52 In Kilmichael Glassary.

Glenaray and Inveraray appeared to be prospering, but none knew better than the leading elder, the Marquess, that dark and difficult days lay ahead.

The Restoration

On 29th May 1660, Charles II was restored to the throne of his fathers. The Marquis of Argyll went to London to seek an interview with the king; he was arrested in the presence-chamber and committed to the Tower. He was executed on 27th May 1661 in Edinburgh and Neil Shaw, Achnagoul, valet to the Marquis, held the napkin to receive his head. Mr. Alexander Gordon had lost his leading elder.

While the Marquis was being tried, the legal basis of the existing Presbyterian Church was swept away by a general Act Rescissory on 28th March 1661. In April, the Synod of Argyll held its normal spring meeting. In September, Charles proclaimed that he was resolved to restore the Church in Scotland to its right government by bishops, as it was by law before the late troubles began, and as it now stood settled by law. On the 18th January 1662, David Fletcher, A.M. was appointed by Charles II to the See of Argyll.[53] His brother Sir John Fletcher,[54] the new Lord Advocate, secured the appointment for him. It is said that he at first refused the See of Argyll "the rent being nought". However, he was consecrated with others in Holyrood Abbey on 7th May 1662.[55]

The two ministers in Glenaray and Inveraray were now in a difficult position.

They received no appointment in the Act of the Scottish Parliament concerning the Chapter of the Bishoprick of Argyll, 1662. The Rev. Alexander was likely to be dealt with more severely, because he had been one of the forty Protesters at St. Andrews in

---

53 Before 1638, David Fletcher had been zealous for Episcopacy and after 1638 for Presbytery. In 1638, he was assaulted and maltreated by several women for no other reason than hesitating to obey the populace of the day. He had many sad strokes from the women. Craven: Records of Argyll, p. 103.

54 It was he who accused Archibald, Marquess of Argyll in common form of high treason. The indictment was mostly a heap of slanders and perversion of matters of fact.

55 Craven: Records of Argyll.

1651; he was one of those who made no secret of their doubts as to whether Charles II was the truly Covenanted king of their ideal. Both Alexander Gordon and Patrick Campbell were deprived by Act of Parliament on 11th June 1662 and by Decreet of the Privy Council on 1st October. Patrick Campbell was allowed to remain. Alexander Gordon was cited before the Council, but was under a dangerous fever. The magistrates of Inveraray sent up a testificate under the physicians' hands, which the Council could not but accept. He was a while forgot as dead, and indeed he was very near death, but the Lord had more work for him; and he upon his recovery continued some years preaching in Bishop Fletcher's time.[56]

Although the position of the two ministers was somewhat insecure, church life in Glenaray and Inveraray went on much as before, at least so long as Bishop Fletcher lived, which was until 1665. The Session of the English Congregation met irregularly and infrequently till February 1663, the last minute signed by Alexander Gordon being dated 29th August 1662. Thereafter the Session continued to be constituted and to perform its disciplinary functions as formerly, but its records for the next decade are not extant.

After the Restoration, there were certain changes made in the form of service. The Rev. Alexander used the Lord's Prayer at all services, the Doxology was sung at the conclusion of each portion of the metrical psalms, the Apostles' Creed was recited, and the Scriptures were read at Public Worship. The Westminster Directory of Public Worship was laid aside and John Knox's Book of Common Order was used. The practice of lecturing for which Mr. Gordon had a particular gift fell into desuetude. In the Gaelic Church, the Rev. Patrick read Carswell's translation of Knox's Liturgy and perhaps such Gaelic translations of portions of the Scriptures as were available, or he may have translated the Scriptures into Gaelic ex tempore.

After the death of Bishop Fletcher in 1665, William Scroggie succeeded to the bishopric in 1666. He married Katharine, eldest sister of Henry Scougal who "is reckoned one of the saints of the

56 Wodrow: The History of the Sufferings of the Church of Scotland, Book 1, Section V.

Scottish church"[57]Bishop Scroggie came to Argyle at Lammas, 1667. The new bishop was not in sympathy with the House of Argyll or with the Presbyterians, as was shown by the fact that in the Scottish Parliament, he entered a protest against an Act in favour of the Earl of Argyll[58] Thereafter Mr. Gordon fell into very great hardships and sore persecutions of which he subsequently drew up a large account. He was an in-dweller at Kilmory on 7th July 1668 and went from there to Ayrshire.

Mr. Patrick Campbell, minister of the Gaelic Church, Glenaray, was more leniently treated, no doubt because he had not publicly committed himself to questions as to whether Charles II was a truly covenanted king. The young minister was allowed to serve in Glenaray and Inveraray, where he would have fellowship with Mr. James Drummond, a man like-minded with himself, who was acting as Chaplain to the Marchioness of Argyll[59] On 3rd August 1669, Patrick Campbell was one of the ministers granted a provisional Indulgence by the Privy Council. He was to conduct himself in an orderly way, attend the Presbyterian Courts and restrict himself to his own parish[60] For this he received the emoluments of his office in whole or in part, and was allowed the use of his manse and glebe. This may have made a difference between himself and Mr. James Drummond, chaplain to the Marchioness. The chaplain did not approve of ministers who accepted indulgence, and he himself attended and conducted conventicles[61]

---

57 Dictionary of National Biography. (Henry Scougal was author of The Life of God in the Soul of Man, a religious classic, republished in 1961).

58 This was in 1670 (Craven: Records of Argyll p. 123),

59 McKerral: Kintyre, p. 96.

60 In Mid-Argyll, conventicles were held at Glasvar and Rudill, Kilmichael Glassary, at the stones known as the Covenanter's Communion Tables. Mr. Campbell was prohibited from attending such gatherings.

61 James Drummond was Tacksman of Kilmichael, Crossalbeg and Kilchousland (Campbeltown) in 1666. Tradition relates that he used his byre as a meeting house. He was imprisoned in 1674 for holding conventicles, and was imprisoned again and sent to the Bass in 1677, but was liberated the same year and allowed to go home. (McKerral: Kintyre, p. 96)

Despite the possible disapproval of James Drummond, the Rev. Patrick ministered in Glenaray and probably in Inveraray also the Rev. Álexander Gordon having taken refuge in the lands of Knock in Ayrshire. The minister of the Gaelic Church presided over the meetings of the two Kirk Sessions, but the records of these meetings are not extant until the 4th September 1677. At that date, William Brown was still a member of the court, Duncan McKenochow continued in office as beadle and Patrick Campbell was moderator.

Although the times were troublous—the ordinances of religion were provided.[62] The Laird of Achenbreck was married in the church in Inveraray. The Session appointed that a collection be made thereat. The monies collected were distributed to the poor and the distribution was recorded in the Session's Book.[63] In public worship, there was a morning service and an afternoon service. Before the service, the bell, for which a rope and block were bought in 1679—the bell was rung by the beadle to indicate that a service was about to be held: this was known as the first bell. At the second bell, the congregation moved into the kirk. At the third bell, the minister entered the pulpit during the singing of a psalm and began the service with prayer. In the afternoon, the schoolmaster caused two of his scholars to repeat the catechism every Sunday between the second and the third bell, and it was intimated that the people should come in at the second bell to hear the repetition.[64]

Church discipline under Episcopacy was just as strict as under Presbyterian church government. In 1679, Neil Campbell in Fisherland was summoned before the Session for lifting his fishing nets on the Sabbath, and Soirle McDowgal was summoned for drunkenness on the Sabbath and for striking his own and other men's wives. Next year on June 1st 1680, the Session laying it to consideration that now the fishing time was drawing near, the

62 This seems to indicate sympathy with the Covenanting Rising of that year: the battle of Drumclog, 1st June 1679 and Bothwell Bridge, 22nd June 1679.

63 The Session Book of the Lowland Congregation, 1677-79.

64 The Catechism was repeated by children in the French Church at Strasburg, during the ministry of John Calvin, and the practice was introduced into Scotland by John Knox after 1560. (Maxwell, W.D: The Liturgical Portions of the Genevan Service Book, p. 65)

town might be filled with vagabonds and rascals, the Session recommended to the elders that they see the testimonials of these fishermen, finding out from whence they came and concerning their good behaviour. The same year, 1680, the English Session, some of the members of which were covenanters from Ayrshire, recommended to the Session Clerk to speak to the Highland Session anent Sabbath breaking in letting their nets lie on the Sabbath day; and likewise to speak to them of the Highland congregation within the town anent drawing of water on the Sabbath day. The next year, 1681, the Session ordained that the elders go through the town every Sabbath to see who was absent from church. This duty was distasteful to the office bearers, so the Session Clerk drew up a roll or rota for the elders and deacons, lest any pretend ignorance of the order in which his turn came. And to make sure that each did his duty, the minister made intimation of the elders' rota from the pulpit and the Session required the office bearers to report diligence.

It was now the turn of the English congregation to have trial of irregular services. In November 1681 it was noted that "there is no regular English sermon yet". In 1682, there were eight Sundays with no English sermon and there is no record of a meeting of the Kirk Session, and in January 1683, the elders met as neighbours, but not as a Kirk Session, which means that there was no ordained minister to act as moderator.

Not only did the Kirk Session or Sessions maintain discipline during the Episcopacy, but they assiduously maintained and improved the fabrics of the churches.

The seats beside the entry to the pulpit were removed and a seat was made up there for those that bring children to be baptised. Foot gangs for the desks, or raised wooden footwalks, being planks on a wooden base between the pews, were made by a carpenter Robert Ross at the order of the Kirk Session. The people sitting in the high pews rested their feet on these boards and were protected from the chill earthen floor and from the puddles of water which gathered upon it. Still enforcing church discipline, the Session ordered a stool for public repentance to be set up.

The roofs of both churches received attention. In 1679 search was made for sclats (slates) and repairs were carried out on the Kirk which were paid for out of the collections. In 1680, John McFarland, sklatter, was instructed to point the Kirk. In 1683, the

Highland Church, which was known as the "old" church at Inveraray, in contradistinction to the English Church, was repaired.

In that year, John Jack, sklaiter (slater) offered to repair the slate work of the old church at Inveraray and to point the same. For this, he received twenty merks Scots, the session providing him with slates, lime and sand, and a workman. He undertook to touch up the work every year for four pounds Scots, yearly.[65]

One of the ornamenta of the church of the Lowland Congregation was the knock or clock. About this time-piece the Session deliberated long and gravely. The knock was set in the steeple and the steeple was kept locked lest any might injure the mechanism. In June 1680, David Carruders was put in charge of the knock and was paid 8 pounds Scots betwixt Whitsunday and Martinmas: he received six pounds for keeping it and two pounds for teaching others to keep it, and to take it asunder according to the skill he had of it. At Martinmas 1680 this commission was renewed and Carruders was provided with candle and oil and any other thing which might be necessary to keep the knock. In January 1681, the keeper of the clock asked the Kirk Session to get leads to be weights for the knock; to close the highest windows of the steeple with boards, stone and lime; and to call on the person who took off the lock of the back door of the Kirk to replace it.

In June 1681, David Carruders wished to be relieved of responsibility for the knock. He agreed to look after it for a fortnight longer; he was persuaded to continue in office till the following Whitsunday and to teach any two in the town who may seem to be fit for it such as John MacNuar and John Walker to work with the clock.

On 4th January 1683, a similar situation rose. David Carruders was still keeper of the knock but was desirous to lay down his charge. Also, he had not been paid for his work during a great part of 1682. (The reason for this omission was that the Session had not met during 1682). The elders, meeting as neighbours but not as a court of the church, desired Carruders that he would keep the knock going during this fourteen days and undertook that the treasurer of the church should pay him sixteen pounds Scots as his fee from Martinmas 1681 to Martinmas 1682, and that out of the first and readiest of the seat rents. David Carruders agreed.

65   K.S.M., 17.1.1683.

A fortnight later the Session met formally. Carruders earnestly desired that his charge be accepted off his hand and laid down the key. Being asked upon his honest word, if he had wilfully wronged the knock or if he knew any of her wheels to be wrong, he willingly took it on his part before heaven that he knew nothing that was wrong with the town knock, neither did he any wrong to it himself.

John McNuar was called upon because he was thought to be fittest in the town for this charge. He willingly undertook it and the same day did enter upon it. All things belonging to the knock were to be gotten from David Carruders before his appointment was terminated and were to be given to John MacNuar his successor in office. The uneasiness of the Session about the safety of the mechanism was not yet completely allayed; and for the security of the knock from anyone who might go into the steeple to wrong it, and for preventing of any suspicion, John MacNuar was desired to get a sufficient lock to be put on the door of the steeple.

This appointment proved to be satisfactory: John MacNuar kept the knock going for more than thirty years.

In 1684, the ministry of Patrick Campbell was seriously interupted. In August of that year, it pleased His Majesty Charles II to give the Marquis of Atholl a commission of Lieutenandry to go to Argyllshire[66] On the second day of September 1684 there compeared amongst others Mr. Patrick Campbell, minister at Innerara and his brother Mr. Duncan Campbell, minister at Knapdell, indulged ministers, in presence of John Marquis of Atholl, His Majesty's High Lieutenant within the shires of Argyll and Tarbet. The ministers having been interrogated anent their observing of the Council's instructions, they ilk and ane of them did confess and acknowledge that they had broken and violated the foresaid instructions, and they signed their confession.

It is not stated in what ways they had broken the instructions. It may be that they had not taken the Test Act of 1681-1682 which required them to swear that the King's Majesty was the only supreme governor, and that they were under no obligation from the National Covenant and Solemn League and Covenant. This Bond or Test was to be taken before 1st August 1684, and it is possible that Patrick Campbell on conscience had not sworn to

66   Chronicles of the Atholl and Tullibardine Families, vol. i. pp. 187, 192.

keep it. It may be that it was simply said of him that he had exceeded the terms of his licence.

At any rate, the Lord Lieutenant in respect of their written declaration and confession declared the indulgence in favour of the said Mr. Patrick Campbell and Mr. Duncan Campbell to be void and null, and prohibited them to preach or exercise any part of the ministerial function in time coming, and further ordained them and ilk ane of them to give bond and sufficient caution to deliver their persons to the clerks of the Privy Council to be disposed upon as the Lords of the Privy Council should think fit, and that in the meantime they should not exercise any part of the ministerial function under the foresaid penalty and ordained them to go to prison till the foresaid caution be found.

As the "outed" ministers from Dumbarton were sent to Edinburgh Tolbooth, Patrick Campbell may have gone with them. The bond for 5,000 merks was found and the Rev. Patrick was liberated on 17th March 1685, but he was ordered to leave the kingdom.

The place of Mr. Patrick was taken by the Rev. John Lindsay formerly of Lochgoilhead. He was presented to Glenaray by James VII on 29th October 1685, on which he received collation and institution. The Rev. Alexander Ruat was minister in Inveraray. (There had been a family of this name in the church for some time - they may have come from Kilmarnock.[67] Hugh Rowat was an elder in 1679 and Alexander Ruat was a member of the Kirk Session in 1680). These two clergymen having been placed, the charges of Glenaray and Inveraray were filled once more.

But this settlement was not to last long. On 5th July 1687, James II for reasons of his own gave freedom of worship in Scotland to all sects, if loyal, in buildings notified to and approved by local magistrates. All penal enactments against dissenters were annulled. This opened up the way for many exiled ministers to return home to become useful pastors again, and among the number was Mr. Patrick Campbell. In the same year, the Rev. Patrick attended a meeting of the Synod of Argyll. There were now two ministers in Glenaray: Mr. Patrick and Mr. John Lindsay, and a minister in Inveraray, Mr. Alexander Ruat.

The situation continued to develop rapidly. By the end of 1688, James II had fled to France and William and Mary reigned in

67   Wodrow: History, Vol. i, p. 296.

Whitehall in his stead. In 1690, Presbyterianism was established and ministers ejected since 1st January 1661 were restored to their parishes whether vacant or not. In consequence, John Lindsay[68] was deprived and Mr. Patrick Campbell was securely settled in the Parish of Glenaray. Similarly Alexander Ruat must needs give way to Alexander Gordon who returned to his charge in Inveraray after an exile of almost quarter of a century. And so the two old colleagues, Alexander Gordon in the Lowland Congregation and Patrick Campbell in the Highland Congregation were together once more.

On 13th October 1691, Mr. Gordon was Moderator of the Presbytery of Inveraray. He was free to resume the practice of lecturing or expounding a whole chapter of scripture, for which he had an aptitude. In other respects, Presbyterianism brought little change in the outward forms of public worship.

Age and increasing infirmities began to weaken these two veteran servants of the Church. Mr. Patrick died "with much peace and rejoicing" in March 1700, and is described as a "faithful minister of Christ, who continued stedfast in the times of persecution." Illness forced Mr. Gordon to demit his charge at the age of 75, between 18th October 1699 and 5th June 1700. He retired to Glasgow where the Rev. Robert Wodrow, minister of the Gospel at Eastwood, had a conversation with him on 9th May 1702. Mr. Gordon published an Account of the St. Andrews General Assembly of 1651, of which he was the last surviving member, and he died Father of the Church, 20th March 1713, aged about 89 years.

The Eighteenth Century - the early years

The eighteenth century was a more settled time for the Church. As the century began, the two veteran ministers who had served for the previous fifty years were discharged from their warfare, and their places were taken by other men.

Daniel Mackay succeeded Alexander Gordon in the English-speaking congregation in Inveraray. His name Daniel, often used for the Gaelic name Donald, seems to show that he was in sym-

68 He renounced Episcopacy and was received into communion by the Synod of Argyll on 16th October 1691. He was admitted minister of Kilchrenan June 1692 (F.E.S., Vol. iv, p. 9)

pathy with the anglicizing tendencies, for which the English-speaking congregation stood. He was translated from Fort William, Gearasdan dubh Inbhir Lochaidh, the Black Garrison of Inverlochy, where he acted as minister to the garrison. Having been inducted to Inveraray he proved himself to be an organiser and administrator. Communicants received communion tickets which were apparently authorised with a stamp.[69] Collections were made for building a bridge, which may have been the Bridge of Leacann.[70]

Poor relief in the congregation was organized. A committee of the Kirk Sesion gave in a roll of the poor divided into two classes: the poor in the first class were allowed a peck[71] of meal, or the price thereof weekly; the second class were allowed half a peck of meal or the price thereof weekly. There was another roll of those by whom the said poor were to be supported. The Earl of Argyll and the Sheriff gave their shares of this weekly allowance of meal to the poor. On 23rd January, 1700, Mr. Zehtrache's relict (or widow) received two pecks of meal. The beddale or church officer was appointed to warn the pensioners to attend frequently the sermon with certificacion that such as will be absent shall want the next week's allowance.

John McVarrich received half a merk weekly for removing strange beggars out of the town. The Session agreed with Angus McNokerd for making coffins to the poor at two libs four shillings Scots money per coffin.[72]

After serving for six years in Inveraray, Daniel Mackay first received a call to Crailing in the Presbytery of Jedburgh and short-

69   These may have been lead tokens. Kirk Sessions obtained two iron moulds or dies; these were fitted into the jaws of a pair of pincers and then the tokens were stamped out from a thin sheet of lead.

70   The River Leacann flows through the modern village of Furnace.

71   At the present time, a peck contains 8 quarts or 2 gallons and is ¼ of a bushel.

72   In value a twelfth of that of the pound sterling, or 1/8d. This devalued state was terminated officially by the Act of Union. R.W. Cochran: Records of the Coinage of Scotland, Patrick, 1876. "On 8 October 1700 there was payed to John Miller, Joyner in Inveraray for makeing a long table with Shulle and turned fraims with lock and key and tuo long furms and a chaire and culloring the Samen green 30.00.0." (Ms. accounts of Rev. Daniel Campbell, Synod Clerk)

ly afterwards became minister of Jedburgh itself. It may be assumed that he was inclined to move away from the Gaelic-speaking area to the South.

The minister of the Gaelic-speaking congregation in Glenaray was Alexander Campbell, one of the Campbells of Duntroon. Born in 1670, he was educated at the University of Glasgow. There he studied under a regent who took his pupils through the whole curriculum from the bajan class on to the final or magistrand class, prelecting through three or four years on Greek, and mathematics, on logic, moral philosophy and natural philosophy.[73] Alexander was in the fourth class in 1689, but apparently did not graduate. He was licensed by the Presbytery of Inveraray in 1691. He may have acted as a schoolmaster in some parish, though not in Inveraray, until 1701 when he was ordained and became minister of Glenaray. He was twice married, his second wife being Elizabeth, daughter of James Campbell of Achnatra, Provost of Inveraray, by whom he had six of a family.

Among his elders were Archibald Campbell of Clonarie, Archibald Clerk of Braleckan and John McKellar of Maam. If it was necessary for the minister of the English-speaking congregation to re-organize the work of the church, it was necessary for the minister of the Gaelic-speaking congregation to repair the fabric. This is not surprising, as the building was old and had been exposed to war, fire, weather and neglect during the vacancies. The fabric of the church was not in good shape: some of the glass windows were wanting and others broken. James Deor (or Dewar) was appointed to see this work done. The roof of the church had very much need of mending, many of the sclats (slates) having fallen off by ye violence of ye weather. Archibald McVicar was instructed to point and mend ye roof.

In 1706, the Session thought fit to build a stone wall about the Gaelic Kirk from the Manse to Archibald Brown's kiln. The length of the wall was to be 2,200 yards and a door of timber was to be made for the same. To carry out this considerable piece of work, the Session appointed every merkland to give a day's work of a horse and of a man for carrying the stones from the quarry to the stone wall. At this period, 1706, the manse was near to the church of the Gaelic congregation, and the glebe consisted of the church

73   Graham, H. Grey: Glasgow University Life in Olden Times, 1901.

lands of Kilmalieu immediately adjoining the old castle of the Duke of Argyll.

The Session also appointed a causeway to be laid at the church door where mud no doubt formed in winter time.

In addition to this care of the fabrics, the spiritual interests of the parish were not neglected. The Session considering the necessity of having catechists in this parish as there were in other congregations, they agreed with Hugh McMartin for the foot of Glenaray and with Martin Walker for Glenshira and the head of Glenaray and they allowed Hugh McMartin nine merks yearly and Martin Walker twelve merks Scots money yearly during their continuance in the said office.

It was the custom for people of neighbouring parishes to gather in whatever parish the communion was being celebrated. On 1st August 1708 many of the people in Glenaray went to the communion in Strachur and there was no sermon in the landward parish of this district on that day.

When Daniel Mackay of the English-speaking congregation was called to the South in 1707, Alexander Campbell was the only minister in Glenaray and Inveraray, and there do not seem to have been any services in the English congregation for two years.

At length in 1711, James Gettie was inducted to the charge of Inveraray, in succession to Daniel MacKay. It must have been a source of satisfaction to the members of the congregation in the Burgh to have a minister of their own once more. Gettie, which is a name found in eastern Inverness-shire and Morayshire, was almost certainly a Gaelic speaker. He studied at King's College, Aberdeen where he graduated on 2nd May 1705 and became a schoolmaster at Kilmallie. Having been licensed by the Presbytery of Lorn, he became minister of the English congregation in Inveraray at the age of 27 years.

Four years later, the Fifteen Rebellion broke out and there was a long interval in the meetings of the English Kirk Session on any business, by reason of the throngness and disorders of the time. The Kirk of Glenaray suffered more than the mere interruption of Session meetings. In 1717, the church was in bad condition through some part of the roof and windows being taken down and broken when the fencible men of the shire were there and the Highland Army. The Session decided there was no way of getting any funds for repairing the same any other way than by their own contributions. They therefore sent for 1000 slates to be procured without loss of time. This trouble continued for some five years. In 1722 the roof of the Gaelic church was still in a decayed state and two elders were appointed to agree with one of the sklaiters who was in the town for its repair.

Despite these necessary expenditures on fabric, the Kirk Session of Glenaray resolved in 1718, in accordance with the Act of the last General Assembly, to take a collection for the Protestant Churches of Lithuania. The members of the Session stirred up the people to be something more free and liberal than upon ordinary occasions and the money collected was twenty three pounds nine shillings, Scots.

In 1722, when James Gettie was minister of Inveraray and Alexander Campbell minister of Glenaray, there was an unfortunate difference between the two Sessions. It appears that the two congregations made use of the same cups, linen and communion table at the Sacrament of the Lord's Supper and that the bread and wine were provided by the Lowland Congregation. In July 1722, however, the Kirk Session of the Highland Congregation were informed that the Kirk Session of the Lowland Congregation had resolved to separate from them and not to share the vessels and the elements. The Kirk Session of the Highland Congregation therefore appointed the minister Alexander Campbell, with Archibald M'Vicar and Niven Turner, elders to provide elements, table, linen, cups and whatever might be necessary for the great work before them.

But they felt so aggrieved that they also appointed a remark or two to be recorded on this occasion. Primo, it was not like the work in hand (the Sacrament) for the Session of the English congregation to divide from the Session of the Highland congregation "only because they have money and one of those homes will give more collections than a hundred of ours. But we are not ashamed of this". Secundo, the new congregation and a lowland minister was set up, much to the detriment of us, the old and only paroch... this erection was for the family of Argyll to encourage strangers to come and set up at Inveraray... they (the members of the English congregation) are poor menial servants who had no more relations in this than in any other place, where they might be called for a while or be given meat and wages...

All which was minuted accordingly.

It is to be hoped that this difference between the two Kirk Sessions was soon harmonized. The bitterness of the language however shows the feelings with which the English-speaking tradesmen and merchants were regarded by the natives.

During the ministry of Mr. Campbell the church bells were recast. In 1725 the two bells in the steeple in the old town were useless. This was a serious matter because the bells had an important part to play in the life of the parish. They were used for the customary purpose, according to immemorial usage, of warning people to proceed to or leave their work, in the morning and evening or on occasions of national rejoicing. The right to fix the hours at which the bells should be rung belonged to the Kirk Session. The heritors of the landward district of the parish, which was partly town and partly landward, were liable to contribute to the expense of the church bell. The bell, having become unserviceable, might be melted down and sold, and the proceeds applied to the purchase of a new one. In Inveraray, it was resolved not to sell, but to have the bells recast. Campbell of Stonefield, Sheriff Depute of Argyll, assumed responsibility. The work was done by Robert Maxwell in Edinburgh, and the new bell bore the inscription: EX BENIGNITATE SPECTATISSIMI VIRI JACOBI CAMPBELL DE STONEFIELD, JUSTITIARII ET VICE COMITIS DELEGATI DE ARGYLL. ROBERTUS MAXWELL ME FECIT EDINBURGHI ANNO 1728. On the bell was the Burgh Coat of Arms.[74]

At this time, in the 1730's, Alexander Campbell in Glenaray required from some persons about to be married the deposit of a sum of money known as consignation money. This caution money or "pawn" was a guarantee of good behaviour till the marriage be celebrated. The consignation money was retained by Alexander Campbell or the Session Clerk for nine months, and if the marriage did not take place or scandal arose before the termination of the stated period, the money was forfeited.[75] On 10th January 1736, a young man in the Parish of Innishael and a young woman in the Parish of Glenaray gave up both their names in order to marriage

74 Inveraray: Official Guide Book; Dunlop: Parochial Law; Black: Parochial Ecclesiastical Law.

75 William Andrews (ed): Bygone Church Life in Scotland, London 1899.

and both parties consigned their consignation money. They were married on the 27th January.[76]

Alexander Campbell, minister of Glenaray died in 1734 and was succeeded by another minister of the same name. James Gettie minister of Inveraray died in 1744 and the way was open for re-adjustment.

Glenaray and Inveraray: A Collegiate Charge

Glenaray and Inveraray were made a collegiate charge in 1745. The two churches were in juxtaposition in the old town. The measurements of the English Church within the walls were 54 feet in length, and 20 feet in breadth; the Duke's Aisle was 16 feet long and 11 feet 8 inches in breadth; there was a Magistrates' Loft which had been in existence since 1681[77] and there was a loft opposite which may have been used for the boys of the Grammar School. The Highland Church was of the same length and breadth as the English Church: it had a west loft and an east loft.[78]

When the two churches were made collegiate, there was a re-deployment of manpower. Alexander Campbell, minister of Glenaray was presented by Archibald Duke of Argyll to Inveraray and was translated and admitted to the Burgh Church in May 1745. This settlement was not altogether in the interest of Alexander Campbell, because the second minister, that is the minister of Inveraray, did not receive any modification out of the teinds of the parish.[79] The Rev. Alexander stated that he considered his interests hurt by the change but cheerfully gave it up in favour of the public utility.[80] The Parish of Glenaray being vacant by this translation, Patrick Campbell, a grandson of the minister of that name in the previous century, was inducted to the First Charge in 1745.

Alexander Campbell was not long translated to the Burgh

76 Marriage Register, Inveraray, 1699-1761.

77 K.S.M., 31.1.1681.

78 Saltoun Mss. 1758.

79 The Teinds of Inveraray in John Connell's Law of Scotland relating to Parishes, p. 149.

80 F.E.S., Vol. iv, p. 11.

Church when he received intimation of big changes to come. Arrangements for the removal of the town of Inveraray from the immediate neighbourhood of the Castle to its present position were under consideration and in 1746 a Summons of Removing at the instance of Archibald Campbell of Stonefield in his capacity of Chamberlain of Argyll was directed against Alexander Campbell, minister, among many other inhabitants.[81]

The Rev. Alexander required to cope not only with possible changes in his place of abode but also with new methods of reckoning time. In 1752, he caused the following entry to be made in the Marriage Register of Inveraray Parish Church: "Upon the third of September this year the computation of time has been changed from the Julian to the Gregorian calculation, so that the 3rd day of September is reckoned the fourteenth New Stile, and all the dates hereafter in this Register are according to the Gregorian or New Stile and all the former according to the Julian or Old Stile." [82]

A week or two after this entry, the English Church in the Old Town was used for an unusual purpose. Between the 21st and the 25th September 1752, from Friday morning 6 a.m. until 7 a.m. on Sunday, the church was used as a Court House in the trial of James Stewart for the Appin Murder.[83]

Two years later, in 1754, Mr. Campbell administered baptism to an unusual candidate. "A native of the East Indies and servant to His Grace the Duke of Argyll, after having been instructed in the principles of Religion and particularly of the nature and end of baptism and having made a publick profession of the faith was baptised by Mr. Alexander Campbell, minister of Inveraray, this twenty third day of October 1754 years by the name of William Campbell before these witnesses, Mr. Lachlan Campbell, minister of Ardnamurchan, Mr. John ffallowsdale, Master of the Grammar School at Inveraray, Mr. Dorret, Mr. Cummin, John Morgan and Sinclair, servants to the Duke of Argyll.[84]

81   MacTavish: Inveraray Papers, p. 55.

82   Marriage Register, Inveraray, 1699-1761.
(The Chancellor of the Exchequer retained the old dates so that the Income Tax year began eleven days after old New Year's Day, 25th March.)

83   Book of Barcaldine, p. 83.

84   Inveraray Baptismal Register, 1699-1761.

In 1758, a young minister, who was to make a name for himself in the Church of Scotland took a service in the Burgh. In October 1758, Alexander Carlyle or Jupiter Carlyle, minister of Inveresk preached to his Grace who always attended the church at Inveraray. The young ladies of the Duke's party told the young man (he was then thirty-six years of age) that he had pleased his Grace which gratified the preacher not a little, as without him no preferment could be obtained in Scotland.[85]

Alexander Campbell, minister of Inveraray, died in 1764 and his library, which was valuable, was sold in Glasgow.

The Rev. John MacAulay, M.A. was admitted to Inveraray in 1765 while Patrick Campbell continued as minister of Glenaray. Mr. MacAulay was father of Zachary MacAulay, an ardent philanthropist who worked for the abolition of the slave trade, and grandfather of Thomas Babington MacAulay, English historian, essayist and politician.

The Reverend John was acquainted with James Boswell, and when Samuel Johnson and James Boswell visited Inveraray during their tour to the Hebrides in 1773, the minister of the Burgh renewed the acquaintanceship.[86] Mr. MacAulay came to the travellers on the morning of Monday, October 25th and accompanied them to the Castle. He also passed the evening with them at their inn. When Doctor Johnson spoke of people whose principles were good, but whose practice was faulty, Mr. MacAulay said, he had no notion of people being in earnest in their good professions whose practice was not suitable to them. The Doctor grew warm and said "Sir, are you so grossly ignorant of human nature as not to know that a man may be very sincere in good principles, without having good practice?" Doctor Johnson was unquestionably right. On the next morning, Tuesday October 26th, the minister breakfasted with the two literary celebrities, nothing hurt or dismayed by his last night's correction.

Another literary giant with whom Mr. MacAulay was acquainted was David Hume, historian, philosopher and sceptic. Meeting Hume at dinner in the Castle, Mr. MacAulay was so bold as to

---

85   Autobiography of the Rev. Dr. Alexander Carlyle, Edinburgh, 1861, p. 382.

86   James Boswall: Journal of a Tour to the Hebrides with Samuel Johnson. Two volumes. London, 1898.

invite Hume to attend divine service on Sunday.[87] Lady Elizabeth, daughter of the Duchess of Argyll undertook to be present and David Hume also agreed to attend. In course of his sermon on the Sunday, Mr. MacAulay spoke about scepticism and the lively Lady Elizabeth indicated to the rationalist that this part of the discourse was for his benefit. When Mr. MacAulay proceeded to address himself to the chief of sinners, however, it was the turn of the philosopher to suggest that this topic was particularly applicable to the lady herself.[88]

While these events were taking place in high society, the two ministers John MacAulay and Patrick Campbell were undergoing various personal vicissitudes. John MacAulay occupied a house in the parish of Glenaray on which he paid one shilling house duty each year.[89] His colleague Patrick Campbell had a less equable existence. Mr. Campbell lived in a part of a house very inconvenient in many respects. He was under the necessity of quitting it and going into one of the little houses in the Gallowgate, a row of cottages facing the loch, to the south west of the new town. He had to lay out money to make the house habitable and he paid rent for it.[90] In 1758, he was put in possession of the farm at Kenmore, agreeable to the tack which had been given him.

In 1773, Mr. Patrick Campbell died and in 1774 Mr. John MacAulay was translated to Cardross.

New Ministries, New Churches and New Manses

Archibald Campbell, the son of Patrick Campbell, succeeded his father as minister of the Highland Charge in 1774, and Alexander M'Tavish was presented by John, Duke of Argyll to the Lowland Charge.

In the same year, 1774, a site was fixed for the churches on a low mound at the head of the Main Street in the New Town.[91] The

87   David Hume regularly attended church at Greyfriars in Edinburgh.

88   The Anecdotes and Egotisms of Henry MacKenzie, 1745-1831, Oxford University Press, 1927.

89   Account of the Rates and Duties upon Houses, Window or Lights in the Seven Parishes of Argyllshire, 1770.

90   The Saltoun Mss, 1758.

91   Inveraray, Official Guide Book.

two churches, Lowland and Highland, in the old town were taken down and services were held on the ground floors of the houses which are now the George Hotel. In 1758, there had been an estimate for building a circular church in the New Town of Inveraray,[92] but this idea was not carried out and a beginning was made with the building of another type of edifice in 1794.[93] Robert Mylne, architect, designed an oblong building to house separate Gaelic and English-speaking congregations under one roof, the two places of worship being separated from one another by a solid partition. The churches were built at the expense and under the close supervision of the 5th Duke of Argyll. The bell which had been recast in 1728 was hung in the South facade, a clock was set on the North facade and there was a slender spire, which the architect regarded as the centre piece of the new town.[94] The church was completed and in use by 1802, the total cost having been about £700.[95]

Of necessity, new manses were built for the two ministers, as the Lowland Manse in the old town was being demolished and the house of the Highland Church minister in the Gallowgate was unsuitable. The two manses built in 1776 were placed in Front Street, on the east of Main Street and opposite the pier, one manse on each side of a larger dwelling house.[96]

About the same time there was a readjustment of stipend. It may be remembered that in 1649 an Act of Parliament was passed appointing commissioners to modify stipends and that in 1651 these commissioners modified to the second minister of Inveraray a stipend of three chalders of victual and 900 merks out of the revenue of the bishopricks of Lismore and of the Isles. The stipend continued on this basis till the beginning of the eighteenth century when the Synod of Argyle obtained a grant from the Crown of the whole revenues which had belonged to the bishopricks and passed

92   Saltoun Mss.

93   D.W. MacKenzie: Inveraray Parish Church, 1952.

94   Department of Health for Scotland: Area Argyll, List of Buildings of Architectural or Historic Interest.

95   MacKenzie: Inveraray Parish Church.

96   D.J. Kellas: Inveraray.

an act giving to the minister of the second congregation a certain stipend out of these revenues. Matters remained in this situation until 1792 when a judgment was obtained from the Court of Teinds finding that a considerable tract of land (Glenshira), formerly reputed to belong to the parish of Lochgoilhead, formed a part of the parish of Inveraray. In consequence, the Duke of Argyll brought a process of modification, with the view that the free teinds of these lands should be appropriated in equal portions to the two ministers of Inveraray. As a result, it was pronounced on 21st June 1792 that each minister receive an augmentation of 30 bolls of victual and £18.6.8d. Scots.[97]

Two very different ministers

The men chiefly affected by these architectural and financial alterations were the minister of the Highland Charge, Archibald Campbell and the minister of the Lowland Charge, Paul Fraser. (Mr. Fraser succeeded Alexander MacTavish in 1789, the year in which the French Revolution broke out).

Archibald Campbell, minister of the Highland Charge, had a sad lot. Having grown up in the cottage of his father, the Rev. Patrick Campbell, in the Gallowgate, Inveraray, he was ordained to North Knapdale in 1759, where the manse had been patched up recently.[98] In 1767, he married Florence, only daughter of Dugald MacTavish of Dunardary, who like many of his neighbours was in danger of getting into financial difficulties.[99] They had a son and daughter while in the Manse at Kilmichael Inverlussa, North Knapdale, the son Dugald dying when he was one year old. In 1774, the Rev. Archibald was translated and admitted to Glenaray or the Gaelic Church. Without doubt, he lodged temporarily in his father's old house in the Gallowgate and conducted services in temporary accommodation in the new town. In 1776 he removed to the brave new manse in Front Street, Inveraray.

By 1792, the Rev. Archibald had left the parish in bad health and the whole parochial duties were discharged by his colleague in the English Church. Nevertheless when the Court of Teinds

97 Connell's Law of Scotland relating to Parishes.

98 North Knapdale in the XVIIth and XVIIIth centuries, p. 152.

99 Ibid. p. 84.

appropriated the free teinds of Glenshira in equal portions to the two ministers of Inveraray, he strenuously contended that he was the only parochial minister and that his colleague had no right to any modification out of the teinds until he the minister of Glenaray "was properly and competently provided". He claimed that he was in a worse position financially after the judgment of the Court on the teinds. But the Court adhered to its decision.

In 1805, the Rev. Archibald accidentally poisoned his only daughter and died from shock. He was one of those unfortunate people for whom happiness is only an occasional episode in the general drama of pain.

His colleague in the English Church was a more robust and happy man. The Rev. Paul Fraser was presented to Inveraray in 1788, the Rev. Alexander MacTavish having died during the previous year. Like so many, though not like all Frasers, he was born in Inverness. He was educated at the University and King's College, Aberdeen, graduating with the degree of M.A. in 1755 when he was twenty four years of age. He probably acted as schoolmaster until he was thirty years, when he was ordained missionary at Glencoe, a district in which the Episcopal Church in Scotland was strong, and which was at that time part of the parish of Lismore. Subsequently, he served as missionary at Fort William and minister at Craignish, marrying Elizabeth Campbell, daughter of Robert MacLachlan of MacLachlan in June 1771. In 1789, he was translated and admitted to Inveraray at the age of fifty eight years. He occupied one of two manses on Front Street facing the pier and conducted services on the ground floor of one of the houses where the George Hotel now stands. By 1792, his colleague in the Gaelic Church, suffering from ill-health had left the parish, and the whole parochial duties were discharged by Mr. Fraser. In that year, he received an augmentation to his stipend of thirty bolls of victual and £18.6.8 Scots.[100] In 1793, he completed the Statistical Account of the Parish of Inveraray and in the next year 1794 he had the satisfaction of seeing the building of Inveraray Church begun at the head of the Main Street of the town. In 1796, the University of St. Andrews made recognition of his abilities by conferring on him the degree of Doctor of Divinity and in 1802 he was conducting services in the newly built Parish Church of Inveraray.

At the same time, Mr. Fraser could not but be affected by the

100   Connell's Law of Scotland relating to Parishes.

troubles of the age. He served as chaplain of the 98th (Argyllshire Highlanders) Regiment of Foot, 1794-1796,[101] which was also known as the Lochnell Highlanders, and his name appears in the list of officers in the Army List of the 1st of January 1795.[102] After this regiment was sent overseas in May, 1795, Mr. Fraser was chaplain to the 5th Battalion, the Argyllshire Regiment of Fencibles. Without doubt he was present when the Argyllshire Fencibles proceeded from Inveraray to Kilchenzie in October, 1798 to repel a French invasion of Kintyre.[103]

Doctor Fraser's family was now grown up and his youngest daughter Caroline was described as "a girl of radiant beauty". The poet Thomas Campbell who met her at Sunipol in Mull, in Tayvallich, and in Inveraray was deeply in love with her[104] but she married Thomas Wingate, Esq., at Stirling on 29 January 1799.

This remarkable parish minister had powers of divination and prophecy or what was known in the Highlands as "the secret of the Lord". In June 1815, when he was eighty four years of age, Doctor Fraser gave thanks for a great victory for our troops, before any one in Argyll had heard of the Battle of Waterloo. He died Father of the Church on 2nd October 1827 at the age of ninety six, and a hall called The Paul Fraser Memorial Hall was set apart in Inverary Church.

The Nineteenth Century

"Men in their generation are like the leaves of the trees."[105] Paul Fraser and his colleague in the Gaelic Church were succeeded by others. James MacGibbon was ordained and inducted to Glenaray in 1807 and Doctor Fraser was succeeded in Inveraray by three ministers, none of whom for a variety of reasons waited any length of time.

101 J.S. Farmer: The Regimental Records of the British Army, London, 1901.

102 Historical Records of the 91st Argyllshire Highlanders, arranged by G. L. Goff, London, 1891.

103 The Correspondence of Lieutenant General Campbell of Kintarbert, 1762-1837.

104 North Knapdale in the XVIIth and XVIIIth Centuries.

105 Homer, Iliad, VI, p. 146.

It is to the credit of James MacGibbon that he was the first minister to take active steps to hold regular religious services in the thickly populated districts of Auchindrain, the Leckan Muir, Furnace, Cumlodden and Minard. It was due to the exertions of Mr. MacGibbon that the Mission of Lochfyneside was appointed. The District and Mission of Lochfyneside extended from Braleckan to Shirdruim. The hearers assembled in the open-air in the most inclement weather or repaired to the school house of Cumlodden, which was never intended for any other purpose than week-day teaching and was limited and confined. As a result of Mr. MacGibbon's representations, a missionary called Mr. MacNab was appointed to this district by the Committee for Managing His Majesty's Royal Bounty.[106]

The most distinguished of the immediate successors to Doctor Fraser in Inveraray was the Rev. Colin Smith. Born in Glen Orchy in 1802, he was educated at the University of Glasgow and became an assistant in the Parish of Glenaray and Inveraray. Colin Smith was presented by George William, Duke of Argyll and ordained and inducted to Inveraray in 1828; he was translated and admitted to Glenaray in 1831. Because of his proficiency in the Gaelic language, he was a member of a Committee appointed by the General Assembly to revise a translation of the Bible into Gaelic in 1840 and afterwards became convener of that Committee.

During the course of their ministries, the Rev. Colin and his colleague in the English Church met with discouragements. In 1837, the two churches suffered serious damage from lightning and were repaired at the cost of trouble and expense in the following year.[107] In 1843, the year of the Disruption, the two ministers were grieved when some two hundred people formed a congregation of the Free Church in Inveraray. This was particularly discouraging at a time when the population of the district was declining.

Mr. Smith, undaunted, soldiered on. By 1845 he had completed the New Statistical Accounts of the Parishes of Glenaray and Glassary, and in 1849 the University of Glasgow conferred on him the degree of Doctor of Divinity. It was said that he possessed numerous accomplishments and excelled in botany. His abilities

106   Fraser, Rev. A: Lochfyneside, pp. 95, 96.

107   F.E.S., Vol. viii, p. 313.

were further recognized when he was nominated to be Moderator of the General Assembly in 1861.

Doctor Smith took an interest in Glenaray School. He generally visited the place after there had been a fight among the boys and spoke kindly to them and urged that they should love one another.[108]

The Reverend Doctor Colin lost his colleague Dugald Campbell MacTaggart, minister of the English congregation in 1865 and he himself died in 1867. They were succeeded by Neil MacPherson, M.A., in the Gaelic congregation and by Donald Carmichael (who married Jeanie, daughter of Doctor Colin) in the English congregation.

Inveraray was visited by an increasing number of people in the summer months, and among these in 1876 were Charles Haddon Spurgeon and Dean Stenley. On Saturday 19th August, Mr. Spurgeon, the English non-conformist divine, was seen accompanied by two of his sons in the streets of Inveraray. On being pressed to stay over the Sabbath and preach, he pleaded an engagement. He left the Burgh at 1 p.m. by the Loch Goil route.

A week later, on Sunday 27th August, Dean Stanley, an English divine, who was visiting the Duke of Argyll, preached in Inveraray Parish Church to a large and attentive audience. The Rev. Neil MacPherson, minister of Glenaray, having conducted the first portion of the service, Dean Stanley, who wore the ordinary Geneva gown, entered the pulpit and delivered a sermon on the Prodigal Son.[109]

It is an indication of Mr. MacPherson's attainments as a scholar, that he was one of the Glasgow Board for examining students entering the Divinity Hall, an office from which he resigned at the Synod of Argyll in September 1877.

Neil MacPherson and Donald Carmichael were followed in turn, first in Inveraray and then in Glenaray by Peter Neil MacKichan. The Rev. Peter was born at Cape Breton in 1837, brought up in the Manse at Daviot, Inverness-shire, educated at the Universities of Aberdeen, St. Andrews and Glasgow, licensed by the Presbytery of Inverness in 1861, and translated from Lochgilphead to Inveraray in 1876. He became Clerk to the Presbytery

108   Richard Lovett: James Chalmers, p. 19.

109   The Oban Telegraph and West Highland Chronicle, 16.8.1876, 2.9.1876.

of Inveraray and his bold angular signature, attesting the minutes of Kirk Sessions arrests the eye of the reader. Mr. MacKichan felt strongly on the divisions of the churches by which his work was no doubt hampered and he published a sermon on "The Evils of Sectarianism" in 1872.

Church Union

For the last seven years of his ministry (1904-1911) Peter Neil MacKichan in the First Charge, Glenaray, had as his colleague John Finlay Dawson in the Second Charge, Inveraray. Finlay Dawson continued to serve in Inveraray while two short ministries took place in Glenaray. Meanwhile great developments were unfolding. Negotiations for Union were entered upon between the Church of Scotland and the United Free Church. The Declaratory Articles of the Church of Scotland (1921) and the Property and Endowments Act (1925) finally created a situation in which all reason for continued separation disappeared. It was a thrilling occasion when on 2nd October 1929 in the presence of the Duke and Duchess of York, the final ceremonies of Union were reverently completed and a single re-united Church of Scotland was constituted.

This great union necessitated re-adjustment in Glenaray and Inveraray. Glenaray was already vacant. The Rev. Donald Campbell Stewart demitted his charge, the United Free Church, Inveraray on 31 January 1930. The Rev. John Finlay Dawson demitted his charge, Inveraray, in the interests of local union 21 February 1930. The First Charge (Glenaray) and the Second Charge (Inveraray) and the United Free charge were united in March, 1930. The Inveraray Church became the parish church and the Glenaray Church after being used for Gaelic services for a time became a hall. The United Free Church was used as a hall for some years.

The first minister of the united charge of Glenaray and Inveraray was Angus McCuish Gray who was ordained and inducted on 24th September 1930. Mr. Gray was an eloquent preacher, able to preach so effectively that men were moved to commit themselves to the Faith. During the War of 1939-1945 he served as Chaplain to the Forces. While Mr. Gray was on active service, the General Trustees of the Church authorised the demolition of the steeple in 1941. The reason advanced was that for many years the spire had given cause for concern and was then condemned by the Trustees' architect. The church and town were thus deprived of a focus of interest and its loss is still deplored.

On the conclusion of hostilities, Mr. Gray resumed his ministry in Inveraray. In 1949 he was translated to St. James's, Edinburgh.

The Rev. Donald William MacKenzie was called to the vacant charge. A graduate of Edinburgh University, he was ordained and inducted to Barra in 1941. From 1943 to 1946 he served as chaplain in the Royal Navy. He was called from Barra to Inveraray, where he served for eighteen years, and visitors spoke appreciatively of the fine tone and quality of his devotions. He was clerk to the Presbytery of Inveraray. Being an enthusiast for Gaelic he taught Gaelic classes in the Night School and helped to promote the study of the language.

Mr. MacKenzie was translated to the Barony Church, Auchterarder in 1966.

The Rev. David J. Kellas, M.A.,B.D., was inducted to Inveraray in the same year. Both Mr. and Mrs. Kellas (who held an Honours degree in history) were remarkable for the qualifications which they brought to their task. Three of Mr. Kellas' forefathers were Doctors of Divinity and he himself had an Arts degree with Honours and a Divinity degree with Honours. With a remarkable knowledge of the finer points of Church Law, he brought a keen, clear, original mind to bear on the work of both parish and presbytery. He did not spare himself in the service of youth and in visitation of the elderly. He was called to St. James' Church, Falkirk in 1972.

The parish of Glenaray and Inveraray has had a varied history. Many notable men have ministered within the bounds, and there is no doubt but that in the future Inveraray will continue to be a centre of Christian work and witness.

The United Presbyterian Church, Inveraray

In 1837, the Secession Church was to be found in the Burgh of Inveraray![110] This body was known as the United Associate Congregation at Inveraray, and it was a member of the United Associate Presbytery of Glasgow. This presbyterian organisation had arisen

110   Inveraray Secession Church Session Minute Book.

out of the working of the patronage system. It was made up of churchmen who were disposed to disregard the presentation of lay patrons and to settle the men desired by the people as ministers. The Secession Church was exclusively a Lowland Church, and its outlook was characterised by theological liberalism. The presence of this church in the Burgh indicates that Lowlanders had come to settle as tradespeople and craftsmen.

In October 1837, the minister of the United Associate Congregation in Kelso, with an elder of the United Associate Congregation, Regent Place, Glasgow, and an elder of the United Associate Congregation, Broughton Place, Edinburgh, ordained three local men to the office of ruling elder in the congregation at Inveraray. The Rev. James Hay was the Moderator and Clerk of the Kirk Session. There was a Committee of Management elected at an annual meeting of members and seat-holders. In the committee there was a preses, a clerk, a treasurer, a precentor and a bell-ringer. Seat rents were paid quarterly in advance at one shilling each sitting. The salary of the clerk was two guineas and that of the precentor five pounds annually. Any cash balance was transmitted to the United Associate Congregation, Regent Place, Glasgow, of which Inveraray was a Station. Admission to communion was by tokens distributed to members of the congregation by the moderator.

In 1841, the Session of this congregation which was also known as the United Secession Church, Inveraray, considered the subject of union with the Relief Churches in Scotland, unanimously decided to approve the steps taken, and transmitted its approbation to the United Associate Presbytery of Glasgow.

In 1846, the state of the congregation was not satisfactory and there was the possibility that it might be dissolved. A committee was appointed by the United Associate Presbytery of Glasgow[111] to meet with the Session of Inveraray Secession Church. The Session asked the Committee from Glasgow to consider the prejudicial effect which the final disbandment of this Station would have on all other stations in the Highlands. They also spoke of the friendly countenance which the Duke of Argyll had given to the congregation, of which countenance the congregation could rest assured. It

111 This should read, The United Secession Presbytery of Glasgow. But the Kirk Session may have been old fashioned enough to use the older title in their minutes.

was agreed by the Presbytery that the Station be continued. A complaint was lodged with the Committee against one of the ruling elders of not performing the duties of his office. The elder resigned.

In 1847, a union was formed between all the congregations of the United Secession Church and 118 congregations of the Relief Churches in what now became the United Presbyterian Church. The local congregation became the U.P. Church, Inveraray.

On 10th July 1849, the Reverend Gilbert Meikle who had just been ordained to the pastoral oversight of Inveraray was introduced and many could not get inside the church because of the crush. As the Session had no funds at its disposal, no treasurer was elected. A roll of membership of the congregation was made up: there were twenty-four members. A congregational prayer meeting was held on the first Monday of each month in the Parish School and a Missionary Society in connection with the congregation was formed. The state of the Congregational Library was considered. As many of the books were out in the hands of the subscribers, all the books were to be given in to one of the elders.

A letter was read from the Synod's Committee on Foreign Correspondence requesting a collection in aid of the ministers who had recently seceded from the Reformed Church of France. The Session sympathised with these ministers, but was not able to recommend a collection.

Next year, July 1850, the Session of the U.P. Church, Inveraray, agreed to address a memorial to the Government against the proposed re-opening of the Post Office on Sabbath; also against the running of the Mails altogether on that day. Twenty five years later, 9th March 1875, the Session was continuing to take an interest in public affairs. It was agreed to petition Parliament against the Contagious Disease Acts[112] The petition, which was signed by the Moderator and Clerk and transmitted for presentation to Sir William Cunningham, Bart., M.P. for the Burgh, stated:

---

112 These Acts provided for the compulsory examination of prostitutes in garrison towns in case of venereal disease.

Your Petitioners strongly disapprove of the Contagious Disease Acts of 1864, 1866, 1869;

1. because they are immoral;

2. because they foster vice by making indulgence in it safe;

3. because they will fail to accomplish the end which was in view when they were passed.

Reverting to more local concerns, the Session was occupied with constant changes in the membership of the Church. A married couple, previously members of the Established Church, applied for admission to the communion of the U.P. Church. A married couple from the Free Church, Inveraray, made application to be admitted to the U.P. Communion. John Redpath, having changed his views in regard to baptism, withdrew from membership of the U.P. Kirk. A woman was suspended from Church privileges for "going wrong through drink". Members of U.P. congregations in Coatbridge, Perth, Cumbernauld, Lochwinnoch, Campsie, New City Road Glasgow, and Bridge Street Congregation Edinburgh presented "lines" or certificates of membership and desired to join the church in Inveraray; as also did members of the South Side Reformed Presbyterian Congregation, Glasgow, and of the Reformed Presbyterian Congregation, St. George's Road, Glasgow. Much of this fluid transference of members indicates free movement of population in search of employment.

In 1858, the Inveraray U.P. Church, belonging to the Presbytery of Paisley and Greenock which met in Greenock, was confirmed in its financial position. In that year, a letter from the Presbytery Clerk was read intimating that the Home Mission Committee had agreed to continue the present arrangement with this congregation for three years, namely £40 to be raised annually by the people of Inveraray U.P. Church and £50 to be given in supplement by the Presbytery. This was agreed by the local congregation.

One of the most remarkable fruits of the work in the U.P. Kirk was James Chalmers, missionary in New Guinea. When he was about ten or twelve years of age, James Chalmers joined the U.P. Sunday School of which the Rev. Gilbert Meikle was superintendent. In 1859, the youth attended evangelistic meetings in connection with the United Presbyterian Church and the Free Church. He became a professing Christian, joined the United Presbyterian Church, served as a Sunday School teacher, addressed religious meetings in the village of Furnace, and eventually sailed as a missionary to the South Pacific Islands.

The United Presbyterian Church like other churches within the bounds received encouragement from the annual influx of summer visitors. In August, 1877 Professor Calderwood of Edinburgh was residing in Poll Schoolhouse near St. Catherine's. On Sunday 19th August in the forenoon, he preached in the United Presbyterian Church at Inveraray. Among the congregation were Lady MacNeill of Colonsay, who was staying at the Castle, and Lady Victoria Campbell. The preacher's text was Romans 6:23. Doctor Calderwood, on account of the storm, had very great difficulty in crossing the loch, there being a gale of east wind and heavy showers of rain.[113]

The ministry of the Rev. Gilbert Meikle in Inveraray was that of a lifetime, and he was held in high respect by everyone. In his manse in what was known as the Newton, to the southwest of Inveraray, he brought up a family, and in 1890 his daughter Susan Carson Meikle married the young minister in the Free Church, Inveraray, Donald Campbell Stewart.

The last ten years of Mr. Meikle's ministry had for their background the conferences between the United Presbyterian Church and the Free Church with a view to union. In 1900, these two churches became one as the United Free Church of Scotland. Mr. Meikle handed over the pastoral care of his flock to his son-in-law Donald Stewart, and his long and faithful ministry of fifty-one years was over.

The Free Church

In 1843, Scotland had been stirred for a decade by what was known as the Ten Years' Conflict, and in Glenaray and Inveraray as in other parishes, the people took great interest in the points at issue. The Duke of Argyll was among landed proprietors who met in Edinburgh three months before the Disruption. These gentlemen assembled for the purpose of uniting to make known their views to

113   The Oban Telegraph, 25.8.1877.

the Government in favour of the Free Church![114] The conflict between Church and State culminated in the protest of 1843 - a protest in the name of the retiring Moderator of the Assembly, the Rev. Dr. Welsh, and 203 members of the General Assembly of the Church of Scotland. These then withdrew and formed the Free Church, which included 474 ministers and of which Dr. Chalmers was elected moderator. In Inveraray, some two hundred people withdrew from the Parish Church and a congregation was formed. Mr. James M. Wright, solicitor and agent of the Union Bank, Inveraray, was prominently identified with this cause![115] A Church was erected in 1844, in what used to be known as the Gallowgate and is now called the Newton district. In the same year Mrs. S. Napier of York Road, London, presented a clock "To the Free Protesting Church in Inveraray". In 1847, the congregation obtained a minister the Rev. Robert Rose, M.A.[116]

Mr. Rose was born at Invergordon, 1813, he studied at the University of Aberdeen, and was ordained at Inveraray. In 1848, the membership of the Free Church, Inveraray numbered 200. In the same year, a Free Church School was built and this school was open to children of any church. In 1851, a Free Church Manse was erected and in 1862 Robert Rose married Mary Clark. Mr. Rose served his congregation faithfully, but the membership of the church decreased as the population of the Burgh and landward parts declined. After forty years, the minister felt himself being overtaken by the infirmities of age; and when he was seventy six years old, he asked for a colleague and successor.

In 1889, Donald Campbell Stewart was ordained and inducted to the Free Church, Inveraray, Mr. Stewart, a native of Argyllshire was educated at the University of Glasgow and the Free Church College. After he had been a year in Inveraray, he married Susan Carson Meikle, daughter of the Rev. Gilbert Meikle, minister of the United Presbyterian Church, Inveraray. Mr. and Mrs. Stewart had two sons, both of whom became ministers, and three daughters.

In 1895, the Free Church built in 1843 was showing signs of

114   Thomas Brown: Annals of the Disruption, p. 461, Edinburgh, 1890.

115   The Oban Times, 9.1.1937.

116   Annals of the Free Church of Scotland, Vol. II p. 111.

decay. Mr. Stewart took action and a new church was built. The clock presented in 1844 was installed in the new building.

The population continued to decline and in 1900 the membership of the Free Church, Inveraray, numbered 140.

In this year, the position of the local churches apart from the Parish Church was affected by events at national level. For some years the Free Church had been in conference with the United Presbyterian Church in the interests of union. In 1893, there was a desire in both churches for an incorporating union; in 1897, the work of constructing a basis of union was begun; and on 31st October 1900 the Free Church of Scotland and the United Presbyterian Church became one Church under the designation of the United Free Church of Scotland.

The Free Church and the United Presbyterian Church in Inveraray became one and the Rev. Donald Campbell Stewart continued as minister of the united congregations.

The United Free Church of Scotland, Inveraray

The union of the two congregations, assisted by the fact that the minister had belonged to the former Free Church and the minister's wife to the former United Presbyterian Church, was harmonious. Mr. Stewart was aceptable to the people and as time passed he was regarded with increasing confidence and respect![117] The accession of the office bearers and members of the U.P. Kirk strengthened the 140 members of the Free Church who entered the Union. Unlike so many United Free congregations Mr. Stewart's flock did not need to face the prospect of building a church and manse. The existing fabrics passed to the U.F. Church. The minister took his full share in the work of the church. For many years, he was Clerk to the United Free Church Presbytery of Inveraray. He was interim-moderator of the Lochfyneside U.F. Church Mission Station and in 1910 a new Church of wood and iron was built and opened in Minard.

Mr. Stewart was for several years a member of the School board of Glenaray and Inveraray, and was chairman for a time. He was also chairman of the Inveraray Parish Council and a member of the Mid-Argyll School Management Committee.

117 It is related that he broke the small finger of his hand hammering on the pulpit boards (Local tradition).

He left a memorial to his scholarship in the lengthy and able introduction which he wrote for the book of poems composed by a noted Inveraray poetess Mrs. Edward MacMillan, who wrote under her maiden name Isabella B. Crawford. The volume was published for private circulation.

On the union between the Church of Scotland and the United Free Church of Scotland in 1929, Mr. Stewart retired in the interests of local union after a ministry in Inveraray of forty years. The local Freemasons purchased the former United Free Church building. Mr. Stewart entered into his rest on 31st August 1932.

Inveraray [Argyll] All Saints

This is a Cathedral Mission of the United Diocese of Argyll and the Isles. The church was built by Amelia, the 8th Duke's second Duchess, who was a devout Episcopalian. Opened for worship and consecrated in 1886, it is seated for seventy people.

The former clergy were J.F. Scholfield, 1885-1887; E.G.H. Little 1887-1916; H.W. Gibson 1916-1925; J.H.C. Macfarlane-Barrow 1925-1928; L.R. Lewis 1928-1931; F.W. Bone 1931-1936; J.P. Collet 1937-52; D. MacIntyre (locum) 1958-1960.

At present, the services are on Sundays at 9 a.m. or 11.15 a.m. Holy Communion is celebrated as and when arranged by the Diocesan Itinerant Priest and is advertised in the Oban Times. The usage is the Scottish Liturgy of 1929.

The church contains the ancient pre-Reformation font formerly in the Chapel of Kilmalieu. The appointments of the church are numerous and valuable, including many old candelabra. The altar frontals and vestments are considered specially beautiful. The late Duke of Argyll (Niall, 10th Duke) gave an alabaster Holy Water Stoup on an ancient stone pedestal in 1932![118]

Niall Diarmid Campbell, 10th Duke of Argyll, was responsible for building the tower of All Saints' Church. In this tower he hung a peal of ten bells (accounted the finest north of the Tweed). The bells were cast in the foundry of Messrs. Taylor at Loughborough, brought to Inveraray in 1921 and housed in a wooden shelter. By 1931, the tower which was 126 feet high was completed. During its erection the Duke himself worked as a labourer, barrowing stones. In September 1931, the bells on each of which is inscribed a prayer

118   Year Book for the Episcopal Church in Scotland 1972-73.

in Latin by John S. Phillimore of Glasgow University, were hung in the tower and in October 1931, His Grace first rang the bells in the Belfry![119]

Appendix

At the end of the year, December 1651, the Commissioners of Parliament modified for a stipend to the minister serving the cure of the Irish (Gaelic) congregation of Inveraray the whole teinds parsonage[120] and vicarage[121] of Glenaray including Tulloch,[122] which extended to five chalders victual and one hundred and ten pounds 13d (Scots) together with four score ten pounds to make two hundred pounds (Scots), along with twenty pounds (Scots) for the communion elements.

For their guidance, the Commissioners had the Commission of Parliament of 1617, which had fixed the minimum stipend at five chalders of victual, i.e. corn or meal, or 500 merks, £27.15s. 6⅓d sterling, "or proportionally part of victual and part thereof in money, according as the fruits and rents of the Kirk may yield and afford, and as the said Commissioners shall think expedient". There was the Commission of 1627 which fixed a minimum stipend of 8 chalders of victual or 800 merks; there was the valuation of the teinds of the various parishes in Argyllshire carried through in 1629; and there was the practice of localling stipends, introduced about 1630, by which stipends were distributed proportionately among the heritors, who thereafter paid their share direct to the minister. The stipend modified to the minister of Glenaray was about the minimum. A sufficient manse and glebe were appointed at the same time.

119   Argyllshire Advertiser, 8.1.1974, 15.1.1974.

120   The great tithes: originally teinds of corn or wheat, barley, oats, pease, etc.

121   The small tithes: originally the lesser teinds of lamb, wool, milk, flax, cheese and eggs. Whales were teinded among vicarage tithes, and certain salmon fishings have been held to be subject to valuation. (Black: The Parochial Ecclesiastical Law of Scotland; Birnie: A Short History of the Scottish Teinds)

122   North and South Tulloch may have provided the endowment for the chapel of Kilmun in Glenaray and this may have been applied later to stipend.

SELECTED REFERENCES

Calderwood: Historie of the Kirk of Scotland, Wodrow Society, 8 vols.

Connell: Treatise on the Law of Scotland respecting Parishes, Edinburgh, Peter Hill & Co., 1818

Craven: Records of the Dioceses of Argyll and the Isles, Kirkwall, 1907 (Craven: Records of Argyll)

Fasti Ecclesiae Scoticanae (F.E.S.)

Knox, John: The History of the Reformation of Religion in Scotland

Maxwell: The Liturgical Portions of The Genevan Service Book, The Faith Press, Westminster, 1965

Minutes of the Synod of Argyll, 1639-1651, Scottish History Society, Third Series

New Statistical Account of Scotland, 1845, Vol. vii, Part 11, Argyll

Origines Parochiales Scotiae, Vol. ii, Part 1 (O.P.S.)

Register of the Kirk Session of Glenaray, 1701-1722 unpublished

Session Book of the English Congregation of Inveraray, 1651

Inveraray Secession Church Session Minute Book

Woodrow: Analecta
    Historical Fragments
    History of the Sufferings of the Church of Scotland,
        Blackie, Fullarton & Co., Glasgow, 1828

Scottish Supplications to Rome, 1423-1428, Scottish History Society, Third Series, vol. xlviii

Local tradition

Register of the Great Seal of Scotland (R.M.S.G.S.)

5

INVERARAY GRAMMAR SCHOOL

The Synod of Argyll was erected by the General Assembly of the Church of Scotland in 1638. At their first meeting in April 1639 they had under consideration the question of extending the educational facilities, such as they were, within their scattered area, and in 1640 they resolved "all in ane mutual voice" that "because the town of Inveraray is most centrically situate relatively unto the rest of the bounds of the province, and therefore it is meetest for the instruction of youth, a Grammar School be erected thereat, seeing that all that are desirous of learning may most commodiously resort thereto". Each minister within the Synod was required to contribute ten merks out of the Kirk penalties of his parish to be a provision to the school master there. Schools were also to be erected at other "considerable places" and to be supported by a contribution of 10 merks from the stipend of each minister within the respective areas served. These financial arrangements made provision only for the salaries of schoolmasters, there being no common fund from which the expenses of students in attendance at the Grammar School or the University could be defrayed, and in May 1643 the Synod referred to the General Assembly to determine whether the vacant stipends, or a portion of them could be employed "for the training up and education of young ones for the ministry". Presumably as a result of this application, an Act of Parliament was passed in July 1644 empowering the Synod of Argyll to employ the vacant stipends "for trayneing up of youthes that have the Irishe Tongue in schooles and colledges."

Next year, 1644, the devastation of Argyll during the Royalist rebellion of 1644-1647 made it impossible for the Synod to take immediate advantage of this concession, but when peace was restored, another fund was made available for educational purposes. During the course of the rebellion, a voluntary contribution "for our distressed brethren in Argyll" had been organised throughout Scotland by the Commission of the General Assembly, who in 1647 appointed a committee representing the Presbyteries of Cowal, Inveraray and Lorn to arrange for its distribution. This committee held their final meeting at Inveraray in December 1648, when, finding that they had still 11,000 merks in hand "and that if the same should be distributed according to the instructions, it would be very small and inconsiderable that would come to everyone's proportion" they recommended the Synod to set the money apart for educational purposes, 2,000 merks to be allocated to the Grammar School at Inveraray and 1,000 merks each to nine parochial schools, three in each of the presbyteries represented on the committee, the sums to be lent out on good security and the interest applied towards payment of the schoolmasters' salaries.

The recommendations of the committee were heartily approved by the Synod and the consent of the General Assembly was eventually obtained, though at first "for want of true information" they considered the arrangements worthy of rebuke. The parochial schools were all duly established, although difficulty was at times experienced in obtaining punctual payment of the interest due, and in one instance Campbell of Auchenbreck appropriated 1,000 merks of the principal. The parish of Dunoon had already been provided for, Charles I, with consent of Parliament, having in 1641 granted 2,000 merks out of the Bishops' teinds as a salary for a schoolmaster there, while the grammar school at Campbeltown was apparently assisted in its earlier stages by the Marquis of Argyll.

In 1649, the Marquis of Argyll added 600 merks to the 2,000 merks allocated to Inveraray, and following the withdrawal of the boys belonging to Argyll from the Grammar Schools of Glasgow, on the collapse of the General Assembly's scheme for their education, the Grammar School at Inveraray became the principal school within the bounds of the Synod. Bursaries payable out of the vacant stipends were regularly awarded to scholars for attendance there from 1651 till the Restoration, the usual allowance for bursars at Inveraray being 1,000 merks.

The interest on the 2,600 merks lent out on good security, which was used to pay the salary of the schoolmaster, was supplemented by the payment of scholars' fees. In December 1655, two of the elders of the Kirk, William Browne and William Loudone were appointed by the Session of the English Congregation of Inveraray, "to go thraw ye towne and desyr the townspeople that (have) bairnes a boarding to wryte to ther parents and others to send money wherewith they shall pay the master and doctour or else to acquent themselves of what they will allow them to give them with all, appoynting them who hev ther owne bairnes at schooll to pay in due tyme ...''.

Not all scholars had parents who were in a position to pay for their children's education, and in such cases the Kirk Session sought to help with their maintenance. On November 19, 1655, ''John McCwall a poor boy at the school having nothing to be sustained by, his father being dead and his mother in povertie, did give in a supplication to the Session for some helpe. In answer to the said supplication, they appoynted Árd. Ritchie treasurer to give to him four pounds Scots for buying clothes and shoone and recommended to ye said Ard. Ritchie to see the money so used.'' In 1656, the Session assisted ''Johne McPhǎll a poore schoiller''. It appears that John McPhail had exhausted the whole money that was bestowed on him by the Session in the year 1655 for buying of clothes in buying clothes. The garments however were not finished and were still lying in the tailor's hands, and John McPhail did not have money to make the final payment. The Session therefore appointed him 19 shillings Scots money to relieve his necessity.

There were conflicts between the school master (at this time Mr. James Fleming) and those who considered that the pupils were not making sufficient progress in learning. On May 22, 1657, there ''compeired Duncan Fisher with a complaint against Mr. James Fleming containing certain scandalous and uncivill expressions uttered by him in a rage and passion, the said complainer being regretting and finding fault with the non-proficiency of some scholars whereof the said Duncan had the oversight. Whereupon the said Mr. James being called for and the Session having heard the matter at length, they appoint the said Mr. James to acknowledge his wronging of the said complainer before the haill school and presence of the said Duncan and to make a fuller acknowledgment thereof befair the Session when he is again called for.''

Apparently, the Kirk Session were not satisfied with the proficiency of the instruction. ''The (same) day the Sessioune upon a regrate that the Scollers of the Grammar School doo not profit in their learning recommended the visiting of the scooll to the Presbitrie at the nixt meeting.''

The conduct of the school continued to be a source of concern to the Kirk Session. On September 22, 1659, ''the Session having observed severall of the scollars distracted from yr. books by folks borrowing of them from the scooll master to goe about their errands and privat businesse, doth admonish the scooll master here anent and desyre him not to lend his scollars to any whom so ever for any ordinar businesse when they should be attending ther books."

The Grammar School was well-attended and the teaching staff consisted of a master (at this time Mr. James Fleming) and a doctor or usher or under-teacher or assistant. Having resolved in 1658 to find a fit doctor, the Session appointed William Cooke as Doctor in 1660 at a salary of ane hundreth and twentie punds Scots money, viz., ane hundreth punds as doctour and the twentie as Session Clerke, beside his other payment of the schollars, and his share out of baptisms and marriages.[1] This appointment, like many similar subsequent appointments, was of short duration. William Cooke resigned as Doctor in September 1660, and his successor Mr. John Burnes did not take up duty till December. It was not long before John Burnes began to feel the difficulties of his situation. In 1661, "the doctor of the schooll and Session Clerke declared unto the Session that because of the smalness and ill-payment of the quarter wages he useth to get of the schollars, being but fourtie pennies quarterly and that he cannot afford the charges except the said quarterly wages be augmented, which the Session considering as also that the smalness of the doctor's maintenance heretofore hath been partly an occasion of so frequent wanting of a doctor to the school and being desirous of the said Mr. John his staying do therefore think it convenient that the quarter wages of each schollar be halfe a merke Scots......" These fees were to be paid by the toune bairnes as well as by those in the countrie.

The restoration of Charles II in 1660 had far-reaching effects. Following on this event, the cause of education was crippled by the

1 His salary would be about six or seven pounds sterling per annum. His share out of baptisms and marriages was what was paid for these in obtaining the order of the Kirk Session for baptism or marriage, and recording it. Dunlop's Parochial Law, 1841. "It was quite reasonable that a small fee should be exacted for registrations. Apart from the fact that it was payment to church officials for work done, the registration of baptisms answered nearly the same civil purposes as are now served by the registration of births. Every person consequently derived a benefit from the registration of baptisms." (Edgar: Old Church Life in Scotland, 1886)

appropriation of the vacant stipends for "the supply and mainten-ance and towards the reparation of the sufferings and losses" of Episcopalian ministers. A special Act of Parliament was necessary to secure for the "poore schoolers having the Yrish language" the bursaries granted to them by the Synod in November 1660, for want of which they represented, they were "not only in hazard to be imprisoned for their bygone buirdeings"[2] but were even in danger of being compelled "to quyte their study for the future". Another Act in 1663 was necessary to make provision for allow-ances to fourteen "expectants" and fourteen "scholars", but no further allocations followed.

Amid the difficulties of the times, provision for instruction continued to be made. In February 1661, a new school house was built at the end of the kirk, with its squat tower, surmounted by a pyramidal steeple. It was appointed that in time coming the master and scholars betake themselves thereto, and that Duncan McKennochow the kirk officer lock the kirk door. The scholars attended public worship; they had their own seat or gallery under the roof, but unauthorised persons sometimes intruded them-selves. On Apryll 23, 1678, the Kirk Session decided that "intima-tion be made that none sitt in tyme of sermon on the south side of the schollars loft but themselves". That there was need for such discipline is proved by the fact that Donald McIntyre, tailor was rebuked by the Session in August of the same year "for molesting and abusing the scholars in their own seats on the Sabbath Day in tyme of sermon". Knowledge of the Catechism was an important part of instruction, and in March 1679, the Session recommended "To the Schoole master to cause his schollers two and two to repeat the catechisme between the second and third bell in the afternoon and intimation was to be made there anent the next Sabbath that the people might come in to hear the same at the second bell".

Some sixteen years after the school was built, it was in need of repair. In 1677, the Kirk Session appointed the treasurer to over-see the schoole doore and seats and to cause mend them; and next year, David Carruders presented ane accompt due to him for some work done about the schoole windows et cetera.

In 1677, as at the present time, some children were unwilling

2   Burdens, debts.

to go to school, and some parents were careless about sending them. In September of that year, it was recommended by the Session to the minister that he speak to severall persones who has children and does not send them to the Schoole.

At this time, from 1677 to 1679, John MacLaurin was schoolmaster.[3] Following upon the succession of William and Mary in 1689, and the re-establishment of Presbyterianism (1689-1690) the Synod of Argyll again got possession of the vacant stipends and a scale of bursaries was drawn up, allowing 180 lib [4] to each student in divinity, 120 lib. to each student in philosophy, and 66 lib. 13.4d. to each grammarian. In 1696, a further fund was made available for education, when the bishops' rents which had fallen into the hands of the Crown were granted to the Synod to be bestowed "upon erecting of English schools for rooting out the Irish language and other pious uses", and from this source provision for assistance to the Grammar School at Inveraray was made.

During the eighteenth century (1700-1750) several elements in the situation of the school master in Inveraray developed. The schoolmaster (for example Tobias Martin 1708-1717) might be a probationer of the Church of Scotland waiting for presentation to a living, and when he had prospects of a charge, he resigned his appointment in the school. (Tobias Martin became a preacher in 1717). The post of dominie was a joint appointment made by the Town Council and Kirk Session: John Montgomery was appointed by decision of the two courts in 1717. To encourage the schoolmasters to continue in Inveraray, their emoluments from various sources were steadily increased. When Tobias Martin took up his duties as schoolmaster, the Kirk Session agreed that he was to receive 20sh. Scots for each marriage and 10sh. Scots for each baptism. On James Barbour being appointed doctor or assistant master in 1720, there was in increase in the scholars' charges: 3sh. quarterly for each grammarian, and 2sh. quarterly from each learning the Rudiments or English. When Mr. Matthew Wallace, Student in Divinity was appointed Master of the Grammar School by the Town Council with the consent of the Kirk Session in 1725,

---

3 Did he become the Rev. John Maclaurin of Glendaruel, author of an Irish version of the Psalms, and father of Colin Maclaurin, the eminent mathematician?

4 Lib. = pound Scots.

his yearly salary was to be £10 sterling: 30 pounds Scots being paid by the Town Council and 90 lib. Scots by the Kirk Session for being Session Clerk and Treasurer, as well as the school wages and other emoluments.[5]

In addition to these financial inducements, Matthew Wallace (and some of his successors) was made "a burgess freeman and guild brother of Inveraray, for the love and favour and respect they bear to him and for the good service they expect of him". Despite these apparently propitious circumstances, Matthew Wallace resigned on 9th November 1726, as at February 9th next, "on account of business calling me to the Lowlands".

The times were troubled; from June 1715 to January 1716, when the country was in the throes of the Rising of 1715, "the disorder of the time and the throng-ness of the place was the reason that there was so long an interval in the Session's meetings." Nevertheless the school continued to be well-attended. In 1714, the schoolmaster asked that a doctor be appointed, "the school being so numerous, that he cannot by himself do a duty to them all", and in 1720, a similar appointment was made for the same reason.

Repairs to the premises continued to be necessary. In January 1721, a great storm blew down the schoolmaster's house in the old Burgh of Inveraray, and the Town Council allotted £20 for its repair. Five years later, in December 1725, the floor of the school house being "utterly decayed", the Kirk Session and the Town Council each agreed to pay half the cost of its renewal.

The Grammar School continued to have the support of men of goodwill. Mr. Archibald Campbell of Stonefield, Sheriff depute of Argyll and doer or factor for the Duke of Argyll did for the encouragement of the school agree to pay yearly 20 lib. Scots during his pleasure. Afterwards several sums were mortified for the benefit of the school both by this gentleman and others to the amount of £283.6s.8d. sterling of which the kirk sessions were constituted the guardians, together with £112.2s. sterling, being the price of teinds in the Parish of Appin, purchased from the Duke of Argyle,

---

5 The school wages, which were re-negotiated almost with every appointment and which rose steadily throughout the century, were in 1725: every scholar learning Greek paid one pound ten shillings Scots, quarterly; for Latin eighteen shillings Scots, quarterly; for English, thirteen shillings four pennies Scots, quarterly.

by Mr. Seaton then of Appin, and made payable by the Duke of Argyle to the Burgh for behoof of the Grammar School. For many years also, and until the teinds were evicted by a late augmentation of stipend, the tack-duty of the treasury teinds of the Parish of Lismore were made payable by the Duke of Argyle to the town for behoof of the school. From these several sources of revenue the Grammar School was supported.

In the middle of the eighteenth century, the incomes of the dominie and usher were supplemented from another source. On the second day of February, Candlemas Day, the pupils all brought candles to school and a gift of money for the master. The master acknowledged the highest gifts with Latin exclamations ... Vivat ... Floreat bis ... Floreat ter ... Gloriat. The pupil contributing most was hailed as King or Queen. Then all the pupils lit their candles and marched round the school and down the street to the Green, where they had built a great bonfire. All stood round, while the king and queen lit the bonfire. The pupils threw in their candles and in a moment, there was a huge fire. This was called the Candlemas Bleeze. Then all the pupils danced round. The Candlemas Offerings formed a considerable part of the master's income. This custom continued till late into the nineteenth century.[6]

In 1736, a second school was opened in Inveraray, alongside the Grammar School. On April 12th of that year, the Session of the Highland Congregation proposed to settle a school for teaching to read English in the Highland Kirk and asked the Town Council to grant their teacher the sole right of teaching to read English within the Burgh. The Town Council considered that it would be to the benefit of the Grammar School that the Master thereof should be freed of the burden of teaching to read English, and enacted that after Whitsunday next no English scholars should be taught in the Grammar School. The master of the Grammar School, George Wilson, agreed and one Patrick Smith appears to have accepted the appointment to the school in the Highland Kirk.

In the same year, 1736, the records first make mention of John ffallowsdale, "one of those stepsons of Fortune, whom she treats with unceasing rigour, and ends with disinheriting altogether".[7]

On August 11th of that year, the Usher of the Grammar

6   The Dunoon Observer, 23.6.1932.

7   Sir Walter Scott: The Heart of Mid-Lothian, chapter XLIII.

School, John Clerk, having resigned, the Town Council and Kirk Session appointed Mr. John ffallowsdale, student of Philosophy[8] to be Usher. His salary was to be £10 sterling to be made up thus: £6 to be paid equally by the Town Council and the Kirk Session; £1.12.4d. from the encouragement promised by Archibald Campbell of Stonefield, Chamberlain of Argyll; £2.6.8d. by the Synod of Argyll. This salary was to be paid in two portions at Whitsunday and Martinmas.

Next year on the 14th October, 1737, John ffallowsdale was certified to be a Burgess and Guild Brother of Inveraray.

He continued in his place as usher for some two and a half years, until 4th February 1740, when the Master of the Grammar School, George Wilson, resigned as from the 4th March. Thereupon John ffallowsdale acted as teacher of the Grammar School, until 10th March 1741, when Colin Campbell, brother german to Duncan Campbell in Lochhead was appointed to the Grammar School. Upon which appointment John ffallowsdale reverted to the position of usher.

The emoluments of the master and usher were reconsidered once more. The salary was £25 sterling of which 3/5 or £15 was paid to the Master, Mr. Colin Campbell, and 2/5 or £10 was paid to the usher Mr. John ffallowsdale. In addition there were the school fees paid by each scholar learning Latin, Greek, Arithmetic and Book-keeping, of which fees 3/5 went to the Master and 2/5 to the usher. There were also the Candlemas offerings, of which ⅔ were paid to the Master and ⅓ to the usher. Also, in 1741, the Treasury Teinds of Lismore, if available, were to be shared on the basis of ⅔ to the Master and ⅓ to the Doctor or Usher.

There was also the complicated question of the Schoolmasters' House. This house was situated in the old Burgh, which clustered around the ancient baronial hold. The house was in need of repair and between 1739 and 1741 the Lowland Kirk Session gave 120.0.0 lib. for expense of the schoolmasters' house. After this renovation, the rent or value of half the house and the garden was estimated at £1 sterling and regarded as part of the salary of the Master. One pound sterling was regarded as the value of the other half of the house, and was counted as part of the Usher's

8 At this time, divinity students were called theologues; art students were vaguely called philosophers.

salary. The house was to be possessed equally by the Master and the Usher. The Master was to have his election (choice) which end to reside in, but "if either Master or Usher shall for the occasion of a wife[9] and family, choose to possess the whole house, in that case the person unmarried shall quit his part to the other upon payment of the half-rent, and the posessors, one or more, shall be holden to keep the house wind and water-tight." This entry in the Minutes of the Town Council was signed by the Provost and Council and by James Getty, minister of Inveraray. It appears that the schoolmaster's house was in need of further repair between 1741 and 1743, and that John ffallowsdale repaired the end of the house, at a cost to himself of £4.16.8d. for which he was subsequently reimbursed.

In 1746, Mr. John ffallowsdale, Usher of the Grammar School at Inveraray and Rachael Brown his spouse, along with a large number of the inhabitants of the old Burgh, received a summons of removal at the instance of Archibald Campbell of Stonefield, in his capacity of Chamberlain of Argyll. He had removed by 1748, having been obliged to leave that end of the schoolmaster's house possessed by him, in repair at his removal therefrom.

In October of the same year, 1748, ffallowsdale, may one say with unexpected spirit? craved some allowance, in respect of the smallness of his appointments, for bygone services, while he taught the school alone and afterwards as usher. The Town Council gave him £12 sterling, being the year's Tack duty of the Treasury teinds of Lismore due for the crop of 1747, in full satisfaction of all his claims and out of this sum he had to pay the debts which he had already incurred in repairing the schoolmaster's house.

Three weeks later, on 27th October 1748, John ffallowsdale suffered a further blow. On that date, His Grace the Duke of Argyll informed the Provost that he would provide a proper person as Master of the Grammar School with ushers for the several branches of learning. The Town Council then called up ffallowsdale with the Master of the English speaking school and dismissed them as from 27th January 1749. John ffallowsdale accepted dismissal and signed the minute.

Nothing appears to have been done about a new appointment, however, and on June 27th 1749 the Town Council met in the Tol-

9   John ffallowsdale was married, his spouse being Rachael Brown (Duncan C. MacTavish: Inveraray Papers, p. 57)

booth to consider the state of the Grammar and English Schools. The Council called on the Rev. Patrick Campbell and the Rev. Alexander Campbell, ministers of the Collegiate Parishes for their advice. In the meantime, as they usually did in such a position, they considered the funds available to pay the teachers.

Both schools were now vacant, and it was decided that they should be kept vacant, till His Grace would provide a master. In the meantime, they nominated Mr. ffallowsdale to be Teacher of the Grammar School. He was to teach Greek, Latin and Church Music till he was warned to remove. He was not to have the use of the school house,[10] but was required to put the house in proper repair. (Apparently the repairs which he had carried out in 1748 had not been sufficient).

Some seven years later, on 16th March 1756, Mr. John ffallowsdale, who was acting as Master of the Grammar School, declared that he would no longer act as Session Clerk and Precentor in the Lowland Kirk, whereupon the Town Council decided to apply his payment for these posts (viz. £2.10s.) to the English school master's salary, for which the English schoolmaster was to serve as Session Clerk and Precentor.

John ffallowsdale yet had about two years to serve. He was continuing to act as Master of the Grammar School, when the Provost intimated on 8th November 1757 that His Grace the Duke of Argyll intended to provide a proper person as Master of the Grammar School. The Town Council decided to give notice to Mr. John ffallowsdale; he was called in and agreed to give up his post at Whitsunday next. On 28th June 1758, it is noted in the Minutes that the Grammar School is now vacant. This stepson of Fortune, having been treated by her with unceasing rigour, was in the end disinherited altogether.

The unfortunate John ffallowsdale was replaced by Mr. Robert Dobson, a man of a different type, on whom Fortune chose to lavish advantages. He was late teacher of Mathematics at Glasgow. His Grace the Duke recommended him and agreed to

10   On 15th February 1749, the west-end of the schoolmaster's house was sett to Mr. Robert Stirling, silversmith for a rent of 40 shillings, sterling yearly, and the east end of the house was sett to Angus Campbell, shoemaker, at a rent of 50 shillings, sterling per year; Campbell was to leave the said end wind and water tight at his removal. The gable end of the schoolmaster's house was· rebuilt at this time, and the roof was thatched.

augment his salary. The Magistrates gave to Mr. Dobson the power, liberty and privilege of keeping a school in the Burgh for teaching English, Latin, Greek, French, Writing, Arithmetic, Book-keeping, Navigation and other branches of education within his knowledge. He was to have the whole salary, fees and endowments, which now amounted to £51.3.4d. He was to have a house, garden and cow's grass in the New Town of Inveraray. He was to be in charge both of the Grammar School and of the English School, having an usher to assist him in teaching the boys Latin and Greek in the Grammar School, and an usher for the English School. He had authority to appoint and dismiss these ushers at pleasure and to pay them such salaries and parts of fees as he might think proper.

Mr. Dobson made the following observations on the position of the schools and on the proposals; he said that the present school was too small for all the scholars, and that the numbers would increase and make the place more inconvenient; he suggested that either of the churches might be used for the scholars learning English, and as both the churches were too far from the present school,[11] for his having constant inspection of boys learning English, he would give up the £5 payable by the Town Council and the £5 payable by the Parish of Glenaray, towards making up a salary for a teacher to the said English School.

After prolonged discussion and correspondence, Mr. Robert Dobson was appointed in 1759: on 11th November 1760 he resigned as from Whitsunday, 1761.

On the resignation of Mr. Dobson, the Town Council appointed a deputation of three to wait on His Grace and ask his permission to advertise the vacancy; they also asked whether His Grace would allow a dwelling house for each of the schoolmasters (that is of the Grammar School and of the English School) with the same accommodation which His Grace was pleased to allow Mr. Dobson.

Apparently a Mr. Watson was appointed Master of the Grammar School at this time although the settlement was not put in writing till 1764. He appears to have come from Edinburgh because in 1764, £4.10.-d. was paid to him by order of the Council as his travelling charges from Edinburgh to Inveraray. Mr.

11   The Grammar School was held in the Court House in the new town.

Watson received £33.6.8d. as his yearly salary in equal portions at Whitsunday and Martinmas.

Not only was the settlement with Mr. Watson put in writing, but the school hours were defined. From 1st April to 1st October, scholars were to receive instruction from 7 till 9 a.m., from 10 till 12 noon; from 2 till 5 p.m. For the rest of the year from 1st October to 1st April, the school hours were to be from 9 a.m. till 12 noon, and from 2 till 4 p.m. The comparative shortness of the school day in winter was no doubt on account of the brevity of the winter's day, and the inconvenience of providing artificial light.

As in 1657, so in 1768, those responsible for the school were anxious about the effectiveness of the teaching. On 30th March 1768, the Town Council, considering that the progress of learning and instruction of youth in the Grammar and English Schools is a matter that merits their serious attention, therefore enact that on the 1st Wednesday of May, and on the same nominal day of each quarter of the current year and all years to come both the said schools shall be publicly examined in presence and at direction of the Magistrates and Town Council to the end they may be better able to judge concerning the diligence and application of the teachers and scholars and make suitable animadversions thereon or give such further injunctions and orders as may be necessary. This was intimated to Mr. John Watson of the Grammar School and to the Master of the English School.

Mr. Watson served as Master of the Grammar School from about 1761 until 1771, when he was appointed to the school at Campbeltown, on the recommendation of His Grace. In view of this impending change, the Town Council and the Kirk Session had already considered the state of the school and what steps would be necessary to get a teacher. The Town Council decided to advertise in the Edinburgh and Glasgow newspapers.[12] They also recommended the Provost and the Rev. John MacAulay, Inveraray, to write to their friends in Glasgow and Edinburgh to look out for a schoolmaster.

The emoluments for the post were not so assured or satisfactory as in former days. The Treasury Teinds of Lismore, which augmented the schoolmaster's salary, had been stopped for this

12 The Edinburgh Evening Courant, The Caledonian Mercury, The Glasgow Journal.

purpose by His Majesty's Solicitor for Teinds; and the garden, house and cow's grass possessed by Mr. Watson, the former master, had been sett to Patrick Campbell, Surveyor of Customs.

Despite these discouraging circumstances, John McKinnon, student in Divinity accepted the appointment of Master of the Grammar School on 15th June 1771. He resigned in 1774, having become a preacher of the Gospel.

After this date, masters succeeded one another, each one having held office for four or eight years. One of these was James Gibson, appointed Master of Inveraray Grammar School at Martinmas, 1786. In 1794, he offered to get a temporary teacher to take his place in Inveraray, because he had been appointed to the Grammar School of Glasgow, which had existed since at least the early fourteenth century, and which had not long been removed from a site on the west side of the High Street to new premises on the lands of Ramshorn.

During his mastership, Inveraray Grammar School was reconstructed. From the time of Robert Dobson 1759, until 1788, the school was held in the Court House in the New Town. In 1788 a building was erected consisting of a parish school and a Grammar School, with houses for the two masters on the upper storey.[13]

James Gibson was succeeded by David Gillespie. His salary was £31.12.8, augmented by the Candlemas offerings. In addition he was allowed a cow's grass and a garden. He had difficulty in obtaining payment of his salary. When he left in 1813 to be rector at Campbeltown, the Town Council owed him £60.[14]

The departure of David Gillespie and the construction of new school buildings appeared to open up the way for re-organisation and changes in administration. In 1815, "it was agreed that the Parish School and Grammar School should be united into an Academy with a Rector of respectability and an Usher for which the very convenient situation of the present schools and lodging houses for the masters affords great facilities."

This was the revival of an idea discussed in 1759, when the

13 This building was only demolished in 1905. The Community Centre now stands on the site.

14 'A Burgh's Schools in the Nineteenth Century' by Donald Mackechnie in The Oban Times, June 22, 1972.

Town Council and the Kirk Session had wished to make Robert Dobson responsible for the Grammar School and the English-speaking School with ushers and under-teachers, a proposal to which Dobson did not acquiesce. The authorities had never lost sight of this plan but there were still difficulties in the way of carrying it out.

Therefore Daniel Stewart was appointed master of the Grammar School in succession to David Gillespie. The Grammar School was suffering from competition by an Adventure School, held in a house by one Duncan McNuier, who taught such subjects as were within his knowledge and who charged a lower rate of fees. In 1816 Daniel Stewart protested that as a result of the activities of Duncan McNuier his income was growing less. "Furthermore," he stated, "in the grammar school the forms and desks are worn out, the windows are broken and some will neither open or shut."

Daniel Stewart left Inveraray in 1823; John Brooks, the old parish school master, died in 1829; and the time seemed ripe to carry out the long deferred plan of uniting the two schools. An attempt was made to unite the two schools, which were in the same building, under one master but this did not work harmoniously. The different ethos of the two institutions, built up over generations, was too strong to be fused. So the two pedagogies continued to pursue different courses under two dominies.

The situation deteriorated in 1848 when there was an unfortunate difference of opinion between the Chamberlain of Argyll and the Town Council concerning the Council's intromission with the school house. As a result the schoolhouse, garden and schoolroom were taken over by the legal proprietor in 1851 and Inveraray Grammar School was in abeyance.

Matters were made more complicated when the Free Church built a school in the Newton which school was open to children of any church.

In the 1850s there were two schools in Inveraray: the Parish School in Church Square under Henry Dunn Smith, M.A., a most able master, and the Free Church School in the Newton. But what of Inveraray Grammar School, dating from 1649? In 1867 the Free Church School in the Newton claimed to be the Grammar School, thereby laying claim also to certain monies, long mortified for the use of Inveraray Grammar School.

This anomalous situation was radically affected when the Education (Scotland) Act received the Royal Assent on 6th August 1872. Thereafter both the Parish School in Church Square under Henry Dunn Smith and the Free Church School in the Newton were administered by a School Board, popularly elected.

The Newton School remained open until 1903. In that year Henry Dunn Smith retired from Church Square School, and the way was open for readjustment. On June 1, 1903, the Clerk to the School Board wrote, "Newton School having been closed, the staff and pupils were transferred to Church Square School, which will be known as Inveraray Grammar School."

In 1905 what had been Church Square School was demolished, a new school was built on the same site and was called Inveraray Grammar School. The building was opened in 1907 by Lord Archibald Campbell and the then Miss Elspeth Campbell, who planted a tree in the playground. Inveraray Grammar School like the phoenix had arisen from the ashes. For many years thereafter secondary education continued to be given in Inveraray. By 1954 the school provided primary education and the first and second years of secondary education. Inveraray pupils who wished to carry on their secondary education beyond the second year proceeded to Lochgilphead, Dunoon or Oban. The school was in charge of a headmaster, Mr. Donald MacKechnie, M.A., O.B.E., J.P., with four assistants and had a roll of over 100 pupils.

In 1962, a new Inveraray Grammar School was built in the vicinity of Inveraray (Argyllshire) All Saints Church, and the old school of 1907-1962, after being unused for some years was reconstructed as a Community Centre and opened in 1971. In 1970, it was decided, on account of declining numbers of children, that secondary education could not be justified in the school. The Headmaster, Mr. MacKechnie, retired. An appeal was made however against the change in status of the Grammar School, and it was continued as a secondary school for a further year, pending a final decision. The decision was confirmed by the Secretary of State for Scotland in 1971 and Inveraray School became a centre of primary education only. The Grammar School set up over three hundred years ago—1649—by the Synod of Argyll ceased to be.

SELECTED REFERENCES

Minutes of the Synod of Argyll, 1639-1651; 1652-1661
Scottish History Society, Third Series, 37 and 38

The Session Books of the English Congregation of Inveraray,
beginning November 25, 1650

The Town Council Minute Book of the School, 1721-1774

MacTavish. Duncan C: Inveraray Papers, Oban, 1939

Chalmers, George: The Life of Thomas Ruddiman, London,
1794

The Literary History of Glasgow, The Maitland Club, 1831

A Burgh's Schools in the 19th Century by Donald
MacKechnie, The Oban Times, 22.6.1972

Inveraray Grammar School. The Dunoon Observer, 23.6.1962

The First, Second and Third Statistical Accounts of Scotland:
The County of Argyll

'Education in Argyll from 1638-1745. An Historical Survey'
by Duncan C. MacTavish. The Glasgow Herald, 15.2.1929

Dunlop, Alexander: Parochial Law, Blackwood, Edinburgh,
1841

Old Church Life in Scotland, Second Series, by Andrew
Edgar, Paisley, Alexander Gardner, 1886.

6

OTHER SCHOOLS

At the present time, the memories and traditions concerning Inveraray Grammar School cause us to forget that this was not the only school in the Burgh and Parish. There were other schools in the district in which good work was done.

The English-speaking School

One such school was the English-speaking school. On 12th April, 1736, the Kirk Session of the Highland Congregation proposed to settle a school for teaching to read English in the Highland Kirk and asked the Town Council to grant their teacher the sole right of teaching to read English within the Burgh. The Town Council considered that it would be to the benefit of the Grammar School that the Master thereof should be freed of the burden of teaching to read English and enacted that after Whitsunday next no English scholars should be taught in the Grammar School.[1] The Master of the Grammar School, George Wilson, agreed and one Patrick Smith appears to have accepted the appointment to the school in the Highland Kirk.

On 17th May 1745, Patrick Smith, Master of the English Reading School resigned at Whitsunday and the Town Council appointed Colin Campbell, son to the deceased Duncan Campbell, writer in Lorn. The appointment was made with the consent of the collegiate Sessions of Glenaray and Inveraray, and the salary was to be made up as follows:— £5 stg., payable by the Parish of Glenaray; £1 stg., payable by the Synod of Argyll; £1.13.4d was promised by Archibald Campbell of Stonefield, Chamberlain of Argyll; £1.5/- being the rent of the house possessed by Patrick Smith; and £1.1.8d. payable by the collegiate Kirk Sessions: all of which came to a total of £10 stg.

1   The Town Council Minute Book of the School, 1721-1774.

The Master of the English-speaking school was entitled to receive half of the christening and marriage monies within the Parish of Glenaray and he was to be precentor in the Highland Church. His school, sometimes called the English-reading school was to be under the inspection of Mr. Colin Campbell, Master of the Grammar School, "and for that end that they remove from the Highland to the Lowland Church."[2]

Scholars learning English or Writing were required to pay 2 shillings stg., quarterly, except the children of tenants living in Glenaray, who contributed to the payment of the £5 stg. to the salary of the master of the English School. When the children paid their fees, half of the money and a quarter of the Candlemas Offerings were paid to the Master of the English School and the remainder of both payments were divided: two thirds to the Master and one third to the Usher of the Grammar School.

On 10th October 1747, the Master of the English School, Colin Campbell, intimated that he was leaving at Martinmas. The Town Council with the consent of the collegiate sessions of Glenaray and Inveraray appointed Mr. John Clerk, late schoolmaster at Glenorchy. A year later, 27th October 1748, the Duke informed the Provost that he would provide a proper person as Master of the Grammar School, with ushers for the several branches of learning. This arrangement apparently applied to the English-speaking school also, because the Town Council called up Mr. John Clerk and dismissed him, and John Clerk signed the minute, accepting his dismissal.

As a result, the English School was vacant, and the Town Council met in the Tolbooth on 27th June 1749 to consider the state of the school, calling on the Rev. Patrick Campbell and the Rev. Alex. Campbell, ministers of the collegiate parishes, for their advice. Meantime they considered once more the funds with which to pay the teacher and took into account the house of the schoolmaster of the English School. It was resolved that both the English and the Grammar Schools would be kept vacant, till His Grace would provide a master. Despite the fact that they had decided to dismiss Mr. John Clerk in January, the Town Council now nominated and appointed John Clerk to be teacher of the English School, until such time as His Grace would make other provision.

2   The Gaelic and English Churches did not adjoin one another in the old town.

John Clerk was to teach English, Writing and Arithmetic, for which he was to charge fees, and the fees were to be his without any division. The children from the country were to be taught gratis. Mr. Clerk was to have a proportion of the Candlemas Offerings in the English School and he was to receive pay as precentor in the Highland Church, but he was not to have occupancy of the school house. His income from all sources was about twelve pounds, sterling.

This arrangement continued for about six years, until on 6th October 1755 The Provost informed the Town Council that Mr. John Clerk had given in his resignation of his post as Master of the English School, to take effect in a month's time. The Town Council accepted John Clerk's resignation and advised the magistrates to look out for a successor.

The English School appears to have been without a teacher all winter and on 16th March 1756, the Town Council and both ministers met together to consider the position. They began as usual by enquiring into the funds which afforded the English teacher's salary. They found that the salary would add up to twelve pounds sterling and agreed that the master would also have the house "in use to be possessed by the master of the English School."

The Provost was to advertise the vacancy in the English Reading School, by means of the public newspapers,[3] to have the School settled by Whitsunday next.

On 28th July 1756, the Provost reported that several had applied for the post of Master of the English School. Among the applicants were Mr. Walter Nicol and a Mr. McCready. Mr. Walter Nicol was the best qualified and was appointed, and one pound sterling was paid to Mr. McCready for his expenses in coming to Inveraray.

Mr. Walter Nicol was to teach English, Writing, Arithmetic, Book-keeping and Church Music. He was to have the house in use to be possessed by the Master of the English School. In the event of his resigning, he was to give three months' notice and to leave the house in good repair.

Some two years later, in 1758, the Duke of Argyll recommended as school master Mr. Robert Dobson to the Town Council

3   The Edinburgh Evening Courant; the Caledonian Mercury; The Glasgow Journal.

and members of the Collegiate Kirk Sessions. It apears that Mr. Dobson was to have charge both of Inveraray Grammar School and of the English-speaking school: he was to have the whole salary, fees and endowments, and was to fulfil the engagements which the Council and Session lay under to Mr. Walter Nicol, Master of the English School.

At this time His Grace was generously pleased to contribute largely to the salaries to be paid to the teachers, and to allow them lodgings with several other conveniences for their accommodation.

In February 1759, Mr. Dobson, inter alia, is to relieve the Town Council and Kirk Session of their engagement to Walter Nicol, whom he can dismiss or retain at pleasure, which was intimated to Mr. Nicol.

Mr. Dobson, however, did not find it convenient to be altogether responsible for both schools. The English-speaking school was held in the Old Town, while the Inveraray Grammar School met in the New Town. Mr. Dobson therefore suggested that either of the churches might be used for the scholars learning English, and as both the churches were too far from the present school for his having constant inspection of boys learning English, he will give up the five pounds payable by the Town Council and the five pounds payable by the Parish of Glenaray, towards making up a salary for a teacher to the said English School. The teacher to be appointed would teach only English and Writing and the first five rules of Vulgar Arithmetic. He would take such fees from his pupils as the magistrates would fix; he was to be considered as one of the ushers; and he would precent in the Highland Kirk.

Walter Nicol being present was informed that after Whit-sunday next, he was not to be considered as in the service of the Town Council and the Kirk Sessions. It appears that Walter Nicol like John ffallowsdale was a stepson of Fortune, whom she chose at last to disinherit.

On 24th May 1759, the Provost informed the Town Council that Mr. Dobson had written to say that he could not find a suitable teacher for the English School. Thereupon the Provost wrote to Edinburgh and found a person who would come, if the terms were suitable. In December of that year, the Provost intimated to the Town Council and Kirk Sessions that he had appointed Mr. James Wright, and that Mr. Wright was teaching English and Church

213

Music in the old School house[4] with general approbation. The appointment which the Provost had made was approved by the Town Council and it was agreed that Mr. James Wright should be paid as from Whitsunday last.

On 12th October 1764, some five years later, the Town Council and members of the Collegiate Kirk Sessions considering that James Wright, Master of the English School, has officiated for some years but that a settlement has not been put in writing, therefore the Town Council and the Kirk Session order the Treasurer to pay Mr. James Wright twenty pounds sterling.

In 1768, Mr. James Wright being Master of the English School, his school as well as the Grammar School was publicly examined in presence of the Magistrates and Town Council on the first Wednesday of May, and on subsequent quarter days. The School was considered to be serving a useful purpose and in 1770 £11.1.8d was spent on its repair.

After having served for fifteen years, Mr. James Wright resigned as from Martinmas, 1774. The Town Council decided to advertise the post, but in the first instance, the Provost Lachlan Campbell and Bailie John McNeill agreed to write to proper persons in the Low Country about finding a person properly qualified. In the month of September, the Town Council and Collegiate Kirk Sessions met together to appoint a teacher to the English School. The Provost reported that his friends in the Low Country recommended to him Mr. Alex. Buchanan, late school master at Whithorn, who on the Provost's invitation had arrived with his family.[5] The Town Council and the Kirk Sessions then appointed

---

4   It would appear that at this time the English Reading School was meeting, not in the Highland Church in which it had been opened, but in the school house, formerly used as the Grammar School, which was adjacent to the English Church.

5   Mr. Alexander Buchanan had a distinguished son, Claudius Buchanan. It appears that before being in Whithorn, Alexander Buchanan had been in Cambuslang, where a son called Claudius was born to him in 1766. When his father was appointed to the English School, Inveraray in 1774-75, Claudius was eight years of age, and he spent the next eight years of his life in Inveraray, till his father resigned his appointment as teacher in 1783. It may be assumed that the boy attended Inveraray Grammar School and that he was instructed in Latin and Greek by Mr. George Gillies. In due course, Claudius studied at the Universities of Glasgow and Cambridge and was ordained according to the

Mr. Alex. Buchanan to teach English, Arithmetic, Book-keeping, Navigation and other branches of education, except Latin and Greek, at a salary of twenty pounds sterling yearly. He was to have the Candlemas offerings and a house, garden and cow's grass in the New Town of Inveraray. He was to precent in the Lowland Church and officiate as Clerk and Treasurer to the Collegiate Kirk Sessions, for which there was no extra salary.

Mr. Alex. Buchanan, teacher of the English School, resigned 1783, and after a brief tenure of office by one Malcolm Campbell, John Brooks,[6] schoolmaster in Kilmarnock, was appointed teacher of the English School. His salary amounted to £19.3.4d. besides quarterly fees and other perquisites. After he had been in office for five years, a new building both for the Grammar and for the Parish School was erected in 1788.[7] On the upper storey were the houses of the two masters. With the house was a garden and grass for a cow gratis from the family of Argyll.[8] Under John Brooks the English School was well-attended: in 1793, there were at an average about 80 scholars in winter, and 60 in summer.[9] In 1795, the master was granted five pounds sterling by the Kirk Session for teaching a Sunday School for the preceding five years.

After so many changes among the masters, John Brooks administered the English School for more than forty years. He was known as "Old Brooks". It is said that he used to repeat a Latin declension to himself, as if it were a song or hum the sing-song words "Arma virumque cano...."[10] His school room was perfumed

---

form of the Church of England at 29 years of age, in 1795. After holding a chaplaincy in India at Barrackpur (1797-99), he was appointed Calcutta chaplain and vice-principal of the College of Fort William. He translated the gospels into Persian and Hindustani. After his return to England in 1808, he aroused public opinion on the missionary question, and by his book Colonial Ecclesiastical Establishment, London, 1813, he helped on the establishment of the Indian Episcopate and the first English bishop of Calcutta was appointed. He died on 9th Feb. 1815. (Encyclopedia Britannica, Fourteenth Edition, 1929)

6   John Brooks is described in Gilian the Dreamer by Neil Munro. Although some parts of Neil Munro's account of the dominie may be fictional, other statements are based on local traditions.

7   This building was in use until 1905.

8   First Statistical Account of Inveraray.

9   Ibid.

10   Virgil: Aeneid, Book 1, line 1.

with the smoke of peat, for the landward pupils were accustomed to bring each his own peat for the fuelling. The peat smoke swirled and eddied out into the room and hung about the ochred walls. Over the fire-place, there was the map of Europe. The master used to sit on a high three-legged stool and his desk, within which were grammars and copy books, pens in long black boxes and the terrible black tawse.

The scholars sitting in rows behind the knife-hewn inky desks hummed like bees upon their tasks and the little ones at the bottom of the room pored over their horn books.[11] During the interval, the bare-legged children played at shinty in the playground, with loud shouts and violent rushes after the little wooden ball. At 3 p.m. in winter and 4 p.m. in summer, Brooks closed the school and went home, one arm occupied by a great bundle of books. It was said that he was so fond of books, that if he had to leave them for an hour or two in the evening, he must have a little one such as the Odes of Horace in his pocket to feel the touch of when he could not be studying its pages.

As Brooks became older, he was given an assistant, George Riddoch. The Town Council decided that on the termination of the old man's mastership, the Grammar School and the Parish School should be united into an Academy with the assistant, George Riddoch as Rector. When John Brooks died in 1829, the Presbytery, the Kirk Session and the Town Council attempted to carry out the plan. There was general dis-satisfaction with the arrangement; the scheme was a failure; and George Riddoch continued as master of the Parish School.

In 1848, George Riddoch left and after another abortive attempt to unite the Grammar School and the Parish School as an academy under Duncan Stewart from Edinburgh, the Parish School was placed under the mastership of Mr. Stewart. He left Inveraray in 1851 and was succeeded in the Parish School by Henry Dunn Smith, M.A. from Aberdeen, who remained in office till 1903.

Henry Dunn Smith had a colleague or rival in the person of the

11 Hornbook, a name originally applied to a sheet containing the letters of the alphabet, which formed a primer for the use of children. It was mounted on a wooden frame with a handle, and protected with a sheet of horn. The frame contained the alphabet in large and, small letters. The vowels then formed a line, and their combinations with the consonants were given in tabular form.

master of the Free Church School in the Newton of Inveraray. The two masters had heard of mortified money, due to Inveraray Grammar School, which was not functioning at this time, and they agreed to apply to the Town Council for a grant. Their application was refused. In 1862, Dunn Smith applied again. As a result, five pounds for prizes were allocated between the two schools. In 1865, the two masters applied for the third time and were granted three pounds for prizes.

In 1872, the Education (Scotland) Bill became law. Two years later, the Free Church School in the Newton was closed, and all the pupils were transferred to the Parish School in Church Square under Henry Dunn Smith. But the master was not given an assistant to help him cope with this influx of scholars. There were now 159 children in tne Parish School; Dunn Smith applied for an assistant, and was refused. The situation was somewhat eased when the Newton School was re-opened in 1879.

The Parish School under Dunn Smith (who was known as "Old Skull")[12] made steady progress and the earned grants rose year by year from £80 in 1883 to £127 in 1891 and £134 in 1896. His passes in specific subjects (what would now be called secondary subjects) were more numerous than those in the Newton School. The subjects which he taught included Latin, Greek, French, English Literature, Mathematics, Geography, Agriculture and Chemistry. In 1884 he wrote: "The chemical demonstrations on alternate mornings excite much interest."[13]

One of his pupils was Neil Munro and in the present Inveraray School, there is a photograph of the future novelist and his classmates with the bearded master. Smith was a notable teacher, and in 1899, he published "An English Grammar Simplified" which reached its third edition in 1901.

In 1893, Her Majesty's Inspector recorded that Smith's school was "conducted with exceptional vigour and ability." In 1902, it was stated: "My Lords award a pension of £30 per annum to Mr. H.D. Smith in view of his prospective retirement." In 1903, Mr.

---

12   Local tradition.

13   'A Burgh's Schools in the Nineteenth Century' by Donald Mackechnie, in The Oban Times, 22.6.1972, passim.

Binnie, H.M.I. made the comment: "Mr. Smith now retires after a long and meritorious career." [14]

During the second half of the nineteenth century, Henry Dunn Smith was a prominent figure in Inveraray. Scholarly and energetic, he was an outstanding member of his profession. His services to the Burgh were not limited to the educational field. He was session clerk, registrar of births and deaths, an officer in the Volunteers, precentor, and for a time a member of the Town Council.

When Henry Dunn Smith retired in 1903, the Clerk to the School Board of Inveraray wrote: "Newton School having been closed, the staff and pupils were transferred to Church Square School, which will be known as Inveraray Grammar School."

The Free Church School

In 1848, five years after the Disruption, a Free Church School was erected in Inveraray.[15] This school was at the southern end of the Burgh, in the part called Newton. It was open to children of any church.

In 1867, under the influence of Provost Scipio MacTaggart, the Free Church School was declared to be the Grammar School of Inveraray.

"In the same year, the Kirk Session of Inveraray Parish Church sued the Town Council of Inveraray for £100, lent by them to the Town Council in 1805. This led to the discovery that the money was the Stonefield Mortification, granted by Campbell of Stonefield in 1755 for behoof of the Grammar School. Provost Scipio MacTaggart now pressed that this money be used for the benefit of the School, which had been established as the Grammar School."[16] Accordingly, Peter Ferguson master in the Free Church School claimed interest on the money on the ground that he was Rector of the Grammar School. The Kirk Session of Inverary Parish Church refused to pay the interest to the Free Church School. A

14   Ibid.

15   See references: Annals of the Free Church of Scotland, Vol. 11.

16   "A Burgh's Schools in the Nineteenth Century" by Donald Mackechnie in the Oban Times, 22.6.1972.

successor to Peter Ferguson, a certain John Wilson, went to law and won the case.[17]

After the passing of the Education (Scotland) Act 1872, the Inveraray School Board took charge of the Free Church School, and on the resignation of John Wilson in 1874, the school in the Newton was closed and all the pupils were transferred to the parish school in Church Square. This created a difficult situation however, and in 1879 the Newton School was re-opened.

The Newton School continued until the master in the Parish School retired in 1903, whereupon the Newton School was finally closed and the staff and pupils were transferred to Church Square School. The former Free Church School is now used as the Scout Hall.

Education for Girls

While the English School was being placed on a business-like basis in 1745, attention began to be paid to the education of girls. By the middle of the 18th century, provision was made to teach girls to sew. For the years 1764-65, half-a-year's salary, two pounds sterling, was paid to Mrs. MacLachlan, seamstress, and in 1765, advertisement was made costing 12s.6d. for a sewing mistress. One Mrs. Frize was appointed, her salary for 1765 being four pounds sterling. By 1771, Mrs. Frize had departed and the sewing mistress was Miss Bell Campbell.

By the year 1793, a female academy had been instituted in Inveraray. His Grace generously made an addition to the salary paid by the Burgh, besides providing a good and commodious house rent free, as an encouragement to the mistress of the academy. It was the purpose of this institution to give instruction in the useful and ornamental branches of female education. In the nineteenth century, this was a Dame School, supported by £20 a-year from the Duke of Argyll, and by £4 a-year from the Town Council. The lessons of the day began with the Shorter Catechism. The pupils were taught in white seam sewing, spelling, and an Italian hand of write![18] It was said that the crochet was never out of the dame's hands in oral exercizes. There were about 23 scholars;

17   Ibid.

18   See References, Neil Munro: The Daft Days.

16 of them girls, the remainder of them boys, who were not old enough to attend the Grammar School.

Further provision was made for the education of girls, when a School of Industry or an Industrial School was established by the Duchess of Argyll in 1841. This institution was supported by a salary for the teacher of £26 per year, with coal, a free house and other perquisites.[19]

The Parochial School at Bridge of Douglas

This was one of the first country schools to open in the Parish of Inveraray. The school was set up about the year 1776 by the Duke of Argyll to meet the educational requirements of children whose parents were working at the woollen factories established at Clonary.[20]

The Duke allowed a salary to the school master in 1793, and in 1845, the school had the statute salary of £25.13.4d. a free house, garden, fuel and grass for a cow.[21] The date above the door of the present building is 1851.

A long succession of capable teachers is recalled by record and tradition. At the end of the nineteenth century, the school mistress was Miss MacLachlan who lodged in Clonary. She was succeeded by Miss Annie Blue.[22] Miss Blue was followed by the Misses Gibson (Miss Barbara the elder, and Miss Agnes, the younger) who had taught in Creggans School. When the Misses Gibson retired to Creggans, Miss Charlotte Gilmour took their place. The last teacher in Bridge of Douglas School was Miss Sarah Omond, who had previously taught in Glenshira. In 1932, the ground around the school and school house was enclosed and necessary repairs were carried out on the school fabric. Latterly, Miss Omond had only three pupils, and the school was closed in June, 1934.

19   The Second Statistical Account.

20   The Oban Times, 23.4.1932.

21   The First Statistical Account, 1793. The Second Statistical Account 1845.

22   Local tradition.

Glenaray School

In 1793, there was a school in Glenaray, maintained by the Society in Scotland for Propagating Christian Knowledge. The children were taught to read the Holy Scriptures and other good and pious books; writing and arithmetic; and such other things as were suitable to their circumstances. The master was obliged to catechize the scholars twice a week and to pray publicly with them twice a day. The number of scholars was about 35 for one half of the year; but a third part of that number did not attend constantly during the other half of the year.

In 1843, this school was supported by a salary of £15 a year from the Society and by a free house, cow's grass and money to the amount of £15 from the Duke of Argyll.

"In 1862, Mr. John MacArthur was head of Glenaray Public School, a post which he held for many years. At that time, there was no room in the school for the scholars to do their writing exercizes together. One half did their writing, while the other half went out to play. Mrs. John MacArthur had a fine lot of girls in her sewing school, among which were six girls from the Maltland and from the Burgh. The mistress was a proficient sewing teacher and had a fine singing voice.

"The school started at 9 a.m. with an hour off at mid-day, and continued till 4 o'clock. At about five minutes to 4 p.m., the boys were drawn up in a semi-circle, ready for dismissal. Mrs. MacArthur came in with the girls' class and the boys came to attention. The mistress started to sing a favourite hymn and all joined in. At the close of the hymn, Mr. MacArthur said prayers and the school was dismissed."[23]

In course of time, a second schoolroom was built at some little distance from the first, which was much too small to contain the number of pupils attending.

In 1932, Glenaray Public School was in charge of a Miss Livingstone.[24] At this time, the school was under threat of closure. It was eventually closed and the children living in the vicinity were conveyed daily to and from Inveraray.

23   The Oban Times, 16.1.1932.

24   Ibid.

The ruins of the schoolhouse, two school rooms and offices may still be seen below Stronmagachan, and one may trace the school road, lined by a hawthorn hedge, and cross the small stone bridge, very strongly constructed, which spanned the stream.

Creggans School

This school was erected by His Grace George 8th Duke of Argyll, K.T. before 1886. It was for the benefit of children of the tenantry in Kenmore and district. It was attended by children from Kenmore, Kilbride, Furnace and Inveraray. The teacher received £8 per annum with a house and garden. The pupils were instructed in industrial work: on 19th March 1886, some girls of ex-Six Standard in Furnace went to Creggans to be trained in this subject.[25]

Unlike Furnace which was a board school, Creggans was variously described as a Voluntary School or as a Private School in receipt of Government grants: the school was not under the authority of the local School Board. Some parents and some children took advantage of this anomalous position. Parents in the village of Furnace who wished to send their children to school occasionally, entered their names in the register of Creggans School and so evaded the Cumlodden Attendance Officer. On 19th March 1897, when the Sheriff convicted defaulting parents from Furnace for not sending their children to school regularly, all children attending Creggans School were exempted from citation, although their attendance was more irregular than pupils in attendance at Furnace School. The pupils themselves were not slow to turn the situation to advantage. On 11th December 1896, several pupils left Furnace School without the knowledge of their parents, and entered Creggans School with a view to share in the forth-coming Christmas or New Year Treat given at Inveraray. A week later, December 18th one of the pupils who had left Furnace School for Creggans called on the schoolmaster in Furnace to say that they would all return after the New Year holidays.

It is not surprising that when pupils removed from Creggans to Furnace, the attitude of the Furnace teacher towards them was critical. On 2nd September 1901, five boys from Creggans School were admitted to Furnace. The master in Furnace noted that "the

25   Log Book, Furnace Public School, passim.

new pupils are very far behind in notation. Pupils from Creggans don't settle to work very well. They need a great deal of attention.''

The last teachers in Creggans School were the Misses Gibson (Miss Barbara, the elder, had no arms:[26] she wrote by holding the pen in her mouth, a fact which made a lasting impression on the pupils.) On the closure of Creggans School, in 1909 the Misses Gibson were appointed to Bridge of Douglas School. When they retired from Bridge of Douglas, they returned to live in Creggans. Miss Barbara died in 1924 and Miss Agnes died about 1930.[27]

Glen Shira School

In the twentieth century, a school was started in Glen Shira at Stuc an Sgardan, the little house above Maam Farm. It was attended by one family who lived at the farm.

The little red-roofed school opposite Ellerig was opened in 1926. It is situated below Stucgoy and near to the strong stone bridge, which carried the old road up the glen from Maam to Drimlee. The school may also be approached by stepping stones across the river. It was built of corrugated iron and lined with wood. The school room apart from the porch measured twelve feet by fourteen feet, and was heated by a "Slowburn" iron stove. There was a porch for the children and a small locked apartment for equipment.

The only teacher was Miss Sarah Omond who was an Orcadian. She lodged at Drimlee during the school week. She was a good teacher, a strict disciplinarian, and some who began their schooling under her tuition became students at Glasgow University. The school was opened for three pupils; there were never more than five in attendance. Stucgoy or Glen Shira School was closed in 1930, and Miss Omond was transferred to Bridge of Douglas.

26 Miss Barbara Gibson lost her arms in an accident, when she was a child. Her father had a mill at Luce Bay, Wigtownshire. The manager asked Barbara to stop the engine in the mill. As she did so, one arm was caught in the machinery and severed. She threw out her other arm to save herself from falling into the machinery, and her second arm was cut off. In later life, with great courage, she overcame this handicap and became a schoolmistress.

27 Local tradition.

These were some of "the other schools", along with schools at the teacher's own adventure, of which there are now only fragmentary records. Thorough work was done in these little school houses and pupils went out from them to the Grammar School, to the Universities and to the colonies. Gradually however depopulation decreased the schoolroll, and modern methods of transport made it more economic to convey the pupils to Inveraray than to maintain three or four teachers in outlying districts. Today, some of these school houses are pleasant dwellings, while others are ruins on the short green turf beside the river, where children once shouted and played long ago.

SELECTED REFERENCES

The Town Council Minute Book of the School, 1721-1774

Encyclopedia Britannica, Fourteenth Edition, 1929

The First Statistical Account of Scotland, Argyll, Inveraray, 1793.
The Second Statistical Account, 1845

Neil Munro: Gilian the Dreamer
    The Daft Days

'A Burgh's Schools in the Nineteenth Century' by Donald Mackechnie. The Oban Times, 22.6.1972

The Oban Times, 23.4.1932
    16.1.1932

Annals of the Free Church of Scotland, 1843-1900, Vol. 11

The Education (Scotland) Act, 1872

Inveraray and Cumlodden School Board, Furnace Public School Log Book

Local tradition

224